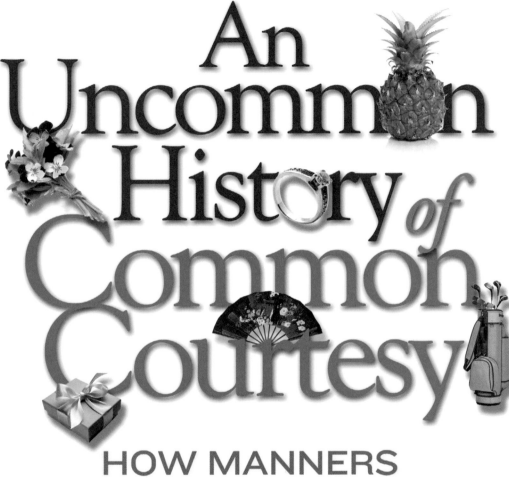

An Uncommon History of Common Courtesy

HOW MANNERS
SHAPED THE WORLD

BETHANNE PATRICK

AUTHOR OF *An Uncommon History of Common Things*

NATIONAL GEOGRAPHIC

WASHINGTON, D.C.

PAGE 1: *Just married: The Duke and Duchess of Cambridge exchange a fabled balcony kiss.*
ABOVE: *1930s WPA Federal Art Project poster from Ohio*

CONTENTS

FOREWORD

This could be a dangerous book. Please promise that you won't use it to decide, from the wealth of customs in the world, that anything you choose to do would be acceptable somewhere in the world. That would be rather like declaring, as some have been known to do, that it is fine to drink all day because it is always cocktail hour somewhere around the globe. Either decision quickly leads to becoming a public nuisance.

There is more sophisticated fun to be had in discovering how other societies choose to live: their everyday gestures; their methods of discouraging people from offending one another; the symbolism of their clothing; and their ceremonies for dealing with birth, marriage, and death. This is the great lure of travel, armchair and otherwise, and travel itself is vastly enriched for those who know the local language of behavior.

To be worldly-wise is to understand that such customs, although neither "natural" nor "logical," are of prime importance to civilization. Etiquette is indeed artificial and idiosyncratic, as its detractors accuse it of being, and it must be learned, not only for every society but also for myriad situations within each society. It cannot be deduced from first principles.

But as varied as particular etiquette practices are throughout the world, their rules can be traced to basic tenets of manners that are universal. These comprise three functions: as a paralegal system, more flexible (not to mention cheaper) than the law for regulating ordinary behavior in the interests of maintaining communal peace; as a symbolic system, using gesture and dress to provide useful information instantly about the status and friendliness or hostility of strangers; and as a system of ritual that expresses cultural cohesiveness and gives supportive community guidance for momentously emotional occasions.

It would be gratifying to find that the particular practices are all equally valid and workable, and that the differences occur because each society has known what would work best for its particular circumstances. Alas, we know, not least from our own history, that the manners principles of showing respect and according dignity to all are not always honored in societies' etiquette rules. While claiming a high degree of civilized behavior, such societies rationalize this deviation by defining whole segments of their populations to be not quite human because of race, gender or class.

There is work to be done everywhere in adjusting etiquette to conform with enlightened principles of manners. And entertainment to be had in the research compiled here.

—JUDITH MARTIN (AKA MISS MANNERS®)

A soldier tenderly kisses the hand of a lady.

INTRODUCTION

Everyone knows the Golden Rule, no matter how it's phrased: Do unto others as you would have others do unto you. But some people might be surprised to know that not only is the Golden Rule not an invention of our Western culture's Judeo-Christian roots, it's not tied to any religion per se. The concept of treating others as one would like to be treated is an ancient and worldwide rule for living that is also referred to as "the ethic of reciprocity."

How we treat other people affects how they treat us. That's also what's meant by the phrase "teach others how to treat you": Humans learn first and best by example. We're mimickers, after all. Practicing common courtesy means applying respect for other beings indiscriminately, across lines of status, wealth, education, gender, age, et cetera. However, the book you are reading isn't simply about the common courtesy you or I practice. It's about different ways common courtesy is practiced and demonstrated around the world, including different cultures, regions, and even time periods.

I have long been fascinated by books about manners and etiquette. One of my most treasured possessions is a copy of Emily Post's *Etiquette* with a special blue dust jacket: her "wartime" edition, published in 1943. It would be special enough for its vintage status and for its meaning to me as I married an active-duty military officer, but the dear friend who gave it to me as a wedding shower gift found one carefully inscribed with the previous owner's first initial and last name: the same as mine. This doesn't indicate a supernatural connection to me—what it does indicate is that people are connected through manners and habits.

Even when I read about a practice that now seems outdated (we've included some of those in our "Archaic Manners" sidebars), I enjoy thinking and learning about why that rule was once followed. Was it due to cultural beliefs? Supply and demand? Basic human kindness? I hope it won't surprise readers to find out that the customs based on the latter are the ones that have stood the test of time. As our "Mannered Lives" biographies will also show you, from ancient civilizations to present-day societies, simple rules work best. Don't complain too much. Keep things clean so that family members are comfortable and guests don't get sick. Tell the truth. Respect your elders.

Another idea that is very important to the Golden Rule is delayed gratification; reciprocation for kindness seldom happens instantly. A group will throw a feast for a birth or a wedding, knowing that a feast will be held when one of their members has a reason to celebrate—even if that's weeks, months, or years in the future. People follow traditions (some that make perfect sense, others that don't) for centuries, and you can see evidence of that in our "Objects of Etiquette." Of course, to err is human—so there are occasions when people attempt to follow rules of traditions and fail, seen in our "Famous Gaffe" stories.

There are many fantastic etiquette books that provide prescriptive advice for how to behave in any situation. This book won't tell you which fork to use or how to dress, or the phrases that will most positively influence your new manager or in-laws, but it will show how people do things in other parts of the world and where our own notions of particular manners come from. You'll be surprised, entertained, and perhaps even relieved to read of the ways in which common courtesy has evolved across the globe. I hope that this volume may provide a window into both ways of looking at manners and mores: the systematic, and the serendipitous.

On a professional note, writing *An Uncommon History of Common Courtesy* allowed me the great pleasure not only of rereading the volumes written by one of my favorite "Manners Mavens" but also working with her. I'm speaking of the incomparable Judith Martin, also very well known as "Miss Manners," whose Foreword now graces this book.

—**BETHANNE PATRICK**
Arlington, Virginia
June 2011

1

SHAKE HANDS, TIP HATS

The earliest origins of making a movement or sound to acknowledge the presence of another human being were probably geared toward personal safety: Early humans might have been unsure of a strange person's motives, and signaling one's approach could ward off an attack motivated by surprise or fear. In some indigenous societies that have remained relatively true to their ancient roots, such as the Wanniya-laeto of Sri Lanka, greeting rituals still include a slow approach to the elder's hut to demonstrate peaceful intent.

However, once the elder of the Wanniya-laeto community comes out to meet a person, he does so with both hands and makes direct eye contact, to express that all people have dignity. In essence, this desire is where modern forms of greeting come from—the wish to provide attention and respect to others.

In this chapter, we examine the courtesies and greetings that smooth all of our paths to what is less likely to be a hut than an apartment building, office complex, school, or single-family home. Likewise, we may no longer take the time to engage in elaborate introductions, but we still greet, shake, bow, clap, and more when we meet or take leave of our fellow humans.

An 1880s American ideal of the male handshake

HANDSHAKES

S HAKING HANDS SEEMS SO SIMPLE, yet can be fraught with so many concerns. Does the other person have germs on her dirty hands? Is the other person forbidden by religious beliefs from putting his hand into a woman's? What if you have terrible arthritis, and a handshake brings pain?

For many reasons you may be in a position to decline a handshake. That doesn't mean, however, that you are allowed to pretend you don't know how common and significant the handshake is, in societies all around the world. As Miss Manners says of handshakes, " . . . the gesture itself has been so well known that a refusal to participate must be explained ('I'm so sorry, but I can't shake hands.') because a refusal to shake hands is a symbolic insult (and thus a handy gesture when faced with tyrants and outlaws)."

There is not a soul who does not have to beg alms of another, either a smile, a handshake, or a fond eye.

—JOHN EMERICH EDWARD DALBERG ACTON

We'll never know for sure if handshakes originated to demonstrate that neither person was holding a weapon. We do know that handshakes are depicted in Greek art as early as the fifth century B.C. However, since our current use of this gesture is in greeting and introduction as a way to show you are "open" to another person, the idea that it came about from two men laying down their arms is not improbable.

Why do we shake with our right hands? Again, we may never know the factual beginnings of this custom, but it may have come about because some cultures consider the left hand "sinister" from associations with demons, or "unclean" from associations with life's less hygienic side.

You cannot shake hands with a clenched fist.
—INDIRA GANDHI

Good Grips

NOBODY WANTS A WIMPY HANDSHAKE. We are judged by whether or not our handshakes are strong and steady; if they're weak and limp, it can make a bad impression, ranging from "She's a business risk" to "He's troubled." Why the concern with a firm grip?

The gesture has always shown trust between two people. A strong, steady clasp meant a person was unlikely to attack, as he was also vulnerable. Some historians think the handshake evolved from soldiers' gripping each other's hands while patting down forearms for concealed weapons. A strong grip on the hand would prevent an adversary from pulling a knife from his breastplate or boot.

Ancient Assyrians keep weapons from handshake.

Countries including the United States, Canada, the United Kingdom, and members of the European Union favor a brief shake. In the U.S. and England, a strong grip is common, but in many other countries, a lighter clasp is preferred. In China, the grip is firm but not too strong, as hands are often pumped up and down for several minutes rather than for a few seconds as in the West.

People in Arab countries may be constrained by religious rules: Many Islamic men do not shake hands with women, and when they shake with men, they prefer a weak or limp clasp followed by holding each other's wrists or forearms. No matter what form a handshake takes, it is a gesture between people who want to show each other at least a modicum of goodwill. Think about that the next time you head into a dreaded meeting; it might make things easier.

This handshake connotes political partnership.

*More history is made by secret handshakes
than by battles, bills, and proclamations.*
—JOHN BARTH

More Than a Handshake

IF YOU TRAVEL IN the Muslim world, you may often find yourself extending your arm in greeting and having your hand enclosed in two. Your hand will be grasped as usual, then covered with the other person's left hand.

Many travelers enjoy this welcoming grasp, part of the gracious enthusiasm of Middle Eastern hospitality. Although shaking hands in greeting existed long before the Prophet Muhammad's birth, he specifically states in the Koran that "there are no two Muslims who meet and shake hands with one another, but they will be forgiven before they part." Shaking hands with fellow believers is part of Islam's etiquette, not simply a cultural mandate but a spiritual directive that many inhabitants believe in very strongly even today.

Like most things in the world's religions, this practice involves a controversy. Are Muslims

Whirling handclasp captured by phenakistoscope

meant to shake with one hand, or with two? Some Islamic authorities deem it against *sunnah* (accepted custom) to shake with both hands. There are long disquisitions about this, with some clergy and scholars believing that two hands is the only proper and scripture-approved method. Depending on how strict these clergy and scholars are, the handshakes discussed will be between two men, because physical contact between a man and a woman who are not married is forbidden in orthodox Islam.

Yet because the countries that make up the Middle East are so diverse, visitors will find many people—male and female, Muslim and Christian and Jewish, old and young—warmly shaking one hand with two. The important thing is to be conscious of the tradition, but open to breaking it when you meet a person who is more modern in his or her approach. Then you'll find yourself truly welcomed.

ARCHAIC MANNERS: Don't Wear White After Labor Day Whether this rule was meant to distinguish those who could afford seasonal wardrobes and good laundering from those who couldn't, given the modern sense of social equality as well as effective stain-fighting detergents, it's no longer universally acknowledged, although some proper people still observe it.

I can feel the twinkle of his eye in his handshake.
—HELEN KELLER

Symbolic Shakes

THE PHRASE "SECRET HANDSHAKE" has long been used to indicate archly that a group or activity involves membership requirements revealed only to a select few. Although many different associations have associated handshakes, the most famous of them all is that of the Freemasons.

The "Masonic handshake" isn't singular; these "grips" and "tokens," as they are known to Freemasons, number at least half a dozen officially and may include many more, depending on the Freemason's degree, lodge, and country of origin (among other factors). The well-known Masonic handshakes have ancient and biblical-sounding names like the boaz, the shibboleth, the jachin, the tubalcain, and the ma-ha-bone that enhance their air of mystery.

The names are memorable, but the differences between them are subtle—a pressed joint here, a raised thumb there—so subtle that an onlooker would not be able to distinguish between them if he were not a Freemason as well. There's a good reason for that. While there may or may not be any real mysteries to Freemasonry, the origin of these handshakes has a firm foundation in history. The original "freemasons" were actually stonemasons; the "free" appended to their name meant that they were not tied to one guild or location, but were allowed to move freely about their regions to work.

However, in premodern times when most people didn't have documents or other printed identification, it could be difficult to figure out who actually had proper qualifications. Building large stone structures can be an exacting and dangerous business, so knowing that a potential mason had been well trained was important, lest someone who had no knowledge of masonry be hired and tragedy ensue. These "secret" handshakes allowed building managers to know quickly and with certainty who had been trained, because if the mason knew his trade, he was given the handshake as his calling card.

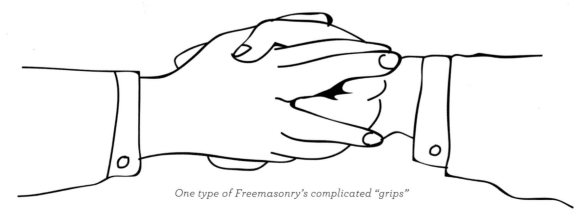

One type of Freemasonry's complicated "grips"

The postman wants an autograph. The cab driver wants a picture.
The waitress wants a handshake. Everyone wants a piece of you.
—JOHN LENNON

Other Clasps and Grasps

WHEN PRESIDENT BARACK and First Lady Michelle Obama touched fists before the 2008 presidential nomination acceptance speech, their gesture set off a storm of controversy in the American media. Why? Because some people believe that "giving dap," as the fist bump is most commonly known, is a symbol of radical race politics.

If they only knew how genteel the gesture's origins might be! Some social historians trace it to cricket players touching their bulky, padded gloves. Others believe the tradition came about through the military during the Vietnam era, and that the term "dap" comes from "dapper." What is certain is that today "dap" is an acronym for "dignity and pride" meant to show members of the African-American community that they had both. With the rise of hip-hop and rap music in the 1980s, nontraditional hand clasps became more widespread.

The Obamas elatedly exchange a "fist bump."

Hip-hop handshakes today can be a simple fist bump or knuckle tap—or may involve an elaborate and choreographed series of moves including slaps, slides, and flexes, and even a fingergrip that looks like the start of a thumb-wrestling match. But the shakes' roots may owe more to the world of sports (see cricket, above) than modern rappers and hipsters might like. "High fives" and "low fives" were exuberant hand slaps that athletes began exchanging in 1950s America when handshakes seemed too formal and old-fashioned.

So dap, bump, tap, slide, or flex. The goal is to exchange warm wishes with a friend for whom the gesture is equally comfortable. Regardless of nomenclature, we say this high-spirited gesture is worthy of applause both on and off presidential turf.

BOWING

EARLY 21ST-CENTURY MEN AND WOMEN in Western cultures are more likely to encounter a traditional bow on a stage than in real life, accustomed as we are to actors, dancers, musicians, and other types of performers "taking a bow" at the end of a performance.

However, bowing was not only once commonplace in the West; it was also primarily the province of men. While many female performers now bow from the waist along with their male counterparts, others still adhere to the long-accepted feminine equivalent: the "curtsey" or "curtsy," which combines a bow of the head with a knee bend. No one knows exactly how this evolved, although we may speculate that it was so women wearing low necklines would not risk unwanted exposure.

While today a curtsey above the footlights looks charming, its origins (as Miss Manners reminds us) come from the practice of an inferior lowering his or her body before a superior. In other words, for hundreds of years, women making curtseys implicitly acknowledged that men had higher status.

At the end of the day when we bow our heads, we are not so different at all.

—JUDY JONES

Fortunately, today women in many cultures, if not equal to men in all aspects of social and workplace life, do have equal rights legally. (This may be one reason that the more egalitarian handshake is popular in global business.) Yet some handshakes are still derided as "feminine" and the curtsey is still for women.

Still, we will see that bowing takes many different forms and has many different purposes, some of which will remain proper etiquette in their realms long after debates about gender equality have ended. The reason performers "take" bows is to acknowledge the audience's respect for their time. All bows, at their best, are meant to indicate respect.

Bow, stubborn knees!
—WILLIAM SHAKESPEARE

Bend or Break

SOME OF THE EARLIEST DEPICTIONS of bows were in reverence to awesome natural phenomena, like thunderstorms or the Northern Lights. The English verb "to bow" does have precedents in Old English, Old Norse, and Goth (*bugen, biugen, buga*), and there are many images of bowing in Indian Mughal-era art. It's hard to say where or why bowing began, but we know some of its uses.

Early humans often bowed down to the divine power and punishment they linked to sunrises and natural disasters. The yogic "salute to the sun" is one such bow.

Bowing at the waist in greeting comes from the Old English verb *bugan*. It means "to bend in submission," which in turn comes from the Old Norse *bjugr*, "to bend."

A bewigged courtier bows in respect.

Theatrical greetings between rogue and ingenue

These words, as well as others (Old High German's *biogan*) come from an Indo-European root, *bheug*. (The Indo-European language family is considered the foundation of most modern Western languages.) *Bheug* does not mean "to bow"; its best modern translation is "to turn to account."

In other words, *bheug* was about acknowledging debt. As time passed and the area we now call Western Europe was settled by tribal cultures like the Vikings and the Goths, the authority of a leader became crucial to survival. As the power of leaders grew, the idea of loyalty to your leader also grew. Verbs derived from the root *bheug* came to denote bending to a leader's will—and eventually, physically bowing meant the same.

I never will, by any word or act, bow to the shrine of intolerance or admit a right of inquiry into the religious opinions of others.
—THOMAS JEFFERSON

How Low Can You Go?

THE TERM KOWTOW COMES FROM Chinese, but it's now part of the English language. You might see the term, which relates to bowing, in a headline about which side is yielding in a political or diplomatic conflict, or you could hear it in conversation, sometimes in a negative respect. Someone might say, "I'm not going to kowtow to his demands," meaning that the speaker does not intend to give in, or plans to buck authority.

However, the idea behind the Chinese origins of the kowtow or *ketou* came from Confucian philosophy and was meant to convey respect and submission rather than mere despotism. (*Kóu* meant "knock with reverence"; *ke* meant "touch upon the ground"—thus, the meaning does alter a bit depending upon which form is used.) The philosopher Confucius (551-479 B.C.) believed that body movements influenced the mind, and therefore a deep bow would remind a person that he or she should be humble.

Should you want to practice the traditional kowtow, start by kneeling. Then, from that position, bend from the waist until your forehead touches the floor. Depending on whom you're kowtowing to, and the amount of respect you want to show, you might repeat this once, twice, or even three times.

Practice of the kowtow reached its height during the Han Dynasty, when an audience before the emperor required "three kneels and nine bows." Although it is much rarer today, the kowtow is still an important part of some ceremonies including martial-arts apprenticeships and after weddings, when the newly married

le Roy monté sur son Elephant.

Subjects in prostration to their king

couple will often kowtow to their parents or visit gravesites to kowtow to their ancestors.

Western negativity toward the kowtow may have developed due to the Chinese court rituals surrounding it, which convinced diplomats from Europe that it was some kind of religious gesture. In China neither Confucianism nor the kowtow is seen as religious; the kowtow is simply another (albeit formal) kind of greeting.

I love you when you bow in your mosque; kneel in your temple; pray in your church. For you and I are sons of one religion, and it is the spirit.
—KAHLIL GIBRAN

A Real Head Turner

An actress curtseys at curtain call.

Debutantes, or "debs," were supposed to be young women of good lineage who were ready for courtship and marriage, so most dances, balls, and cotillions still take place when the young women are about 18 years old, even though most 21st-century 18-year-olds are far from walking down the aisle.

At these occasions, the debs are still scrutinized—and some have developed elaborate curtseys. The "Dallas Dive" or "Texas Dive" is a quadricep-challenging dip to the floor with a final turn of the head to the left so no lipstick stains her gown.

SOME BOWS NO LONGER HAVE much to do with their original invention—and (since we're equal-opportunity here) the same goes for curtseys.

Women curtseyed often when they were legally dependent on men. A curtsey (from "courtesy") showed respect and deference. (Of course, this is technically also what a man's bow should show to a woman.)

Curtseys became highly ritualized at European courts, where a lady's curtsey before a monarch could make or break her social standing. Everything from her hairstyle to her posture was scrutinized. The United States of America emulated the Old Country tradition by presenting young ladies to society at "debutante balls."

A ballet dancer's curtsey-like pose

MANNERED LIVES

Ptah-Hotep of Ancient Egypt

Move over, Emily Post: The first doyen of good manners lived during the Egyptian 5th dynasty and first formed his etiquette guide around 2880 B.C. He was Ptah-Hotep, the vizier (first minister) during the reign of Pharaoh Djedkare Isesi (Tanchares, in Greek). He was attributed by his grandson Ptahhotep Tshefi as the author of *The Maxims of Ptah-Hotep*. The oldest surviving copy of the manuscript, known as the Prisse Papyrus, is now on display at the Louvre in Paris.

Many of Ptah-Hotep's writings sound remarkably contemporary: "Follow your heart as long as you live"; "Do not covet more than your share"; "Do not vex the heart of one who is burdened." Others, from rules about gender roles to dictates concerning superiors, are products of a specific era. Some seem so obvious to our modern sensibilities that it's hard to imagine that people needed such reminders. Consider Ptah-Hotep's thoughts on visiting a home: "If you desire to excite respect within the house you enter, for example the house of a superior, a friend, or any person of consideration . . . keep yourself from making advances to a woman, for there is nothing good in so doing."

However, even when Ptah-Hotep's rules seem outdated, their overall concern is for the oppressed and the weak: women of his era, the sick or afflicted, servants, and children.

While it's doubtful that anyone's living room contains a papyrus scroll of Ptah-Hotep's maxims, the Egyptian administrator nonetheless is the oldest existing source of the sort of collected advice that everyone's parents like to make sure they do keep somewhere handy on a shelf. Behave like *this* Egyptian and you'll give new meaning to the phrase "old-fashioned good manners."

Ancient Egyptian bureaucrat Ptah-Hotep authored manners guidelines.

The savage bows down to idols of wood and stone,
the civilized man to idols of flesh and blood.
—GEORGE BERNARD SHAW

Bowing to No One

ONCE UPON A TIME, everyone bowed to the king and queen because they ruled absolutely. If you didn't bow—say, in Han China—you could be beaten or even executed.

Today people in most cultures understand that no particular class has divinely granted powers over others, and no set of rulers has been empowered by a heavenly force. The "divine right of kings" is as much a fairytale as anything the Brothers Grimm wrote. No human ruler has the right to execute someone simply for failing to perform a bow.

At different points in human history, people have challenged absolute authority. One revolt that has had a great impact is the American Revolution. In 1773 American colonists who called themselves patriots refused to submit to the British crown's authority. In their first act of subversion, "The Boston Tea Party," patriots who opposed the royal tax on tea dumped chest after chest of imported tea leaves into Boston Harbor.

The American patriots knew that refusing to submit to authority would literally mean not bowing to authority. Once the Declaration of Independence had been set down on paper, Americans were officially recorded as a nation that considered all persons equal. (We can argue later about women and minorities.)

If everyone is worthy of equal respect, then a simple handshake should suffice as a greeting. Americans have long believed that when a foreign monarch is on our shores, no American President should bow to him or her.

In 1773, U.S. patriots defied the British by throwing tea chests into Boston Harbor.

KISSING & HUGGING

KISSING AND HUGGING OFTEN FORM PARTS OF INTIMATE, romantic moments—but they also happen in public. Like other greetings and gestures discussed in this chapter, kissing and hugging have rules governing when, where, how, why, and to whom they are bestowed.

Unlike other greetings, kissing and hugging involve coming into close contact with another person—and that can raise all sorts of mannerly questions. Do I know this person well enough to hug her? Why is this man's breath so terrible? When will Aunt Hilda stop pinching my cheeks? There's no ignoring another human's smell and feel when you lean in, but getting closer can provide pleasant information, since our lips have a high density of nerve endings.

While anthropologists debate where the instinct for kissing comes from (is it instinctual, or learned?), most humans receive first kisses from a mother, father, or other caregiver. "Kisses of affection" get us used to the warm feelings that they engender, which is a good thing; as adults, romantic kisses encourage the brain's release of dopamine.

> *Man is deceiv'd by outward Show—/'Tis a plain homespun Truth I know;/ The Fraud prevails at every Age,/So says the School-boy, and the Sage:/Yet still we hug the dear Deceit . . .*
>
> —NATHANIAL COTTON, PHYSICIAN AND POET

Scientists are not sure whether other animal species actually kiss—but they are convinced that other species hug (although dog owners should be aware that pack animals usually interpret any gestures involving limbs as dominance). Of course, some species that hug also publicly groom each other, picking fleas from body hair and cleaning each other's ears. We suggest getting to know Aunt Hilda extremely well before attempting any of these feats. In the meantime: How about a hug?

I don't know how to kiss, or I would kiss you.
Where do the noses go?
—INGRID BERGMAN IN THE FILM *FOR WHOM THE BELL TOLLS*, 1943

20 Kinds of Kisses

SOME CULTURES—including England and America, until relatively recently—do not have a tradition of social kissing. In these societies, handshakes and sometimes hugs are the most common greetings.

But many other cultures have been kissing in greeting for hundreds of years, and have evolved particular habits. Most fall under the ancient Roman category of *osculum*, or a kiss on the cheek. (Those classification-happy Romans also delineated *basium* as a kiss on the lips and *savolium* as a "deep kiss.")

Gustav Klimt's "The Kiss"
shows an osculum.

Unlike the other types of kisses (some historians specify 20 kinds of kisses, but they refer to purpose, not physicality), the kiss on the cheek is usually given in friendship, greeting, comfort, or respect. In France, the tradition is known as *faire la bise* and generally refers to a kiss on each cheek. However, the number of kisses given varies

widely according to region in France—and it also varies in other countries. In Brazil two kisses are standard, but a third might be offered for "luck" if the recipient is unmarried. One of the most entrenched traditions is in the Netherlands, where kisses of greeting between friends and relatives always number three. Women kiss both males and females three times in succession, but men generally reciprocate only with women. With other men, they confine physical greetings to a handshake. Although the three kisses can look like an awkward head-bobbing dance, it is terribly impolite to refuse.

Why? "It's a Dutch thing," is the answer.

But wait! Kissing three times on alternating cheeks is also traditional in Egypt, Russia, Slovenia, Serbia, Bosnia, Herzegovina, Macedonia, and Montenegro. Hmmm. Maybe not such a "Dutch thing" after all.

FAMOUS GAFFES: George W. Bush winks at Queen Elizabeth II In a 2007 speech welcoming Britain's Queen Elizabeth II, U.S. President George W. Bush made it sound as if she were alive 200 years ago. Trying to mitigate his verbal gaffe, the President made a physical one: He winked at the monarch. Her Majesty glared at the world leader, who later remarked that she "gave me a look that only a mother could give a child."

A kiss can be a comma, a question mark or an exclamation point.
That's basic spelling that every woman ought to know.
—MISTINGUETT, *THEATRE ARTS*, 1955

The Penalties of Public Kissing

SOME OF THE MOST FAMOUS IMAGES in world art are of people engaging in "PDA"—a humorous English abbreviation of the phrase "public display of affection." Think of the V-J Day photograph of a nurse and a soldier kissing in Times Square, or of Gustav Klimt's oil painting "The Kiss."

Even simpler: Think of lovers kissing all over Paris, a city celebrated for its open displays of smooching and hugging. While no one wants to see overtly sexual acts on streets, in parks, or in other public spaces, many people are cheered to see happy couples kiss and embrace. Today in many countries around the world opposite-sex and same-sex couples stroll hand in hand or cuddle in restaurant booths, and no one looks askance.

However, there are still cultures in which the simplest peck on the cheek between a man and a woman can cause an outcry if seen in public. Actually, the consequences can be much stronger than an "outcry"; in early 2010, a Saudi Arabian man was given 90 lashes of a whip and four years in prison for kissing a woman in a shopping mall. Later that year, the vice chancellor of a Nigerian university threatened severe punishment for anyone hugging female students. In 2009, a British couple was arrested for kissing at a resort in Dubai.

Today, strict segregation of the sexes is the law in some Islamic states, but it's worth remembering that at different times in history, penalties for PDA have seemed extreme in other places, too: Think of Puritan America, where a wayward embrace might result in a woman spending hours in "the stocks," or of Oscar Wilde's years in Reading Gaol for kissing Lord Alfred Douglas. We change our attitudes regarding what is permissible in public all the time, and it bears thinking about before condemnation is involved.

LIFE *magazine's classic Times Square WWII VJ-Day clinch from 1945*

A hug is like a boomerang—
you get it back right away.
—BILL KEANE, "FAMILY CIRCUS"

Manly Hugging

HUGGING—PLACING ONE'S ARMS around another person—is not only a universal gesture signifying everything from friendship to comfort to love, but also healthy. Hugging can lower stress, generate hormones, and reduce blood pressure, according to researchers.

Such findings support the idea that human animals are meant to have frequent physical contact (the jury's still out on flea-picking). Yet the amount of hugging, hand-holding, and the like varies greatly between cultures. The same scientists looking into the health benefits of hugging found that Parisian couples have up to three times more physical contact than American couples. (A few cultures, like the tribal Himba in Namibia, do not hug at all.)

Yet hugs are not always romantic or sexual, as anyone who has been hugged by her best friend or by a child knows. Some of the most vital "hugging traditions" are greetings.

The Latin American *abrazo* transcends boundaries: Unlike cheek kisses in other parts of the world, which people use to greet both friends and acquaintances, the abrazo is a warm hug between intimates. Men practice it with particular gusto, enfolding friends and relatives of both sexes in an all-encompassing "bear hug" that lasts for as long as a minute. There are even variations: *un abrazo muy fuerte* is a tight hug. The abrazo is such a close embrace that it is the name given to the "tango hug" in the traditional ballroom dance.

*A compliment is something like
a kiss through a veil.*
—VICTOR HUGO, *LES MISÉRABLES*, 1862

Ring Kissing

IN 2010 DR. BILL MURPHY, the Bishop of Kerry, made news when he said he was "embarrassed" at being expected to kiss Pope Benedict's ring. He called the practice "out of touch with modern thinking."

Ceremonial kissing of the pope's ring may not be modern, but it does have a specific tie to Christian doctrine. In the New Testament, disciples of Christ are instructed to "greet each other with a holy kiss," a tradition that continues today in Christian churches as the "sharing of the peace." Today this involves kisses on the cheek, brief hugs, or handshakes. It is still meant as a sign of mutual forgiveness.

A Roman Catholic or Episcopal communicant who kisses a bishop's ring (or, in the case of the Catholic, the pope's) is certainly acknowledging a cleric's authority, but that authority is

The longest-reigning pope, Pius IX, served as pontiff from 1846 to 1878.

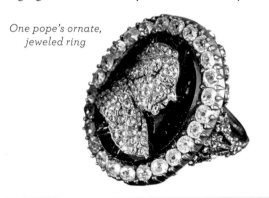

One pope's ornate, jeweled ring

meant to stand for Jesus Christ's own and for forgiveness in the same way.

In other words, someone kissing the pope's ring is not worshipping the pope. However, this doesn't mean that the tradition of kissing the "Ring of the Fisherman," as each individually cast ornament is known, should continue. Clergy members like Dr. Murphy understand the pope's role, yet would prefer not to kiss his ring.

ARCHAIC MANNERS: Hand Kissing Although the kissing of a lady's hand by a gentleman was once an ultimately genteel (although sometimes seen by North Americans as "too Continental") expression of good manners, today hand kisses are usually avoided in favor of the more egalitarian handshake. In the case of "Continental" manners, a double-cheek kiss is often the substitute.

GREETINGS & SALUTATIONS

ACKNOWLEDGING THE PRESENCE OF ANOTHER PERSON is a universal instinct, in fact it's so universal that the worst way to insult another person in many cultures would be to fail to acknowledge that person. However, while the acknowledgment is universal, the ways in which we manifest it are many and varied. From a baby's first recognition of its mother or parents to a simple wave of greeting on to formal kowtowing of Chinese subjects and the complex dance of diplomacy, greetings and salutations make the world's interactions go much more smoothly.

What is the appropriate behavior for a man or a woman in the midst of this world...What's the proper salutation between people as they pass each other in this flood?

—BUDDHA

In this section, we've collected a number of ways that humans begin to communicate. That communication may be done in person, in printed correspondence, by phone, or by such electronic means as texting or email. When two or more people meet face-to-face, words, gestures, and facial expressions can all combine to enrich the meaning of a greeting, while the same words conveyed by phone, in ink, or on a screen may be construed somewhat differently.

The most important thing about all greetings and salutations is that they are meant, by their very existence, to smooth over differences and conflicts between people and make it easier for communication to take place. That communication might be as simple as inquiring about someone else's health or as complicated as negotiating a treaty, but if all involved start off on the right foot—or with the right attitude—things will be easier. That's what good manners are about, after all.

So when you're in Hawaii,
you should just hang loose.
—HAMANA KALILI

Sunny Salute

EVEN MANY PEOPLE WHO HAVE not been lucky enough to visit Hawaii are familiar with its ubiquitous "shaka" greeting, which consists of a hand with thumb and pinkie fingers extended and three middle fingers curled towards the palm, wiggled from side-to-side. The gesture indicates everything from "Hello" to "Everything's cool" to "See you later."

Hawaiians consider the shaka sign to be a symbol of what they call the "Aloha Spirit," which includes an easygoing attitude toward life and work, as well as an understanding of the diversity of people who inhabit the eight large tropical islands that make up Hawaii. Several sources, including the Polynesian Cultural Center, trace the origin of this distinctive gesture to a man named Hamana Kalili (1882-1958) who lived in the Laie area, on the northeastern shore of Oahu, nearly 40 miles north of Honolulu.

Kalili worked at the Kahuku Sugar Plantation and, although some have suggested he lost his middle fingers while battling with a shark over a fish or when he was fishing with dynamite, his hand was most likely injured when something went wrong at a sugar mill. At that time, sugarcane was fed through powerful rollers to extract its sweet juice, and according to an interview his nephew gave to the *Honolulu Star,* Kalili got his fingers caught in the mechanism one day. After the accident, he waved to people by holding up the hand that had only a thumb and a pinky finger. Eventually, something about Hamana Kalili's new wave would catch on.

Kalili spent a great deal of time at his local Mormon church, a touchstone of the Laie community. When young people who enjoyed his spirit began imitating Kalili's hand movement, a local car salesman named Lippy Espinda decided to feature it in his television commercials. Soon, people of all ages around the islands were bending their middle fingers into their palms and waving their pinkies and thumbs; the shaka sign became a casual greeting. Through surfer culture, the gesture has spread to Florida and parts of Latin America as well.

*Alas! it is true: "Be polite to bores and so
shall you have bores always round about you."*
—EMILY POST, *ETIQUETTE IN SOCIETY, IN BUSINESS, IN POLITICS AND AT HOME* (1922)

"How Do You Do?"

IF YOU RESEARCH "How are you?" in English, one of the first things you'll learn about is the British construction "How do you do?" That phrase has long been considered the proper way for upper-class Britons to greet each other, the plebeian "Hello" being relegated to the hoi polloi.

Dig a little deeper, however, and you'll find that it wasn't simply the shoutlike "Hello" (derived from the Old English "Hallo" and more of an announcement than a cordial greeting) that was under siege. It was the growing 19th-century and early 20th-century practice of saying "Pleased to meet you" to new acquaintances.

As pretentious as this might sound to modern ears, arbiters of manners like Emily Post and her British counterparts believe that it is presumptuous and false to tell a stranger that you are pleased to meet them. The only exception Mrs. Post made was when you had "through friends in common, long heard of a certain lady, or gentleman, and you know that she, or he, also has heard much of you."

A charming illustration of mannerly children

Interestingly enough, what experts feel is false in English doesn't hold true for other languages and cultures. In French and German, for example, it is common and polite to say *"Enchanté de faire votre connaissance"* or *"Es freut mich, Sie kennen zu lernen"* ("I am delighted to make your acquaintance"). Perhaps it is the formality built into those languages, with their *votre* and *Sie* second-person pronouns, that differentiates the exchanges. In French or German you might use a different word for "you" when addressing a superior than you would use for addressing a friend, but in English anyone—even a famous etiquette doyenne like Mrs. Post—can be addressed in the same way.

Today, of course, "Hello" has become a standard and accepted greeting, and is often followed by "How are you?"—a perfect example of how the status quo can effectively merge with newer practices. But if you see a member of the Post family, try not to blurt out "I'm so pleased to meet you!"

ARCHAIC MANNERS: Wedding Invitations Issued Only From Bride's Parents   Once upon a time, when the princess accepted the prince's proposal, her royal parents could foot the bill for the whole wedding extravaganza, and their names came first on the invitations. Nowadays, regular folks tend to split the bill and share top billing on invitation cards. The rule is that whoever hosts, issues the invites.

A man never knows how to say goodbye;
a woman never knows when to say it.
—HELEN ROWLAND

We'll Meet Again

SOMETIMES WE SAY "HELLO" to someone for the first time; sometimes we say "hello" to the same person many times. Similarly, we don't always say permanent words of leave-taking; often, the person to whom we wave "goodbye" is someone we'll see the next morning at the bus stop, conference table, or when we're picking up our bread, milk, and eggs from the store.

It was not ever thus. In more primitive times, when dangers ranged from catastrophic (wild animal attacks, natural disasters, frequent bloody battles) to domestic (disease, household accidents), taking leave of someone could be quite solemn and serious. It could also be an occasion for hope and good wishes

"Goodbye" in English comes from variations of "God be with you" ("until we meet again" is the understood second half of the phrase). Other languages also mention a deity, such as the Spanish *A dios*. In some Latin American countries, people use as *adios* as a quick greeting—it can be hello and goodbye and, literally, "to God" all at once. The word also makes neither party feel compelled to stop and chat. It might be said while passing a neighbor in the street, or called out to a passing motorist you'll never see again. But in some of those instances the meaning of leave-taking words that evoke a higher power is closer to a significant parting, perhaps one in which two or more people will not meet again for some time. In that case, quite a few languages offer alternatives to divine intervention, including "Strength to you" in the indigenous Mam language of Guatemala, and the Turkish "Stay in peace."

While modern life does has its pitfalls, changes in communication methods mean that most of us assume that if we say "See you tomorrow," that it will happen. Many languages include " 'til tomorrow" valedictory phrases, from Chechen to Hausa to Uzbek. Perhaps as the centuries have rolled by, people have become more confident in being able to see their friends and family "tomorrow."

A soldier's goodbye asks for strength.

That farewell kiss which resembles greeting, that last glance of love which becomes the sharpest pang of sorrow.
—GEORGE ELIOT

Where's the Beef?

THERE'S "GOODBYE" and then there's "farewell," which indicates that you don't know when you'll see someone again—but it could be soon.

At least one global "farewell" has a set ending, and that's the late-winter/early-spring tradition of Fat Tuesday/Mardi Gras/Carnival. While the festival may well have taken place for centuries before the Christian religion was established, it was the church's conception of a liturgical season symbolizing Jesus Christ's 40 days in the wilderness prior to his Crucifixion that led to the modern meaning.

The word "carnival" most likely comes from the Latin phrase *carne vale:* "farewell to the flesh" or "to the meat." Faithful members of the Christian Church were supposed to forgo anything rich, fatty, or fleshy during the 40-day period before the Easter holiday.

Because Christians (much like Jews before Passover, who cleanse their homes of anything leavened) are supposed to clear their pantries of all fats, sugars, meats, and dairy products before Lent begins, a tradition evolved in which communities gathered to eat as many of these foods as possible before the official "Ash Wednesday" start to the penitential season.

The day before Wednesday? Tuesday, of course—which began the Mardi Gras (Fat Tuesday) custom. In England it's known as Shrove Tuesday (when churchgoers are shriven, or absolved, of their sins) and in Germany as *Fasnacht,* derived from the name of a deep-fried pastry that's gobbled up in anticipation of the coming fast.

The irony in all of these celebrations is that the minute Easter Sunday arrives, meat, fats, and all manner of rich pastries are back on tables around the world. Not every "farewell" is "goodbye forever."

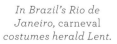

In Brazil's Rio de Janeiro, carneval *costumes herald Lent.*

HONORIFICS & NAMES

AN "HONORIFIC" ISN'T SPECIFICALLY an honorary degree or a title from British nobility; it's a noun (and, rarely, an adjective) placed before or after a person's given name to confer honor and respect. Some cultures have multilayered systems of honorifics linked to different levels of speech; Korea has seven different traditional speech levels (several of which are losing ground, but they still exist).

In some societies, the system of honorifics seems deliberately obtuse and meant to keep people of lower status in ignorance; for instance, the British peerage includes not just ranks for men and their wives, but also specific rules for referring to ranks followed by first—or first and last—names.

For centuries, most people did not travel far from their hometowns and lived in fairly homogeneous communities, so using honorifics to distinguish between one powerful person and another with the same name could be very important. In places where there were many similar names but very little power to go around, like Welsh mining towns, two men of the same name might be called by their talents: "Evan carvings" and "Evan songs."

> She certainly has a wonderful faculty of remembering people's names, and forgetting their faces.
>
> —OSCAR WILDE, *A WOMAN OF NO IMPORTANCE*, 1893

Now that so many people wind up living far away from their close relatives and often do not share the same values and systems of honorifics as those around them, honorifics have lost some power. In an age when adults sometimes tell children, "Call me Jane," there is a pull between recognizing the adult's wish and training the child properly. We still teach children to address adults using dignified titles, but experts in manners advise teaching children flexibility by instructing them to call adults by the titles the adults prefer. In this way children learn that showing respect for adults' wishes is more important than adhering to rigid rules.

If you want to save face, keep the lower half shut.
—ANN LANDERS

Go-betweens

MANY WESTERN CULTURES have business etiquette that is, if not informal, at least quite direct. An executive from one country who needs to meet with another from a different country will either make contact herself or through an executive assistant, using one or more forms of media (email, telephone, the post), depending on the situation. (Of course, the dance between the administrative assistants of two different executives can be its own complicated thing.)

However, in China business culture is quite a bit different. To the Chinese the concept of "face," loosely meaning honor and reputation, is of utmost importance and is given careful consideration during meetings, negotiations and other types of business discussions and arrangements. The Chinese prefer to do business and make introductions through intermediaries, meeting directly only after agreeable terms have been reached.

Intermediaries verify an outsider's credentials, beginning by receiving packets of information in advance and continuing by receiving business cards and letters of recommendation as requested. Companies or individuals will also often use an intermediary to ask questions that they would prefer not to address directly, such as details of financial transactions.

An intermediary holds a very respectable and public position in China. Businesspeople who come to that country use the intermediary's services to meet new contacts as well as to smooth over difficult and complicated

A Chinese opera mask "saves face."

negotiations with known contacts. When contacts do meet, introductions can be quite formal and always begin not with the highest ranking, but the oldest person present.

Aside from brief handshakes, no other physical or emotional contact will be made—that means no smiling and no laughing, and no attempts to be overly friendly. Sometimes, people will even avoid eye contact. Most important, one should never frown in disagreement during one of these real-life interactions. Treating someone with disrespect (negativity, informality, too much jokiness) is seen as embarrassing them in front of their peers.

A word, in a word, is complicated.
—STEVEN PINKER, *THE LANGUAGE INSTINCT*, 1994

An Unmarried Woman

IN THE EARLY 1970S when *Ms.* magazine came out in the United States, many people were offended. Why would a woman need to be referred to as anything other than "Miss" if she were single and "Mrs." if she were married?

Well, for a number of reasons—but here let's just note that men, regardless of what kind of relationship they're in or out of, are always called one thing: "Mr." in English, *"Monsieur"* in French, *"Mijnheer"* in Dutch, *"Signor"* in Italian, and so on and so forth.

For some reason, while all of these languages and many others had special terms for an unmarried woman—from *"Fräulein"* in German to *"Señorita"* in Spanish—very few had terms for an unmarried man. In English, the term "Master" is often used for boys, but usually just until they are about 12.

Even today, more than 30 years after feminists proposed "Ms." as the English alternative for women, there are people who dislike it. Meanwhile, during the second half of the 20th century around the world, cultures were quietly eliminating the use of "Miss" for adult females. For example, *"Fräulein"* is rarely heard as a term of address anymore in Germany; all women over the age of 18 are called *"Frau."*

Perhaps the most interesting fact in this controversy is that "Ms." is hardly a modern construction. The term is a contraction of "Mistress" and was originally meant to be used as a way of addressing a woman that carried no marital status—just like "Mister" for men.

Ms. magazine founders Gloria Steinem and Pat Carbine in their 1980 office

A language is a dialect with an army and a navy.
—LINGUIST MAX WEINREICH

Formal Feelings

FORMER FRENCH PRESIDENT Charles de Gaulle and his wife were married for more than 40 years. However, when they addressed each other (at least in public), they always used the formal *"vous"* second-person pronoun.

While this might sound in keeping with de Gaulle's post-World War II era, it hasn't vanished. In more recent years, President Jacques Chirac and his wife also use the formal "you."

French adults still use *"vous"* with professional colleagues and mere acquaintances. Close friends who use *"tu"* often ask each other *"On peut se tutoyer?"* ("May I address you informally?").

We speak about being "on a first-name basis" with other people, but in some countries, you may be on a first-name basis but still reserve the personal "you" for only your closest friends and relatives. Nonetheless, in some places, using a formal pronoun could sound cold to someone

The de Gaulles formally used "vous."

who considers herself a friend. At one time, the English language included "thee" and "thou," but contrary to what many people think, after Middle English, these words had grammatical and not reverential significance: "Thou" is nominative case, and "thee" is objective case.

In order to hear contemporary instances of the formal and informal "you" we need to look across the Atlantic. The "T-V distinction," as it is known by linguists, comes from the Latin *tu* and *vos*, which were originally simply the singular and plural of the second-person pronoun. The Spanish, *tu* and *vosotros* are still informal, and in some Latin American countries you'll hear people address friends and family as *vos*. In French, however, the informal and formal "you" are *tu* and *vous*. Generally, French children are addressed with the informal *tu* until they are about 16 years old, when both their teachers and colleagues will begin to use *vous* when speaking with them. Adult family members often call children *tu* no matter their age.

Spaniards say "tu" *and* "vos" *among friends.*

MANNERED LIVES

Confucius

In the West, we hear "Confucius" and think "Chinese philosopher," believing that name to be analogous to a moniker like "Erasmus" or "Jefferson." However, the name "Confucius" is actually a Western conglomeration of the Chinese characters for the great teacher's given name, Kong Qiu, and the title Fuzi, for "master." Regardless of his title, the name Confucius has become virtually synonymous with ideas of Chinese wisdom.

Master Kong Qiu was born in the sixth century B.C. to a poor family that had once been prominent and wealthy but had fallen on hard times, according to contemporary records. A lifelong autodidact, Confucius did manual labor (stablekeeping) and clerical work (bookkeeping) while learning the six arts of ritual, music, archery, charioteering, calligraphy, and arithmetic.

His own course of study convinced Confucius that education was the best form of self-improvement, and that self-improvement was the best route to true nobility and societal stability. At some time during his 30s, he began to teach, both in one place with students gathered around him, and on travels to other regions of China, where he was received by heads of state as an expert in the art of diplomacy.

Today, Confucianism is considered a religion by some, although unlike many other major world religions, it is less concerned with matters of spirituality than with matters of behavior and intellect. However, the *Analects*, Confucius's major work, contains models for developing and demonstrating values that are echoed in many other religious and philosophical systems, such as the belief that human life is the most important thing on earth.

The learned Chinese philosopher Confucius wrote extensively on manners.

What's in a name? That which we call a rose
By any other name would smell as sweet...
—WILLIAM SHAKESPEARE

Who's Your Daddy?

ICELANDERS ARE VERY STRICT about first names. So strict that any name a parent wishes for a baby must be on an approved list, or be signed off on by the Icelandic Naming Committee, which decides whether names fit with Icelandic grammar (they conjugate nouns along with verbs). When parents of a newborn recently proposed "Magnus," it was rejected; however, the Committee approved "Magnús." The difference may be only an accent mark to us, but to Icelanders, it represents their linguistic heritage.

The degree of scrutiny Icelanders apply to first names is no surprise given the role first names play in determining surnames. While surnames are not subject to approval, they follow a long tradition: Everyone—and that means everyone—in this homogeneous society has a last name that is one of their parents' first

names along with a gender noun. So, for example, if dear old dad was named Jon, then Jon's son will have the last name of—Jonsson. His daughter? Jonsdottir. Likewise if a son elected to choose his mother's name he could be known as Sigridsson; a daughter, Sigridsdottir.

Historically, other Scandinavian countries followed this same tradition of patronymics, but have now adopted the more common practice of inheriting father's surnames (as in the United States). Only Iceland still adheres to the custom. Although patronymics were the traditional model, they are now just as often matronymics (e.g., Karla's daughter has the last name Karlasdottir). In rare cases, a person will use a patronymic and a matronymic together, like former mayor of Reykjavik Dagur Bergþóruson Eggertsson.

Because this system can be confusing and because Icelanders do not use honorifics like Mr. and Mrs., many of them address each other using full names or with first names and abbreviations of their last names. If there are two men in a meeting named Einar, they might call each other "Einar Olafsson" and "Einar Sigursson" or "Einar Olaf" and "Einar Sigar."

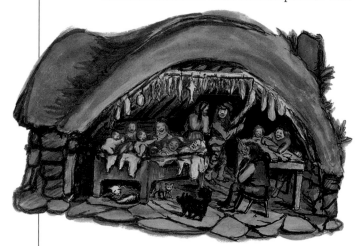

Icelandic families use patronymics.

GESTURES

G ESTURES COMMUNICATE SPECIFIC MESSAGES–sometimes more than one, depending on the gesture and where it is used. These forms of nonverbal communication are often quite specific, from the shape signifying a single letter in American Sign Language to a battle command.

Gestures can take the place of speech, as when someone places his hands at his throat to indicate that he is choking—or they can be used in conjunction with speech, as when a person holds her hand up while saying "I've heard enough!"

Human gestures can involve nearly all parts of the body, but one of the most important to discuss is the face. The eyes and mouth can be involved in specific gestures, but all of the facial features and muscles can be employed when, for instance, someone pleads (outstretched hands, raised eyebrows) or threatens (raised fist, tightened mouth). Sometimes a person gesturing will keep her face as neutral as possible deliberately, but in other instances the emotional range of human facial musculature can make a gesture more emphatic.

Gestures can be friendly, formal, celebratory, instructional, funny, or obscene. They can be made with one hand, two hands, shoulders, arms and wrists, legs, feet, and even the torso. Gestures can also be made together with other people, something that any Jimmy Buffett fan who has ever raised his arms to "Fins" will understand.

Since those "Fins" in the song are referring to a big fish, it's worth reminding everyone that gestures don't distinguish us from animals—they make gestures, too, especially during mating rituals. Is it any surprise that Buffett compared men trying to attract a single woman in a bar to circling sharks?

> *Grace was in all her steps, Heaven in her eye, In every gesture dignity and love.*
>
> —JOHN MILTON, *PARADISE LOST*

It is absurd to say that there are neither ruins nor curiosities in America when they have their mothers and their manners.
—OSCAR WILDE

Sole Offense

IN 2008 U.S. PRESIDENT George W. Bush was holding a news conference in Baghdad when an Iraqi journalist took off his shoe and flung it at the American leader. "This is a goodbye kiss from the Iraqi people, dog!" he yelled before throwing his other shoe as well. Bush ducked and the Secret Service tackled the television reporter.

The event puzzled, amused, and disturbed folks back home—and in Iraq a shoe sculpture was later built in honor of the shoe-throwing journalist—but the incident also exposed U.S. citizens to a taboo that's common in other countries: Shoes are considered extremely dirty, and exposing your feet or footwear to others can be highly insulting. In numerous cultures it is very impolite to show the soles of your feet or shoes to another person, whether by stretching your legs

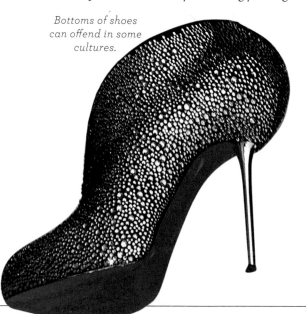

Bottoms of shoes can offend in some cultures.

out on the floor, crossing your legs, or pointing your foot up so that the sole becomes visible. In some places, such as Thailand, it is even ruder to have the bottom of your feet facing an image or representation of the Buddha. In Iraq, the country where President Bush dodged flying shoes, people also expressed their hatred for Saddam Hussein by beating their shoes and sandals on his toppled statue in 2003.

This isn't the result of a superstition or ritual as it is of common knowledge. Human beings walk upright on two legs anchored by feet, which means that the feet are the most likely body parts to come in contact with the dirt, garbage, and effluvia found on the ground. Even the most modern and industrialized nations have dirty sidewalks, streets, and buildings. No one's feet are immune from filth. Even if you arrive at a restaurant and immediately wash your hands, the soles of your feet or shoes will track in all sorts of bacteria. Feet keep us anchored to the earth, but they also unfortunately come in contact with all of the things that give us diseases.

Whether it is because the bottom of the foot is unhygienic or not, showing the sole to strangers is considered the height of disrespect in numerous places. This is true in Thailand, in Turkey, in Arabic-speaking nations, in Korea, in parts of Africa, and in China—in fact, in so many places that it is a good idea to learn to sit with your feet flat on the floor wherever you travel. Why risk being considered rude or threatening if you don't have to be?

No notice is taken of a little evil,
but when it increases it strikes the eye.
—ARISTOTLE

The Evil Eye

PEOPLE AROUND THE WORLD understand the phrase "evil eye," but different cultures interpret it—and its evil effects—differently.

Ancient peoples believed eyes were windows to human essence; a person casting an "evil eye" might transmit dangerous, ill humors. Socrates was said to have a "demon eye." His followers were called Blepedaimones, or "evil looks," as people believed they were under the Greek philosopher's spell.

The Hellenic concept of the evil eye was likely brought East about the time of Alexander the Great. Perhaps cemented by the Islamic belief in the evil eye, the idea stuck in what is now modern Turkey.

Hamsa amulets ward off the evil eye.

Turkey produced the famous *hamsa* or talisman against the evil eye, the *nazar boncuğu*—a representation of a blue eye. Folklore says these charms reflect or send the evil to its source. Speaking of source, it's pretty clear that the Turkish evil eye has Greek origins; in Greece it's called the "Eye of Medusa"—Medusa was a female monster in Greek mythology.

The concentric circles of the *nazar boncuğu* appear on walls, in jewelry, and on boats—but now also on airplane tails and on beads hanging from mobile phones.

A Turkish glass "evil eye" ornament

In defeat unbeatable; in victory unbearable.
—WINSTON CHURCHILL

Victorious

IF YOU'VE LISTENED to the distinctive and dramatic opening bars of Ludwig van Beethoven's Fifth Symphony—three short tones followed by a longer low tone—then you actually know a bit of Morse code: The three dots and a dash that signify the letter "V."

During some of the darkest days of World War II in early 1941, several people at the British Broadcasting Corporation (BBC) realized that if large segments of the Allies' populations displayed courage and conviction through a "V for Victory" hand gesture that the Axis Powers might be psychologically shaken. The "V" could stand for "victory" in English, *victoire* in French, and *vrijnheid* ("freedom") in Dutch and Flemish.

By midsummer of 1941 the "V for Victory" sign had gained widespread acceptance, so much so that British Prime Minister Winston Churchill began to flash it, often between puffs

Churchill flashes a "V for Victory" in 1940.

of his beloved Havanas—so his "V" sign was palm-in, cigar held between third and fourth fingers.

Unfortunately, Churchill—from an upper-class background—didn't realize that the palm-in "V" sign had a much different meaning for his less privileged countrymen, who had long used it to signal a strong, rude aversion to authority. This may have come from English longbowmen in medieval times showing French soldiers that their "trigger fingers" were intact, but by the early 20th century the sign's vulgar intent was cemented in the culture.

Today, the palm-in "V" sign can still get athletes sidelined in the United Kingdom, but the palm-out "V" sign experienced another metamorphosis. The sign's two-fisted use by U.S. President Richard Nixon to laud his 1968 election win was co-opted by "hippies" and other people who opposed Nixon's Vietnam War policy—and became the ultra-iconic "Peace" sign.

ARCHAIC MANNERS: Servant Bell For hundreds of years, wealthy homeowners could summon a member of their household staff by ringing a bell. Over the centuries, the handheld bell evolved into a bell fixed to the wall, activated a floor or more above by an unseen hand. Today, these bells have all but disappeared, with staff summons likely to arrive via mobile phone.

...Oh, maybe just whistle. You know how to whistle, don't you, Steve?
You just put your lips together, and blow.
—LAUREN BACALL, IN THE FILM *TO HAVE AND HAVE NOT*, 1944

Moscow Manners

WESTERNERS AT A MUSICAL CONCERT or play might clap their hands, shout "Bravo" and "Encore," or even yell and whistle. Loud, appreciative whistles are normal, whether on Broadway or at La Scala.

But at the Bolshoi, keep your pinkies out of your mouth and unpurse your lips. The whistle that shows praise in England is *nyekulturny* to Russians.

Nyekulturny loosely translates as "uncultured," and applies to many customs. For example, Russians never wear overcoats or snow boots past the entry way of a home, feeling that outside precipitation and dirt belong outside.

Also *nyekulturny:* slumping in chairs or sprawling on sofas, standing with hands in pockets, publicly mentioning a restroom visit, or lounging on a museum's steps.

Whistling isn't the only *nyekulturny* noise— speaking or laughing too loudly is frowned

In Russia the arts are highly respected.

Russian boots stay outside.

upon by sophisticated Russians. Part of the "nyekulturny" idea derives from the highly class-oriented pre-Russian Revolution czarist culture in which fine manners distinguished the nobility. Another part comes from the long decades of Communism when public decorum made long waits in shop lines and bureaucratic offices more bearable.

So, while in some places "whistle while you work" is a lighthearted way to pass the time, in Russia? Nyet to whistling and other forms of *nyekulturny!*

SAY THE MAGIC WORDS

Even if you never throw a dinner party, send out a formal wedding invitation, or meet the monarch of another country, in the course of your life you'll have to communicate with other human beings. That's why two of the sections in this chapter are titled "Saying Please" and "Saying Thank You." Communicating those words makes almost any interaction in any part of the world smoother and easier.

Likewise, while the previous chapter covered the sorts of physical greetings easily recognized by humans, this chapter's greetings are the verbal kind that make it possible for strangers to acknowledge each other with a certain degree of civility. Just as certain types of bows and waves indicate differences in status, so do the communications here convey meaning: There are several reasons for "saying please," and many ways of asking after someone's current state of being. (Who knew, in fact, that various cultures interpret "How are you?" in so many ways?)

Whether you are issuing a formal thank-you or saying a quick farewell, the quirks and customs in this particular chapter will remind you of how powerful it can be to state your manners. No wonder your mother told you that these are "the magic words!"

Work Projects Administration 1937 poster exhorts park visitors using "please."

SAYING PLEASE

FOR YOU—THEY ARE GIVING THEIR LIVES OVER THERE

FOR THEM—YOU MUST GIVE EVERY CENT YOU CAN SPARE

2nd WAR FUND—May 6-11

W HEN WAS THE FIRST "PLEASE" UTTERED? Could it have been "Eve, please give me a bite of that apple?" Perhaps—but according to etiquette experts, it's far more likely that the act of asking evolved along with rituals of "giving and taking." Humans started to acknowledge that they were taking something from another human in order to keep communal reciprocity working. In other words, you've got to ask to partake of someone else's whale blubber or crust of bread, and you also have to be ready to share your own when you've got it.

The important thing to know about this reciprocal behavior is that in many tribes and cultures, "please" and "thank you" are seen as unnecessary: Everyone gives and everyone takes because that is the only way everyone survives. When people began to ask for things consciously, it was the beginning of consciously acknowledging differences in importance among community members.

If this is coffee, please bring me some tea; but if this is tea, please bring me some coffee.

—ABRAHAM LINCOLN

We may never know who said "please" for the first time, but we do know that the verb "please" was a regular part of language in ancient Rome, a society that has had a great influence on the modern West. Saying "please" indicates to others that you understand the effort behind their actions. Acknowledging effort, of course, is pretty important when you aren't able to reciprocate. When we learned to say "please," we were also beginning to understand that sometimes we were going to wind up in someone else's debt. Want to be released from obligation? You'll have to ask nicely. You might want to say, "Please!"

When the world says "please, let us help,"
extraordinary things begin to happen.
—BRUCE WILLIS

Pleasing the Public

PEOPLE HAVE ENJOYED collecting things for centuries—and probably longer. One of the latest ways to showcase a collection of photographs (even photographs of collections, but that's for another book) is online, in a "pool" or through a "meme" that people follow. You can see the relative popularity of things and the interest in them through how many contributions are made to the meme (a collection in and of itself).

On the popular photo-sharing site Flickr. com, one of these pools is devoted to "Keep Off the Grass" and "Please Keep Off the Grass" signs from around the world (a Google Images search will show similar photos). The signs are

round, square, rectangular, oval, even shaped like various objects and creatures, and made of wood, stone, metal, ceramics, paper, and plastic. But they all carry the same phrase.

While "Please Keep Off the Grass" is, like "Please go ahead" (page 51), a phrasal verb, its inclusion here is due not to its grammatical construction but to its inflected meaning. "Please Keep Off the Grass" really means "You Are Not Allowed on This Grass, but We Aren't Here to Police Your Actions." Some of the collected photos cheekily nod at the lack of supervision, showing one or more people standing on the grass behind the sign.

The truth is, sometimes we say "Please" not just to a single person, but to many and various people, as a way of maintaining something that's good for all. Libraries ask us to "Please speak softly," and hospitals hang signs saying "Please turn off your cell phones," but none of these mean "It's your choice." Instead, they mean "We're Counting on You to Behave." You might say that this use of "Please" is an appeal to the superego.

Etiquette is the science of living.
It embraces everything. It is ethics. It is honor.
—EMILY POST

The Favor of a Reply

DURING THE GILDED AGE, as Europeans visited the estates of magnates like Cornelius Vanderbilt and Andrew Carnegie, and rich Americans visited London, Paris, and Rome, some "foreign" ways caught on.

Entertaining grew more formal. Invitations to dinners and luncheons quickly changed to include the fashionable French abbreviation "R.S.V.P." It stands for *"Répondez s'il vous plaît,"* or "Please respond," although many a hostess used the properly American "The favor of a reply is requested" (a phrase still seen on many wedding invitations).

While the French abbreviation was an affectation, in the late Victorian era it was not useless. It

Print invitations required large machines.

Personal, handwritten notes are appreciated.

could be embarrassing for a hostess's guests and troubling for her staff if extras arrived. Even today a host might want responses to determine how much food to order or to ensure that there are enough guests to welcome a visitor.

Most Americans still know what R.S.V.P. stands for, but, unfortunately, people tend to ignore it today. Manners are more casual in the 21st century, but if someone requests a reply, you should honor it—though today you might do so by phone or via email, instead of with a fountain pen and engraved stationery.

OBJECTS OF ETIQUETTE: Copper Plates For years in Anglo-American culture the term "copperplate script" meant your handwriting was highly desirable. It mimicked the beautifully even script of printings made from copper plates. These plates were etched by expert calligraphers and set the standard for printed text.

Please all, and you will please none.
—AESOP

Go Ahead

PORTUGAL IS KNOWN AS one of the politest nations in Europe; men wear suits to the cinema and restaurant patrons greet newcomers with a spontaneous *"É servido?"* ("Have you been helped?") Good manners are stressed, down to the smallest interactions. At an impasse in Lisbon, the other person will inevitably step aside and say *"À vontade!"* ("Please go ahead").

While the actual Portuguese phrase literally translates as "As you wish" or "Be at ease," its routine use has made "please" an implied part of what, in English, is a "phrasal verb"—a verb combined with a preposition that conveys an idiomatic meaning. In Japan, "Please, go ahead" is conveyed simply by *"Dozo,"* while in Egyptian Arabic, it's "itfaDDal." In English, phrasal, or multiword, verbs include common usages from "bring up" children to "fill out" a form. The preposition is part of the verb's meaning.

Many phrasal verbs are used in mannerly situations, from "run into" (to meet) and "call on" (to visit) to "get along with" (to cooperate) and "put up with" (to tolerate). From a manners perspective it's fascinating how the prepositions can portend behavior. For example, "with" connotes linking and cooperation. With "Please, go ahead," the speaker's use of "ahead"—whether it's spoken aloud or built in to the verb phrasing itself—shows that she is deferring to another.

The Portuguese are polite even during the briefest interactions.

MANNERED LIVES

Louis XIV of France

He was known as the Sun King, and after taking the French throne at the tender age of four still holds the record for the longest documented reign of any European monarch in history: 72 years, 3 months, and 18 days.

Those seven decades gave King Louis XIV ample time to observe, learn, master, and codify courtly manners. He is widely credited with inventing the notion of "etiquette," or the refined and stratified system of manners used at court to denote rank, status, good or ill favor, and even fashionability.

The French word *étiquette* means "tag" or "label," and regardless of how good or ill you consider what we now refer to as etiquette, it helps to remember that it's a bit more rigid than simple good manners. The Western version of etiquette that Louis XIV and his court developed has had lasting effects on society. Etiquette focuses not on how best to treat any person, but on how best to treat the "best people."

Of course, defining "the best people" requires having one person who is most important, and Louis XIV was it. (Contrary to popular belief, he probably did not say *"L'état, c'est moi"*; in fact, on his deathbed he said "I depart, but the State shall always remain.") Court etiquette centered on his daily schedule, which began at 8 a.m. and involved as many people (or "courtiers") as possible, since everyone was vying for tasks that included the dubious honor of wiping the perspiration from the King's body. With royal etiquette like that, no wonder the French had a revolution!

France's King Louis XIV held high standards in behavior and in attire.

SAYING THANK YOU

WHAT WE CALL "GOOD MANNERS" MEANS, at its simplest, the manner in which we treat other people. The "Golden Rule" (which does not belong to any particular faith tradition, although several traditions espouse it) calls for us to treat other people as we would like to be treated. Most of us would prefer not to be insulted, or caused physical pain, or given less than everyone else, and so we learn early that we should not insult, strike, or cheat anyone else.

However, learning to say "thank you" is about more than how we treat others. Yes, we all like to be thanked for our efforts—but in the act of thanking, we also acknowledge that we are interdependent. To more "primitive" societies (that is, those groups who live more closely to their earliest roots than others do), interdependence is a given, but to those of us who are more accustomed to emphasizing our individual success, a reminder of how much we owe our fellows can be important.

> *As we express our gratitude, we must never forget that the highest appreciation is not to utter words, but to live by them.*
>
> —JOHN F. KENNEDY

Sometimes we say "please" when we're asking, sometimes when we're commanding, sometimes when we're giving, and sometimes when we're entreating. In all of these cases, we need someone else to fulfill, follow, take, or answer a request. No one does anything completely on his or her own, and remembering to say "thank you" forces us to reconsider our innate vulnerability. Is that perhaps why some people have trouble remembering to write thank-you notes? (That's not an excuse, Mom, I swear it isn't!) In any case, saying "thank you" is one of the most basic and humbling statements that "good manners" entails.

How small a part of time they share
That are so wondrous sweet and fair!
—EDMUND WALLER

No, Thanks

LONG AGO, AN INUIT MAN might have known his comrades by the cut of ring-tailed seal meat he regularly gave them—one might be "Flipper" and another "Middle Haunch." They participated in an ancient system of food sharing known as *piqatigiit,* in which nonrelated hunters received the same parts after each slaughter. No one was thanked for the meat. "Seal brothers" were bound not by DNA but by community ties.

The Inuit ensured that everyone had the resources to survive in their harsh environment. Food-sharing networks independent of family relationships not only keep one group from gaining too much power; they may also have prevented the monopoly of one bloodline and resulting genetic problems like those suffered by 19th-century European monarchs.

Payuktuq, another sharing network, distributed seal parts to families not in the original hunter's group. While piqatigiit and *payuktuq* were tied to seal hunting, a similar system managed other foods—and continues today.

Today, "commensalism" (meal sharing) involves community freezers with meat, fish, and "southern food" (as non-Inuit groceries are called). Asking is still unnecessary. Taking a salmon from a friend's freezer is still part of survival, no thanks needed.

Inuit villages are small and isolated; food-sharing groups are important.

Mercy I ask'd; mercy I found.
—WILLIAM CAMDEN

An Obligation

WHEN SOMEONE THANKS YOU in Japan, you may hear the expected *"Domo arigato,"* literally, "Thank you very much"—but just as often, you may hear *"Domo sumimasen"*: "I am very sorry."

Why does "I am very sorry" equal "Thank you"? In Japanese culture when someone does something for you it is both a burden to that person and an obligation to you. (A proper apology is *"Gomen nasai,"* by the way.)

Part of this relates to hierarchy. In *The Anatomy of Dependence,* Tadeo Doi, M.D., writes that during his American residency he refused to say "thank you" to a mentor because, in his Japanese psyche, "thank you" implied equality; he preferred to say, "I'm sorry" to his superior. Gift-giving in Japan is based on rank

In Japan gift-giving has long been important.

(sons get more than their sisters), and so much responsibility is tied to receiving that many Japanese write *"Osoreirimasu"* ("I am overcome with shame") on what we would call "thank you" notes.

But in this tightly packed, largely homogeneous society, social anthropologist Margaret Visser notes that the Japanese learn early that "apology not only repairs but enhances a relationship." Frequent apologies help everyone get along.

When I'm not thanked at all, I'm thanked enough.
I've done my duty, and I've done no more.
—HENRY FIELDING, *TOM THUMB THE GREAT*, 1731

We're Not Worthy

MODERN AMERICANS ARE TAUGHT that the proper response to a compliment is "Thank you." That's that. Witness the response Miss Manners gave to a woman who worried about how to respond when told she has a pretty face: "To be told that you have a pretty face is very nice, but a mere pleasantry. You need only reply, 'Thank you.' It is not necessary to point out that you did not make it on your potter's wheel."

How very straitlaced that seems, almost Puritan, in fact, when compared with how our British forebears respond to kind words—responses that have trickled across the pond, too, as linguists and sociologists have found. Very often, compliments are met with responses that downgrade, reject, or qualify them. The British tendency toward self-deprecation is famously manifest in these reactions. An Englishman is told, "You did a wonderful job," and he says, "Oh, well, anyone could have done it"—or to cite a popular culture reference, in English author Douglas Adams's *Hitchhiker's Guide to the Galaxy,* after a character named Arthur is praised for saving everyone's lives, he says, "It was nothing."

This reaction isn't because the British as a whole aren't grateful for kind words—instead, it's a national tendency toward not allowing anyone to think too much of themselves. They can also give compliments sparingly; one British teacher who moved to the United States blogged that frequent and earnest compliments from Americans confused her. That need to be modest—or at least to appear so—is very English, according to British psychologists. Arrogance and self-satisfaction, after all, threatens to unbalance the status quo, and in the English social structure, keeping the status quo balanced was important.

English courtly humility hasn't disappeared.

ARCHAIC MANNERS: The "At Home" Day   In a custom starting in England and later spreading to the U.S., urban ladies of the "best sort" once reserved a day of the week as their "at home" day on which any of their friends and acquaintances might come to call and stay for a cup of tea and conversation. This is one custom that was hard-hit by technology: Once the telephone became common, younger people started to use it to confirm meeting times, and the use for "at home" days diminished.

One can pay back the loan of gold,
but one dies forever in debt to those who are kind.
—MALAYAN PROVERB

Loads of Baggage

IN SOME CULTURES, the concept of "thank you" does not exist as it does in ours. For example, one African mother told an anthropologist that while "Thank you, sir" would be said to a stranger, "To one's own people one does not thank, not at all!" In a traditional society where everyone is considered to have obligations to one another, being thanked is tantamount to being released from obligations. Not only would that imply an excuse—it would imply separation from the community that supports survival.

That doesn't mean that no occasion for thanks exists, however. Anyone who has ever visited Africa, or even has just seen an airport departures lounge for a flight, say, to Lagos, knows that Africans returning home from a stint abroad often bring back large amounts of goods to distribute as gifts. One family's travelogue to South Africa includes mention of a suitcase full of gifts for the family weighing

Going back to Africa means sharing new things.

about 30 pounds "that would be empty on the way home." That pales in comparison with a Senegalese woman's 70-pound load of gifts: "I had a long, exhaustive list to make sure I covered everyone, cousins, uncles, aunts, friends, imams, and babies."

Gifts are meant to be handed out to everyone in the community, and it is preferable to bring many smaller items than to bring just a few expensive goods for the immediate family. If you, as a Westerner, pay a visit to Africa, remember that giving gifts is the best way to say "thank you" there, as it does not carry any overtones of noblesse oblige or pity the way actually saying "thank you" sometimes does.

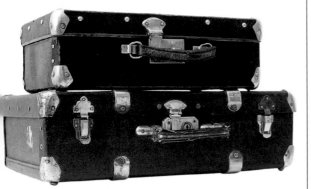

Expatriates traveling home often pack gifts.

SAYING YOU'RE WELCOME

IN MANY LANGUAGES, THE WORD OR PHRASE equivalent to our English "You're welcome" is either the same as or another form of "please." The correct response to the German *"Danke"* ("Thanks") is *"Bitte"* ("Please"), while in Spanish, *"Gracias"* is followed up with *"De nada"* (meaning "It was nothing.") Similarly in French, the phrase is *"De rien"*.

The reason for this isn't that the person being thanked actually did nothing—it's a little more complicated than that! Once you've thanked someone—and acknowledged your debt to him or her—you then put that person in your debt. Complicated? Well, interpersonal relationships tend to be so; think of your last Thanksgiving with family.

> *Feeling gratitude and not expressing it is like wrapping a present and not giving it.*
>
> —WILLIAM ARTHUR WARD

Therefore, a "thanks" must be either ignored entirely (which, as you'll see, tends to be the English way) or responded to with some kind of demurral. Perhaps receiving gratitude is just as unnatural a behavior as giving it is: Although humans have taught each other to acknowledge these actions with words, they go against our most innate self-interest so much that we haven't found a natural, gracious way to express them.

However, once we've learned to say please, thank you, and you're welcome (as most of us do from our parents), we do remember them. As author and social anthropologist Margaret Visser points out in her 2009 book *The Gift of Thanks*, these phrases become "so ingrained" that after aphasic strokes and through senile dementia, people can still respond to and repeat these words when all other words have left them. They're more than "nothing" after all.

*One word or a pleasing smile is often
enough to raise up a saddened and wounded soul.*
—THÉRÈSE OF LISIEUX

Double Meaning

IT'S EASY TO REMEMBER the Russian words *"Na zdorovie!"* from the musical *Fiddler on the Roof.* Before a Jewish man sings "To Life!" (*"L'Chaim!"*), several Cossack soldiers say *"Za va'sha zdorovie!"* ("To your health!")

In its entirety, that Russian phrase does mean "To your health." *"Na zdorovie"* on its own, however, is not—like *"Zum Gesundheit"*—the toast that many assume it is. The words "Na zdorovie" are actually an old-fashioned way of saying "You're welcome."

Yes, *"zdorovie"* means "health" in Russian— but "Na zdorovie!" will only earn bemused glances if you say it while lifting a glass of vodka in St. Petersburg. It's quite easy to make this error if you've traveled in countries close by; the Polish *"Na zdorowie"* does mean "To

Another Russian tradition: nesting dolls

your health!" To make matters worse, a popular restaurant in St. Petersburg serves traditional Russian dishes and is decorated with folkloric motifs—and the restaurant is named Na Zdorovie.

If you're stumped, instead of saying "Na zdorovie!" shorten the Cossacks' phrase and say *"Za Vas!"* ("To You!"). You can't go wrong with simplicity—and no one will think you mean "You're welcome." Oh, and if you do want to say "You're welcome" in Russian? *"Ne za chto."*

In Russia, even a cup of tea can be festive.

This is an age of lazy moral relativism combined with aggressive social insolence.
—LYNNE TRUSS, *TALK TO THE HAND*

Don't Be Negative

MANY OLDER AMERICANS OBJECT to a current fashion for people to say "No problem" in response to "Thank you." Those who object prefer "You're welcome" or "It's my pleasure," believing that "No problem" indicates a condescending attitude, especially when people say it quickly and without much thought.

Technically, saying "No problem" to a "Thank you" is quite correct and quite polite, too. It's one variation on the "It's nothing" response we see in other languages (*"De rien," "De nada," "Es war nichts,"* and so forth). However, "No problem" is not synonymous with "It's nothing," is it? And it is also not synonymous with "You're welcome," as some younger people who have grown up hearing it may have thought.

Why? Saying "No problem" implies that there could have been one in the first place— and when, say, people go to a restaurant or a fine shop, their presence is never supposed to be a burden. To have a member of the waitstaff say "No problem" grates on the nerves of those who remember the saying "The customer is always right."

The "white glove" approach wins people over.

Cracking the manners code can be tough.

That same waiter saying "You're welcome" makes a big difference, because she is saying "It is my pleasure." However, if you still balk at being remonstrated for using "No problem," think of it this way: A phrase that starts out with "No" is bound to be heard more negatively, and if you're trying to be polite, you're probably also trying to be positive.

But just using positive words isn't always enough, especially in a word where sarcasm— often employed by people who have forgotten their manners—is quite rampant. Have you heard the one about the linguistics class? A professor is explaining to the class that in some languages two negatives can be grammatically correct for negative statements, while in others, double negatives cancel each other out. ("I don't have nothing" means I do have something.) But, the professor says, two positives can never equal a negative. At that moment, a student in the back raises his hand and says, "Yeah, right."

So, the lesson? Be positive and mean it.

You give but little when you give of your possessions.
It is when you give of yourself that you truly give.
—KAHLIL GIBRAN, *THE PROPHET*

The Three-in-One

IN AT LEAST ONE long-standing cultural tradition, the phrases "please," "thank you," and "you're welcome" are rolled into a single object: the ex-voto, an object known in Latin America as a *milagro*.

The actual *milagro* is a small object representing a prayer that the giver believes has been granted by the Christian deity. These objects, often made to look like the result of the prayer, can be made from wood, metal, wax, or clay, and are left in places of worship, sometimes beside statues or pictures of saints. Originally fashioned by the supplicant, ready-made and even manufactured *milagros* are now available for purchase to leave in churches and cathedrals. They can represent wished-for objects, like cars and houses; healed body parts, from ears to legs to whole skeletons; and sometimes even places that have been avoided, like jail. Some even include personal photographs demonstrating the answered prayer.

Simple milagro *symbolizing the Sacred Heart*

So, they reflect a request and a response, but what about a "You're welcome?" Due to cultural and religious beliefs, that phrase, too, is represented in these small offerings: The people who place milagros are doing so in order to show others that a spiritual power has granted them something. While no one expects that power to say "You're welcome" out loud, everyone in the community understands that gratitude expressed receives a favorable response. Since Roman Catholics believe in a triune god—Father, Son, and Holy Spirit—this three-in-one votive offering is a symbolic reflection of theology, as well.

Rosaries are another tool for prayers of gratitude.

He who has health, has hope;
and he who has hope, has everything.
—THOMAS CARLYLE

Reading the Tea Leaves

SOMETIMES WE GET SO CAUGHT UP in a cycle of "Thank you"; "No, thank YOU" that something needs to end things—that is the idea behind a flavorful Burmese tradition.

Centuries ago, warring kingdoms in what is now Myanmar (formerly Burma) presented salads of pickled tea leaves as peace offerings. The salad, known as *lahpet* or *laphet,* is now a national dish—and it is still offered to end disputes and also when a "You're welcome" might be said.

In lahpet pickled tea leaves (sometimes simply salted, sometimes spiced) are surrounded by foods like crisp fried garlic, peas, peanuts, toasted sesame, dried shrimp, preserved shredded ginger, and fried shredded coconut (one rare delicacy is lightly fried grubs from an isolated lake). Variations include *lahpet ohk,* a "ladies' lunch"–style version that has fresh tomatoes, garlic, green chilies, and fish sauce.

The dish is an important part of many Burmese celebrations, including the Buddhist *shinbyu* novitiation of boys under 20 into monastic life, but its most common appearance as a "You're welcome" comes during the wedding-invitation process. Families deliver invitations from house to house; when someone accepts—the "thank you for the invitation"—the person accepting is offered lahpet. By sharing something tasty and tangible, the inviting family immediately discharges themselves from any obligations to say "Thank you for accepting."

Myanmar's traditions include the shan costume.

FAMOUS GAFFES: Hans Christian Andersen, bad houseguest to the Dickens family   Invited as a houseguest for two weeks at Gad's Hill Place, the Dickens residence south of London, Danish author Hans Christian Andersen didn't budge for five weeks, complaining and talking constantly during his visit. After he finally left, Dickens wrote on the guestroom mirror: "Hans Andersen slept in this room for five weeks—which seemed to the family AGES!" The ungainly Dane so annoyed the entire clan that daughter Kate Dickens called him "a bony bore."

SAYING HELLO

BIRDS DO IT, BEES DO IT … no, not "fall in love," silly, "say hello"! It's true: Many animals greet each other. With humans, however, the greeting ritual is not universal. Every known culture has some way for people to share greetings.

We discussed waving in Chapter One, but here our concern is mostly with verbal greetings. Even so, there are ways of "saying hello" that don't involve the word "hello," or in at least one case, any words at all. The goal is to make people feel safe and welcome. There's even a linguistic reason: Humans need to hear just two syllables to distinguish one voice from another. "Hel-lo" and its equivalents give a listener just enough time to recognize a new speaker (with very familiar friends we tend to use the monosyllabic "Hi," because we don't need the same "warning").

…The older I get, the more I see that it's the little things you do that make a difference to people. Even just saying hello can brighten someone's day.

—FRAN CURRY

Variations in greetings can seem as multifarious as snowflakes: Some cultures stand, some sit, some take a long time, others have many steps (like the Maori haka). In the modern United States of America, saying "hello" is the most common greeting, but as we will see, that wasn't the case before the telephone.

This brings up another important element about greetings upon meetings: Any time we encounter another person, one or both of us may be doing something else. A proper and sincere greeting shows that we know that, and that we respect the other's boundaries, as well as our own. "Hello" can be the prelude to anything from hospitality to hostility, but it marks a transition in and of itself.

Hello, this is a recording. You've dialed the right number,
now hang up and don't do it again.
—FRANK SINATRA, IN THE FILM *OCEAN'S ELEVEN*, 1960

Party Line

TODAY, IN THE UNITED STATES, greeting another person with a "Hello" is routine. It wasn't always so, however.

"Hello" comes from the medieval French interjection *"Ho la!"* meaning both "Stop" and "Pay attention!" It remained an interjection and shout in English, changing from "holla" (1523) to "hollo, hollow" (1542) to "hillo, hilloa" (1602) and sometimes "halloo" (1568) and "hulloo" (1707), and also to "hallo, halloa" (1847) and "hullo, hulloa" (1857).

Why would a shout become our telephone greeting? Alexander Graham Bell first used "Ahoy!" when he called down his "speaking tube"; it was actually Thomas Alva Edison who first said "Hullo" on the phone. Both used these "shouts" because it was hard to be understood on early telephones.

It's easy to shout the "u" and "oo" of "Hulloo," but harder to yell the short "e" and long "o" of "Hello." The early phones were manned by enthusiastic boys who shouted at people, but by the late 19th century, telephone exchanges were "manned" by "hello girls."

The softer diction of these young women fixed the spelling and pronunciation of our most common greeting. They were so renowned that author Mark Twain mentioned them in *A Connecticut Yankee in King Arthur's Court:* "The humblest hello-girl along ten thousand miles of wire could teach gentleness, patience, modesty, manners, to the highest duchess in Arthur's land."

Alexander Graham Bell shouting down the line

OBJECTS OF ETIQUETTE: Calling Cards Engraved calling cards were once de rigueur in polite society, properly left on a hall tray to indicate one had paid a call. Sometimes through card shapes, turned-down corners, and written abbreviations people also indicated leave-taking, sympathy, and more.

You make your guests feel welcome and at home.
If you do that honestly, the rest takes care of itself.
—FROM THE TV SERIES *NORTHERN EXPOSURE*, 1994

Message in a Dumpling

SOMETIMES "HELLO" ARRIVES on a plate instead of from the tongue. Such is the case with Chinese dumplings, which were often originally prepared for a celebration like a wedding or the birth of a child. Eventually dumplings became the "welcome" food of choice, demonstrating hospitality.

Of course, many cultures have traditions about serving guests. Enter an English home in late afternoon and you'll receive a cup of hot black tea and a biscuit; go to a Japanese home at the same time, and you may be offered green tea and a quartered orange. Much depends on local resources, tastes, and customs.

Getting back to China: There, foods definitely have a hierarchy and a place in *guanxi* (relations). Fried rice has absolutely no business next to a fine broth, and that's why it's a bit amusing that the homely dumpling has acquired such a lofty position.

"Coffee, anyone?"

Chinese dumplings signify welcome and joy.

Another amusing example of food-and-beverage hierarchies comes to us from the U.S. military, where rigid protocol once even held sway over the refreshment table. If ladies were present, the highest-ranking officer's wife would pour, as a sign of her elevated station—but the Service Etiquette Guide made sure to specify exactly what she would pour. Not cocoa, not tea, but coffee. Why? "Coffee outranks tea." It isn't simply that coffee is stronger than tea; it's that more people of both genders take coffee, and so the coffee service enabled the ranking spouse to greet more people.

Language tethers us to the world;
without it we spin like atoms.
—PENELOPE LIVELY, *MOON TIGER*, 1987

Speaking in Tongues

EVERYONE HAS A PERSON—sometimes more than one—in her life to whom respect must be paid. Often that respect is freely given, and modern people consider that the norm. But in premodern societies, sometimes that respect had to be reinforced, even through different ways of saying "hello," depending on who was in earshot.

While a modern spouse probably need not worry if her speech is slangy and informal, some cultures used to carefully adjust their speech to the situation. Centuries ago, indigenous tribes in Australia, Africa, and even North America developed distinct modes that are more respectful and/or subdued than everyday speech; taboos prevented men and women from speaking to or even looking at certain relatives, and they spoke differently in the presence of those relatives.

These modes are known by linguists as "mother-in-law languages" because the grammar and pronunciation are usually the same as those of the common language, but the vocabulary can be distinct. In the Aboriginal Guwal language, there are at least four different words for different kinds of grubs—but in the Dyirbal language, the "avoidance" tongue, just one word for grub exists. The different words and

Australian Aboriginal symbols on boomerangs

the immediate switch to them helped speakers reinforce the required "arm's length" distance between themselves and their relatives.

Most "avoidance speech" languages have declined sharply in use since the early to mid-20th century, when modern explorers brought more cosmopolitan ways to the furthest reaches of the globe. Today, only five speakers of Dyirbal remain.

FAMOUS GAFFES: Prince Philip Britain's Prince Philip, the Duke of Edinburgh and consort to Queen Elizabeth II, has long been famous for his offensive verbal gaffes, which include saying "Do you still throw spears at each other" to an indigenous Australian businessman and "If you stay here much longer, you'll all be slitty eyed" to a group of British students in China.

*I bow to the lotus feet of our great teachers
who uncovers our true self and awakens happiness.*
—ASHTANGA YOGA MANTRA

Such a Poser

EVERY MAT-TOTING WOMAN exiting a yoga studio can tell you how to slide into "downward-facing dog," but does that same woman know why that stretch was originally performed?

Some greetings, of course, are made to divinities, from the monotheistic to the multifarious—but few have evolved into a modern fitness craze the way yoga has. The ancient (perhaps even prehistoric) origins of this Hindi practice are probably most firmly rooted in the Vedic era, during the first millennium B.C. when the sacred Vedas were being composed. While some yoga fanatics insist that the "sun salutation" series of poses originated along with the rest of the discipline, others trace it to the early 20th-century raja of Aundh (a former state in India, now part of Maharashtra state).

Today the typical sun salutation consists of eight different yoga poses, including mountain

Yoga poses originally greeted the gods.

The "downward-facing dog" yoga pose

pose, plank pose, and both upward- and downward-facing-dog poses. Also known as Surya Namaskar, almost any yoga class begins with this series, as the gentle, flowing movements synchronized to careful breathing are a good warm-up for more challenging poses.

But the true purpose behind these exercises is spiritual, if not specifically religious. The "salute to the sun" is a way of welcoming a new day's beginning, as well as our planet's source of energy. Even if you are not interested in yoga's deepest meanings, the mythic and symbolic connotations of its poses can be interesting. When you begin an hour of moving and bending and stretching with the sun salutation, you are, in effect, connecting with the energy around you, greeting it as surely as you would greet a friend with a warm verbal salutation.

SAYING "HOW ARE YOU?"

INQUIRING ABOUT ANOTHER PERSON'S STATUS is nearly as common as uttering words of greeting. Different cultures and language groups have many different ways of forming this inquiry, from the quotidian "Did you sleep well?" to the more complicated "How is your family?"

The idea behind these questions, of course, is that once greetings have been exchanged, a new level of sharing is appropriate. It may be that in the earliest instances of humans saying "How are you?" the respondents actually told the truth: "I could be better. The cave was awfully chilly last night, and I think there might have been something a bit 'off' with that haunch of mastodon we ate." Over the ensuing centuries, however, the reactions such replies got must have made the cave dwellers think twice, because the responses to "How are you?" have now become as standardized as the question. "I'm fine, and you?" is the most common, although the occasional "Could be better" and "So-so" are allowed.

There is nothing so dangerous for anyone who has something to hide as conversation!.... Every time he will give himself away.

—DAME AGATHA CHRISTIE

Even in our modern era of abbreviated communications, when the already contracted "Wassup?" has been further contracted into "'Sup?" we are still holding on to the verbal routine of asking after each other's health and well-being. It's never a bad idea to at least try and gauge another's status. Finding out if the person you're talking to is willing to abide by social conventions (or not) can be an important step toward a successful interaction, whether that interaction last seconds or hours. At the very least, saying "How are you?" shows the other person that you care enough to say the very least—even if you're not willing to stick around for the answer.

Good manners have much to do with the emotions.
To make them ring true, one must feel them, not merely exhibit them.
—AMY VANDERBILT

Class, Dismissed

IN HER LANDMARK 1922 book *Etiquette,* Emily Post says, "Do not use the expression 'pleased to meet you' . . . on any occasion." According to Post, the correct greeting upon meeting another person is "How do you do?"

Post, herself a product of America's upper class, had learned its British-centered etiquette. A member of British aristocracy would never assume that on encountering another person either party would necessarily be "pleased." How could you be? Either you have never met the person before and therefore could not be pleased or displeased, or you have met the person before, so you can only be "glad to see you again." "Pleased" was not a logical or truthful option. And proper people had no interest in pretending they were glad to meet their sister-in-law's gossiping niece or their new gardener's red-faced wife.

Even in more recent years, the class-conscious British have clung to the idea that upper-class people say "How do you do?" while people of the lower class, or "non-U," say "Hello" or (gasp!) "Pleased to meet you." In a society still marked by economic and social strata, "Pleased to meet you" can not only be technically incorrect, but

Primers helped to erode class distinctions.

also appear to be overly striving or condescending. If a working-class person says "Pleased to meet you" to a blue blood, she might be trying to ingratiate herself, while if the blue blood says the same to her, she might be miffed, believing him to be phony in his interest.

Of course, anyone in the United States who makes a habit of saying "How do you do?" certainly wouldn't impress any of us Yankees. We might find the expression silly, maybe snobby, or perhaps we'd briefly feel sorry for someone whom we thought was simply trying too hard. These days, "How do you do?" feels foreign, almost of another era. It conjures up images of women in petticoats, men with top hats, and a formality we Americans aren't terribly interested in embracing.

Of course, when it comes right down to it, everyone should be saying "How do you do?"—even as our own society is founded on the notion that everyone is equal. However, since that is not the case, and "How do you do?" means "How are you doing?" perhaps we can all dismiss any preconceptions about class, and simply and sincerely make a point of asking others when we meet them, "How are you?"

Cleanse your emotions, passions, impulses, attitudes, and reactions.
That is the essence of spiritual discipline as laid down in all Faiths.
—SRI SATHYA SAI BABA, INDIAN GURU

Their Sole Concern

FOOT WASHING IS IMPORTANT in Hindu spirituality. Worshippers at a Hindu temple are expected to clean their feet before entering. Washing someone else's feet is a sign of respect and hospitality, both of which are demonstrated during the foot washing at a Hindu wedding, where the bride's parents do the washing (mother to bride, father to groom) before applying red *kumkum* paste and giving flowers.

India's caste system is, even today, a sad reminder that prejudice can exist even among members of the same ethnicity and race. To promote equality some groups, both religious and social, encourage people to wash the feet of members of the lowest castes.

Many devout Hindu households routinely wash guests' feet, indicating the same respect and hospitality of religious ceremonies. Instead of asking "How are you?" they assume you are ready to be honored through this simple but meaningful practice.

Muslims in India and across the globe also practice ritual foot washing, especially before meals—but this foot washing is part of the Islamic prayer ritual, and has caused controversy when Muslim populations have asked to have footbaths installed in certain areas. In Christianity, washing another's feet is an act of respect and humility meant to mimic the actions of the disciples at Jesus Christ's Last Supper, and it is mostly done at Easter season services.

Shoes must be removed or covered before entering the Taj Mahal's mosque.

10 RLS AJMAN AIR MAIL

They recognize a false smile and a false greeting.
Be gentle and be yourself.
—AUBURN UNIVERSITY BASKETBALL COACH SONNY SMITH

Greetings for All

SOMETIMES JUST SAYING "Hello, how are things?" just doesn't express enough sentiment—at least in German Switzerland. Is it because the Alps make it difficult to meet in person, so every encounter must be formalized? No one knows for sure, but we do know that politeness is everything in *der Schweiz,* where even the briefest encounter will be characterized by a number of conversational routines, including a greeting, a conversation, and a farewell. Contrast that to our America habits where, in many offices, colleagues passing each other on the stairwell might greet each other "Hi! How are you?" and won't be surprised or disappointed if the other person simply says "Hey!" and makes no effort to answer the question. Often, the "How are you?" question is perfunctory, and anything beyond "Great!" or "Fine," or even the grammatically suspect "Good" disrupts the superficial greeting and prevents us from getting on with our day.

But, in the Alps, failure to offer or reply to a greeting in a substantial way isn't simply a lack of good manners; among these mountain folk, it is viewed as arrogant, possibly hostile, and

Even in greetings, the Swiss are well equipped.

maybe even a serious insult. Unfortunately, the form of the greeting is also important. One respondent to an academic study of Swiss etiquette and manners noted that her group had discovered that you could not say *"Guten tag, Frau"* to a *Schweizer* woman; her full name absolutely had to be included if you were not to be considered rude.

However, the Germanophone Swiss take things even further, offering greetings that are classified by activity, like *"Gelegenheitsgrüsse"* (specific to an occasion, such as a birthday or a graduation) and *Arbeitsgrüsse* ("work greetings," such as when one is in the office or occupied in the garden) and even *"Zeitgrüsse"* ("time greetings" that might be specific to a season, a day, or even a particular hour). While some of the traditional Arbeitsgrüsse have died out, a researcher found that younger people in the region have come up with new forms of these greetings, including the *"Hip-Hopper-Grüss,"* the *"Skater-Grüss,"* and even the *"Gimme-Five-Grüss."* In Zurich, at least, specific and personal greetings are still relevant—no doubt someone there is already thinking about a *"Smartphone-Grüss."*

*Learning what the greeting is in the language
of the culture you're in is already a good start.*
—DAVID SOLOMONS, CEO OF CULTURE SHOCK! CONSULTING

Time Is Money

ANY U.S. CITIZEN USED TO giving colleagues a quick smile as he juggles a latte and a laptop bag might struggle with the pace of greetings in many African countries. If "Time is money," then the cash-poor continent displays its true wealth with lengthy minutes spent welcoming even casual acquaintances.

In Kenya people exclaim *"Jambo!"* then shake hands energetically for a while before chatting. Talk covers health to travel, and is serious, even amid jokes and pleasantries.

Another time- and patience-intensive social ritual is the *lobolo,* or bride-price negotiations. These were protracted, probably because the outcome had such an effect on societal wealth. Working out potential problems meant not only the best deal *and* the best knitting together of families.

Today, African business remains slow and dignified, and anyone seeking to contract an African company should put down his coffee and briefcase and get ready for some proper conversation. Whether your host begins with *"Jambo!," "Bonjour," "Salaam aleikum,"* or even "Hello," you can expect a change of pace.

Kenyan greetings are delivered enthusiastically—and patiently.

MANNERED LIVES

Erasmus

Dutch humanist philosopher Desiderius Erasmus is probably most famous today for his saying that adorns many a tote bag: "When I have a little money, I buy books, and if any is left, I buy food." Unfortunately, that quotable quote does little justice to the man's long and illustrious career as a scholar and theologian whose commonsense approach to Christian living put him at odds with the more famous Martin Luther.

However, Erasmus's practical approach to life also led him to write what is widely regarded as the first set of manners for child-rearing. *A Handbook on Good Manners for Children* was published in 1530 and included guidance that sounds remarkably modern, like "Young bodies are like tender plants, which grow and become hardened to whatever shape you've trained them."

His treatise was an immediate best seller, translated into more than 130 editions; evidently, even in an age marked by violence and chaos, people agreed with Erasmus that a child's education by his or her family in

Renaissance luminary Erasmus took care with his books and his manners.

communal devotion and good manners could have an effect on society at large. The 17 sections of the book include all aspects of life, from posture, to behavior at the table.

While we might recognize rules like never blowing your nose at the table, Erasmus does address some practices that have changed. He advises children never to put bones back on their plates—because it was once common to throw those bones on the floor for the dogs so they would have something to eat, too.

Despite living hundreds of years ago in a world still constrained by feudal codes, Erasmus believed that while no one can choose his or her parents or place of birth, everyone can shape his or her own character and behavior. What could be more modern—and more important, relevant—than that?

SAYING GOODBYE

WHEN SHAKESPEARE SAID "PARTING IS SUCH SWEET SORROW," he cannot have been thinking of houseguests. (This may be why Australians customarily walk visitors all the way to the curb and wave as the car moves down the street; it's the best way of making sure those guests really are gone!) Saying goodbye can, at times, be a happier occasion than saying hello.

But saying goodbye, for better or worse, is just as important to humans as saying hello. We social animals crave signs and signals that tell us when we're starting, ending, and continuing things. Even whales and porpoises hold funerals, and what is a goodbye if not a sort of temporary burial? That's not morbid—that's just psychology. Any farewell might be a permanent separation, because anything can happen—so while saying hello can be a dangerous proposition, saying goodbye can be fairly serious.

It is never any good dwelling on good-bys. It is not the being together that it prolongs; it is the parting.

—ELIZABETH BIBESCO

This is why people often prolong their leave-takings: Even if you're ready to be alone again, you have no way of knowing if you'll ever see the other person again. Even if you do, someone on either side will probably have changed. A first impression may be lasting, but a last impression might be final. No wonder some traditions draw goodbyes out for as long as possible. While familial and romantic farewells may be filled with hugs and kisses, those between the less intimately acquainted may consist of a mere handshake. Regardless of the form these goodbyes take, they can be equally significant.

The story of life is quicker than the wink of an eye.
The story of love is hello and goodbye.
—JIMI HENDRIX

Quick Takes

The more formal form of farewell in Italian

IF YOU WENT TO COLLEGE with someone who had the good fortune to spend junior year abroad in, say, Bologna, you've probably heard that someone say *"Ciao, bella!"* at least once, or *"Ciao, ciao!"* on parting; this seems to be the equivalent of that same person's buying lots of scarves in France, or developing a life-long taste for schnitzel in Germany—just one of those affectations that lets the world know you're worldly.

But that someone (maybe you, this time?) should be at least a tiny bit cautious when returning to Italy before tossing *"Ciao!"* around with abandon. Yes, it means "See ya!" in a most casual way; however, its etymological origins tell a more sinister tale. *"Ciao"* derives from the phrase *"Schiavo vostro,"* literally, "I am your slave." Its Latin equivalent, *"Servus,"* is still used in some parts of Central Europe.

Of course, no one in Italy will think that you're actually avowing your servitude if you say *"Ciao, ciao!"* at the end of an evening. The phrase long ago came to connote "I'm with you; you can count on me," then morphed into the breezy "So long!" that your undergraduate chums heard. However, in European societies, the distinction between formal and informal discourse still has some meaning. Just as you wouldn't call just any new Continental acquaintance by his first name immediately, you should use more formal words of farewell with those who aren't close friends. *"Arrivederci"* takes a tiny bit longer to say, yes; but the goodwill you engender will carry you much further than a casual college night in a smoky café.

No one ever wants to say goodbye to Italy!

Could we see when and where we are to meet again,
we would be more tender when we bid our friends goodbye.
—MARIE LOUISE DE LA RAMÉE

God Be With You

IN ENGLISH, "GOODBYE" IS a contraction of "God be with you," once the shortest way for people to wish each other safety and health until their next meeting. In some faiths, part of regular worship is saying goodbye to a deity.

The Jewish havdalah ceremony marks the end of each week's Shabbat, which begins at sunset on Friday and ends on Saturday when three stars appear in the sky. Havdalah marks the end of sacred time and the start of secular time, which is stated in the final blessing: "Blessed are you, Lord, who separates between the sacred and the secular." (*"L'havdeel"* means to separate in Hebrew.)

However, the steps before that prayer demonstrate that while the Lord entreated separates

Elaborate spice boxes demonstrate reverence.

between the sacred and the secular, the humans doing the entreating need to keep a little of the sacred in their daily lives. The prayers encourage participation through the five senses: taste (wine), spices (smell), touch (heat), sight (flame), and sound (recited prayers). Those gathered are meant to share these experiences, much as Christians share a communion ritual.

This communal ceremony also reminds participants that they are meant to return. The original phrase was "God be with you, until we meet again," because anything might happen to a person while away from loved ones. The weekly havdalah blessing is a reminder that a community exists.

A 17th-century Jewish havdalah ceremony

Happy trails to you, until we meet again.
—ROY ROGERS

Departures

IN *THE AMERICAN WAY OF DEATH* British-born Jessica Mitford excoriated her adopted nation for its hands-off, sanitized approach to burial rites. Funeral homes in the United States (sometimes still called by the Victorian name of "parlor," suggesting that nothing untoward happens there) tend to keep loved ones far away from the dead person.

Not so in Japan, where modern funeral homes exist to make it easier for families to help prepare a body for its final voyage. The encoffination, or *nokanshiki* ritual, was witnessed by Western audiences when *Departures* won the Academy Award for Best Foreign Film in 2008. Before the 1960s, most burial preparation in Japan was done at home. When the process became more commercialized, however, it did not become one in which family were entirely separated from their dead relative. During the encoffination ritual, family members can do everything from give the corpse its "last drink" (water on a cotton swab) to its final clothing.

While the "last drink" might seem whimsical, most of the *nokanshiki* process is no different from what societies all over the world have done for centuries: making the deceased look his or her best before interment. The final touch

Sometimes origami cranes are placed in coffins.

may be the most folkloric. Before the wooden coffin (usually built with a small window on top for viewing the deceased's face during the funeral) is shut, the gathered family is offered a basket of folded paper (origami) cranes to place around the body. Cranes were traditionally regarded as spirit guides.

OBJECTS OF ETIQUETTE: Funeral Wreath   Wreaths of fresh flowers are rarely seen except at funeral homes, perhaps because these *corona fuberis* have been in use at funerals since Roman times. The commoner's "crown" of flowers and leaves was a memento mori to all gathered. Because the wreaths are now so closely associated with funerals, few people would dream of using them to decorate for a party, special event, or wedding.

Fare thee well! and if for ever,
Still for ever, fare thee well.
—LORD BYRON

Fare Well

MANY WESTERN MILITARY CUSTOMS have evolved from the military of ancient Rome, one of the first professional military classes. The Roman Army became an all-volunteer professional organization later in the republic's history, but its traditions caught on quickly. Soldiers were comrades, serving and dying alongside each other, and as their ranks experienced times of peace, they also celebrated and commiserated together as family.

That family feeling is expressed in a poetic phrase by the Roman poet Gaius Valerius Catullus, *"ave atque vale,"* or "Hail and Farewell," in which the speaker refers to a deceased fellow as his "brother." In military organizations since, it has become traditional to formally gather when soldiers arrive or depart. In the U.S. military, an event like this is called a "Hail and Farewell," and allows soldiers, commanders, and in many cases their families, to acknowledge service done or about to start.

Deployments call for formal farewells.

The "Hail and Farewell" has a serious purpose, particularly in countries like the U.S. that follow the Roman model of an all-volunteer military: When soldiers (or sailors!) leave or join a unit, they need to feel like part of an existing team. Of course, in peacetime, these events can seem both less serious and unnecessary, leading military families to label them as "mandatory fun"—but when there is a war on and soldiers are deploying, "Hail and Farewell" gatherings once again take on a more solemn aspect as comrades face the prospect of prolonged separations from their families, injury, and death.

ARCHAIC MANNERS: Jewelry Caskets "Coffin" means basket in Greek, and the word wasn't used in its funerary context until the 16th century, when it acquired such a dour feel that some people tried to substitute "casket" instead. Unfortunately, this meant that fine examples of cabinetry, like jewelry caskets, acquired their own dour feel. Now, we usually say "jewelry box."

*I think the dying pray at the last not please but
thank you as a guest thanks his host at the door.*
—ANNIE DILLARD

Funeral Pyres

MANY MODERN PEOPLE associate funeral pyres with the outdated Hindu practice of *suttee* in which a widow voluntarily is burned alive on her dead husband's cremation tower. (The practice has been outlawed in India since 1829.)

However, funeral pyres have been used by various civilizations for thousands of years. The ancient Romans built *ustrina* of four tiers, with the pyre itself (which they called a *rogus*) at the bottom, sending enough heat upwards to incinerate the body at the top. At its most basic, the practice of building a pyre is a form of what we now call cremation: Reducing dead bodies to their simplest elements of bone fragments and gases.

Crematoriums in the West have become quite streamlined, but not so much that they actually do the job quickly. In the U.S. and Western Europe, modern laws forbid the construction of crematoriums capable of incinerating more than one body at a time. This is a direct result of what is one of the most horrendous criminal uses of a pyre ever: the Holocaust. While it may not be pleasant to be reminded of this assembly-line genocide perpetrated on six million Jews (as well as many other targeted groups, including Roman Catholics, homosexuals, and dissenters) by the World War II German Nazi regime, it is important.

The use of ovens to burn bodies was not simply gruesomely efficient: It was a special affront to Judaism, whose practitioners held anciently derived beliefs against cremation, as do other world religions including Christianity and Islam. While many cultures and faiths have now moved toward accepting cremation in recent decades, the practice is still not universally accepted, and understanding that may make it less likely for people to commit faux pas when hearing of others' funeral plans.

Modern Hindu funeral pyres burn along Nepal's holy Bagmati River.

ELBOWS OFF THE TABLE

When Neanderthals learned to handle fire, their eating and dining behavior changed. Raw food can be eaten at any time, but cooked food requires waiting. Just as with other human habits, the delay of gratification requires a higher level of functioning around which rituals can develop.

Yet it's not cooking food that separates Neanderthals from primates, or modern humans from all of the animal kingdom, but table manners. That's right: Some scientists suggest that cooked food allowed our stomachs to shrink and reduced the volume of food needed and the blood flow the stomach required for digestion. Our brains were able to grow because blood previously sent to the stomach went to the brain. We stopped simply eating and started thinking and talking about food and how to serve it.

Even if the first dinner table looked more like a Flintstones prop than heirloom mahogany, the principle was the same: We eat while seated, usually facing each other, and we share our meals. These developments make what we do while eating significant; we're usually in fairly close proximity while we dine. No wonder that table manners are some of the first things we teach children. It's only human.

So many bad manners at once, it's farcical

HOSTS

WHEN WE IMAGINE A HOST OR HOSTESS, we think of a jovial man proffering a freshly shaken martini, or a smiling woman passing around a tray of hors d'oeuvres on toothpicks. Hosts might be friends, relatives, colleagues, or strangers you only just met. In some early cultures, however, hosting other people was about equalizing power. When a possibly unfriendly visitor arrived, providing shelter and a bite to eat could go a very long way toward making the visitor feel more the equal of the host—and therefore happier.

We should look for someone to eat and drink with before looking for something to eat and drink, for dining alone is leading the life of a lion or wolf.

—EPICURUS

As Western civilization progressed, threats from strangers lessened, and hosting became part of entertainment: Putting out a spread of food and drink, even for people who had not necessarily traveled long and far, was a way of communicating goodwill (and sometimes, of course, status as well—we can't keep up with the Joneses until we've seen what's inside their house).

Nowadays, whether it's "Minnesota nice" or "Southern hospitality" here in the United States, people understand that certain slices of society have certain ways of hosting, as well as certain expectations of their guests. While these expectations include things that seem superficial—putting napkins in laps, passing dishes to others, and properly buttering your bread—underlying all of them is an older idea. As Garrison Keillor's Lake Wobegon radio stories about Minnesota show, being "nice" means "no confrontational verbs or statements of strong personal preference, you know." In other words, let's make sure you're friendly—here, have some egg coffee and some hot dish! We're proper hosts, after all.

What is there more kindly than the feeling between host and guest?
—AESCHYLUS

Consider Yourself at Home

MANY CULTURES AND RELIGIONS have elaborate codes of behavior, like the Ten Commandments or the teachings of Confucius. However, one of the world's oldest codes of conduct has never been written down: the ancient Pashtunwali, or "The Code of Life" according to the tribal Pashtun people of the regions now divided into Pakistan and Afghanistan.

Pashtunwali, which predates and is unrelated to current Islamic law, embraces nine principles, including bravery, loyalty, justice, and trust in a divine creator, but the first and perhaps most important is hospitality, or *melmestia* in the Pashto language. *Melmestia* is required regardless of a visitor's status (race, religion, nationality, class, and gender) and freely given, without hope of payback in any form. Although the honor-based Pashtunwali can include fierce struggles for leadership, its basis is egalitarianism—so hosts and guests are equal at all times.

Along with hospitality comes the ultimate hosting obligation, *nanatawai,* or the right of sanctuary. Any person who asks for shelter and safety from harm is taken in, no questions asked. While modern people may assume sanctuary is tied to crimes (a victim fleeing a killer; a criminal evading the law), for the once wholly nomadic Pasthun, sanctuary was a basic right that could mean the difference between life and death when someone was without basic resources.

Nanatawai can also mean "repentance," often involving a feast between two neighboring families that have been involved in a blood feud. In this case, the original aggressor funds the meal and gives sheep, cloth, and sometimes even a few young women as brides to his former enemy.

Pashmina shawls from the Pashtun

ARCHAIC MANNERS: Women's Menus   Imagine dinner in a 1950s fine restaurant: A man and a woman sit down together, and are handed leatherbound menus, his with prices, hers without. The assumption was that men always paid for everything, so women didn't need to see the cost. Nowadays, this tradition persists in a few old-fashioned temples of gastronomy such as The Four Seasons in New York, which keeps a few on hand for the occasional request.

*No rule of etiquette is of less importance
than which fork we use.*
—EMILY POST

Just the Right Blend

DON'T SERVE "KOREAN TEA" at a Korean Tea Ceremony. The former is what we call an "infusion": Herbs, leaves, flower petals, fruits, and spices steeped in hot water, often for medicinal purposes. While some "Korean tea" mixtures are quite delicious (e.g., ginger and honey), they are a homely remedy.

In contrast, the Korean Tea Ceremony (often referred to as *darye,* or "way of tea") usually involves green tea of the "five tastes" (saltiness, bitterness, astringency, sweetness, and sourness). Pottery or porcelain resembling natural objects like leaves and branches is used in a centuries-old protocol—in which Koreans have taken a new interest—that dictates gestures, actions, and, in some cases, guests for the 15 types of ceremonies. Women often wear the traditional *hanbok,* a long, voluminous silk robe with a shorter bell-sleeved blouse tied on top.

The *Naebahng Darye,* or "Ladies Tea Service" was a two-hour rite performed only for the Queen, her court, and relatives (sometimes the

A Korean shopkeeper mixes tea for customers.

Crown Prince could attend) in the 19th century. As the Korean royal family no longer rules, the ceremony is relegated, along with martial arts, swordplay, and marriage ceremonies, to the popular "royal soap operas" that dramatize Korean history.

Just as you wouldn't serve "Korean Tea" at a *darye,* you wouldn't invite men to a "Ladies Tea Service." The guests—and their gender—are as important to the occasion as the food and drink.

*For ceremonial use,
loose tea is essential.*

*At a dinner party one should eat wisely but not too well
and talk well but not too wisely.*
—W. SOMERSET MAUGHAM

The Right to Lie Down

IN MANY CULTURES, the host of a meal (usually male, but not always) takes an honored chair at the head of a table or dais, seated so that all guests can see who is providing their meal and watch his behavior as they dine. Even though today a host might just be the guy microwaving the nacho cheese and passing out cans of cold beers, the seating arrangement evolved from the long-ago era when royalty ruled the table and no one lifted a turkey leg or a goblet before the monarchs had taken their first bite or sip. A vestigial remnant of this tradition is the fact that most dining rooms contain just two chairs with arms, for either end of the table: These chairs represent the symbolic seats of the king and queen.

However, other societies never adapted to chairs as mealtime thrones. In ancient Rome, hosts—and the most honored guests—reclined on raised and cushioned platforms and ate by propping themselves on one elbow so that they could reach food and drink on a smaller platform set up in front of them.

Until quite recently, many African tribes honored their chieftains during meals by allowing them to lie down at a distance from the other members of the tribe, who would sit on the ground so that their heads could not possibly be lower than their leader's.

While today only a small portion of chiefdoms remain in sub-Saharan Africa, some of those still derive from traditions in which the leader was considered a descendant of the gods. The chief's honored mealtime repose and separation from his people symbolized this godlike status. He is served only by his wives and children, and everyone else is allowed to eat and drink only after he has done so.

Roman nobles often reclined for entertaining.

ARCHAIC MANNERS: Dressing for Dinner   For several centuries, changing clothes before the evening meal, or "dressing for dinner," allowed the wealthy to show that they had better garments to wear. Evening gowns, dinner jackets, and jewels to match were de rigueur in aristocratic circles, and the practice evolved into a sort of evening ceremony. Today, the custom is still followed in rare instances—for example, formal nights on cruise ships.

MANNERED LIVES

The Duchess of Orléans

In the pre-Revolution French court, illegitimate birth was no barrier to obsession with etiquette. One of the chief early 18th-century arbiters of royal behavior was Françoise Marie de Bourbon, daughter of Louis XIV and his mistress the Marquise de Montespan (familiarly known as Madame de Montespan).

The Duchess of Orléans, as she was known after marriage, was so very status-conscious that courtiers joked that she remained a "daughter of France" even while attending to the call of nature—and since life at Versailles revolved almost entirely around etiquette, she may well have needed to be on her toes even when on the toilet. After all, the toilet, or *chaise percée* (pierced seat) was a chair—and who sat in which particular type of chair at Versailles was extremely telling. Only the king and queen were allowed to lower their royal selves into armchairs. Their children and other close relatives could sit in armless chairs with backs, while high-ranking nobles perched on padded stools known as *tabourets*.

Everyone knew their place—and everyone else's places, as well. The Duchess of Orléans was particularly mindful of the ups and downs in people's reputations. One letter she wrote venting her frustrations to the Duchess of Hanover in 1704 is worth quoting:

Once the Duchess of Orléans took a seat, she did not give it up easily.

The Duchesse de Bourgogne's ladies . . . tried to arrogate the rank and take the place of my ladies everywhere . . . They got the King's Guards to keep their places and push back the chairs belonging to my ladies . . . I went immediately to the King and . . . Although these ladies are high in favour, the King, nevertheless, sent the majordomo to find out how things should be done . . . These women are becoming far too insolent now that they are in favour . . . I shall not lose my rank nor prerogatives on account of the favour they enjoy.

One cannot think well, love well,
sleep well, if one has not dined well.
—VIRGINIA WOOLF

It's on Me

IN THE MIDDLE EAST, especially in Saudi Arabia, Iran, and Iraq, many dimensions of daily life are segregated by gender. Men and women not only stay apart in communal situations; they often have entirely separate routines. These include social events, too. While Western men and women, married or not, will routinely attend dinner parties together at private homes, Arab women are accustomed to holding "women-only" dinner parties, which can be quite elaborate and festive affairs.

Even in the few places in the Arab world where women are no longer segregated, female-only gatherings continue a long tradition of women entertaining themselves while men were either on the other side of a wall, in a completely different building, or otherwise distanced from the

Scents are part of the sensibility in Arabia.

ladies' party. One of the most intriguing customs at these parties comes toward the end, when the hostess will bring out her box of perfumes (once these might have been various essential oils; today they are just as likely to be designer brands). Each guest is allowed to try the fragrance she prefers—sometimes they spritz on more than one scent. Part of this is due to religious constraints: Muslim law has firm words for women who wear perfume in situations where they might encounter men. For devout Muslim women, sharing the perfume chest among women is a safe way to experience a little luxury with friends.

For guests who wear robes (burkas or chadors), one last ritual awaits. The hostess will light a cone of incense, and each woman will stand over it, holding out her robe. In this way, her entire person will be scented—and when she returns home, her relatives will say "Where have you been this evening? You smell so lovely!"

But these Muslim women aren't alone in building social customs around nice scents. In Japan, you'll find the *kodo* ceremony, something similar to that country's tea ceremony, but inspired by incense instead of a hot drink. In one variation, different scents symbolize particular images, phrases, or ideas. Ceremony participants try to identify the meaning behind each scent and connect the smoky fragrances to a poem or well-known story. Mastering the kodo ceremony is considered an art. The most beautiful detail of the custom, however, is that no "smelling" is done. Instead, inhaling the various scents is referred to as "listening."

GUESTS

Hosts have obligations to guests—but the reverse is also true. Guests aren't the same as family. There is a deliberate protocol in every society for what a guest should expect, and what a guest is allowed to do. In an Asian home, guests are expected to remove their shoes at the door, and are sometimes provided with special slippers or indoor footwear. For a guest to clomp in wearing mud-encrusted boots or to leave with the host's slippers would be considered terribly rude.

> *Men that can have communication in nothing else, can sympathetically eat together, can still rise into some glow of brotherhood over food and wine.*
>
> —THOMAS CARLYLE

Part of the social contract between host and guest is that neither should embarrass the other. For example, in Western cultures, a guest should generally leave a bit on her plate to show that she was given enough (often phrased by grandmothers as "Leave a little on your plate for Miss Manners," which is where Judith Martin got her *nom d'etiquette,* if you will), which prevents the host from feeling embarrassed about not serving sufficient food. Meanwhile, the host should not take away dishes without asking if everyone has eaten their fill. This can result in humorous situations of guests and hosts trying to accommodate each other—as anyone who has ever attended a family Thanksgiving celebration will attest—but the goal is that both hosts and guests feel respected.

However, the greatest part of a guest's contract is to remain engaged and interested. If you are receiving someone else's hospitality, you need to be conscious of that fact and be charming, even if you'd much rather be at home in bed. Act as if the simplest bowl of stew is filet mignon and you will not only honor your host—you may be asked to return.

The manner of giving is worth more than the gift.
—PIERRE CORNEILLE, FRENCH DRAMATIST, *LE MENTEUR*

You Shouldn't Have

MOST NORTH AMERICANS take great care, when wrapping a gift, to remove all evidence of its cost. Tags are removed, prices scratched out, and stickers carefully unpeeled, even when the object's value is known to all (like an iPad). That's not the case in Japan, where price stickers are often proudly displayed on the outside of wrapping paper!

That's because gift giving in Japan is less about surprise and delight than it is about gratitude and respect. The ceremony of giving a gift is more important than the actual item, so knowing the price does not "spoil" the gift, but enhances its presentation. The gift wrap, whether it is elaborately prepared paper or *furoshiki*, a lovely, reusable fabric that is folded around a gift like origami, lets a host or hostess know that you took time and trouble on their behalf. That's also why a Japanese person will never open the gift in front of you, preferring instead to display it for as long as possible.

Appropriate gifts, therefore, are not one-of-a-kind artifacts. It's best to choose name-brand liquor, good candy, or fruit rather than anything for home décor or personal adornment. (This is in part because Japanese homes are small and a consumable good won't require long-term storage.) Your relationship with the recipient is more important than the gift;

present it with both hands and a slight bow to indicate that you remember this. It will probably be refused at least once and usually twice, so keep offering until it is accepted. And should you be offered a gift? It's also polite to demur once or twice, then receive it in both hands, with a bow. While it isn't traditional to open the gift in front of the receiver, if you end up doing so, be careful to remove the wrapping neatly and set it aside.

Because both objects and their wrapping have a great deal of symbolism in Japan, it's easiest to buy hostess gifts at a department store. That way you needn't worry about the significance of red or the unlucky status of items in groups of four. You can relax and concentrate on what's most important: your friendship with the people who have chosen to entertain you.

In Japan, fine wrap can mean more than a gift.

*Food comes first,
then morals.*

—BERTOLT BRECHT, *DIE DREIGROSCHENOPER*, 1928

Hearty Appetites

JULIA CHILD, TELEVISION'S FRENCH CHEF, had a significant impact on American cuisine, and in addition to *Julie & Julia,* a 2009 film about the chef and a young New Yorker, Julia Child's distinctive voice has been imitated over and over again, sometimes even on comedy shows such as *Saturday Night Live.* Fans may remember her gregarious presence and her honest portrayal of what cooking takes. Upon dropping a chicken on the floor, she picked it up, kept cooking and famously reminded viewers, "You are alone in the kitchen." One particular Julia Child saying that stuck was her signature *"Bon appétit!"* the French phrase used to signal the start of a meal.

Many cultures say a kind of "secular grace" just before everyone starts buttering their bread and cutting their meat, by diners wishing each other a good repast. In Germany, one diner will say *"Guten Appetit! Prost Mahlzeit!"* and the rest of the company will quietly repeat *"Guten Appetit"* or *"Gleichfalls"* ("Likewise"). In Slovak-speaking regions, people say *"Dobro chut,"* meaning "Enjoy your meal." In Japan they say, *"Itadakimasu"* ("I graciously accept this") before the meal, and *"Gochisosama deshita"* ("It was delicious") after the meal.

Julia Child had an appetite for life.

In Spanish-speaking countries, the phrase is *"Buen provecho"* ("To a good meal"), but the tradition is carried one step further. A person dining in public is honor bound to ask a stranger nearby to share in his "good meal." While modern Spaniards and Latin Americans rarely follow this custom, the idea is there, and reminds people in Ecuador, Bolivia, Argentina, Chile, and Paraguay that saying "Buen provecho" is a sign that we are bound to others by our daily bread.

Unfortunately, there is no common equivalent phrase in English. Could this be due to the centuries-old rivalry between France and Great Britain? Regardless of the cause, it is a shame that in a language gaining new speakers all over the world all the time that we do not have a simple way of wishing each other "good appetite."

Julia Child

Mastering
the Art
of French
Cooking

Louisette Bertholle
Simone Beck

Cooking is like love.
It should be entered into with abandon or not at all.
—HARRIET VAN HORNE, *VOGUE*, 1956

Just Smashing

GUESTS SHOULD TREAT THEIR host's belongings with utmost care and respect. If you spill a glass of red wine on a white carpet or break a beautiful serving dish, you should immediately apologize, offer to pay for the repair or replacement, and perhaps leave a little earlier than you'd planned.

But imagine a scenario where your host and hostess handed you your plates and begged you to smash them into bits! That's what might happen if you're asked to take part in an old German tradition called the *polterabend* ("noisy evening"). A polterabend is held right before a wedding (in some parts of Austria and Switzerland it is the equivalent of a bachelorette party), and is often a very casual affair, with invitations passed by word of mouth to all relatives and neighbors—a wider circle than is actually invited to the ceremony.

The couple and their families greet guests and then pass out pottery and crockery; if there is old, unwanted china about, they'll use that, too, but glass and mirrors are off limits because breaking glass symbolizes bad luck. Once everyone has a few mugs, plates, and platters, everyone has a merry time smashing them on the ground. While the origins of this chaotic tradition are unclear, who cleans up the mess isn't: It's always the bride and groom, because sweeping up the shards of broken household goods is supposed to teach them about how to work together in the years ahead.

Of course, other groups also break things at times of celebration. Jewish weddings end with the groom stomping on a glass (though, these days, it's more likely a lightbulb wrapped in a cloth napkin). While crushing the glass appears to be joyous, it's actually intended to remind the couple and their guests of the destruction of the Temple in Jerusalem and the suffering that Jews have endured. In another wedding tradition, the mothers break a plate, symbolizing the changed relationship with their children.

Smashed crockery signals a fine wedded start.

At every party there are two kinds of people—those who want to go home and those who don't. The trouble is, they are usually married to each other.
—ANN LANDERS

The Women's Room

AT ONE TIME, when a meal had finished, an English or American hostess of the upper classes would rise as a signal to the other ladies at table that it was time to leave the gentlemen to their port and cigars. What this really meant—besides stinky stogies and drained decanters—was that the men were "ready" to talk about matters they believed the women did not understand or might be offended by hearing. Politics, coarse gossip, bawdy jokes, and the world of ideas were what the men considered lively conversation. They just didn't realize that most of the women had equally lively conversation of their own.

For a variety of societal and cultural reasons, the generations of Westerners who separated after dinner (and the practice continues in a few far-flung places even today) believed, or at least paid lip service to, the idea that women

Ladies were once sent off to sew after dinner.

were less intellectual and more delicately sensitive than men.

As women became more likely to hold advanced degrees, professional positions, political offices, and business clout, men and women had much more in common to discuss. Colleagues encountering one another—with spouses in tow—at dinner parties might just as likely be opposite genders; separating would deprive each of lively "shop talk" or interesting policy debate. Men also found they had much to lose by ignoring highly intelligent women.

Eventually men and women decided against separating after dinner, as well as in the boardroom, for that matter. Today, both genders congregate for coffee—although the cigars, in our modern nonsmoking world, are definitely optional.

FAMOUS GAFFES: Sir Paul McCartney at a Washington banquet In June 2010, former Beatle Sir Paul McCartney made gossip column news when he supposedly switched the place cards at a dinner being held in his honor at the Library of Congress in Washington, D.C. He did so in order to be seated next to his love interest Nancy Shevell. No one knows who took his original chair between Representative Nancy Pelosi and Lady Sheinwald, the wife of the British ambassador.

TABLES

S ITTING DOWN TOGETHER AT SOME SORT of surface to share dishes is an ancient practice. After thousands of years, most tables have evolved from low wooden circles to chic designs such as sleek metal oblongs; all are now raised off the ground and have legs. But regardless of their form, their purpose is to help people gather and eat.

Now that we've got the table structure figured out, the social part should be easy, right? Wrong. Remember that family Thanksgiving celebration? Any group of people headed toward a meal can have any number of problems: Not enough food. The wrong kind of food. An uneven number of chairs. Relatives who don't want to sit close to each other, and lovers who want to cuddle through dinner. And those are the simple problems. Who knows what might happen if someone is holding a grudge—or bearing a weapon?

Fortunately, dinners rarely involve bloodshed these days. However, the long-lasting effect of extreme behavior at the table is that dining etiquette has become an important delineator of social class. Men and women with excellent table manners

It is so beautifully arranged on the plate, you know someone has had their hands all over it.

—JULIA CHILD

are accorded the kind of respect that a person who left sword and scabbard at the door might have been given hundreds of years ago.

Refinement in table manners signals that a person has taken time to consider what best suits other people, whether they're seated at left or right, or across the table. No wonder that elaborate dinners are often a precursor to being hired in large, formal companies— he or she who demonstrates deft precision with cutlery will usually practice the same when faced with a crucial deal.

It isn't so much what's on the table that matters,
as what's on the chairs.
—SIR W. S. GILBERT

Get Carded

IN THE 21ST CENTURY, the most common occasions requiring seating plans are business functions and weddings. At a business event, planners want to be sure that people at certain professional levels are accorded the highest places. At a wedding reception, planners must account for both family hierarchy and social hierarchy.

Basically, seating arrangements at social events (as opposed to ticketed, stadium and concert hall events) have always been and probably always will be a matter of etiquette rather than simple good manners. If we went by simple chance, the oldest, youngest, and most socially awkward might get seats next to the bride and groom, and junior employees could potentially cozy up to the boss. That won't happen except at a handful of very progressive tables, and so people continue to use place cards. At some modern weddings, however, place cards themselves are less formal and more whimsical. A creative bride might write your name and table number on a smooth river stone, a card perched on a wine glass, or perhaps, on a tag tied to the branches of a tree.

The fascinating thing about modern seating arrangements is that what was once a laborious duty of the chatelaine and head housekeeper (traversing a ballroom, pen in hand) has been transformed by modern technology. Software programs, web sites, and applications for various mobile devices allow people planning events from bar mitzvahs to dinner parties to endlessly experiment with table sizes and configurations—right up until the moment those place cards (or river stones) must be printed. The element of early decisiveness has been eliminated—or at least delayed. Yet even as seating charts go online, the hostess has more opportunities than ever to buy leatherbound planners, seating guides, and entertainment journals with pages of schematics for building perfect seating arrangements. Everything old is new again.

At a royal wedding, protocol matters.

Laughter is brightest where food is best.
—IRISH PROVERB

Dig in

IT'S AN HONOR TO BE A GUEST, and in many cultures, honored guests are served food and drink before anyone else at the table. However, this is not a universal practice.

In many Balkan countries, the family is the fundamental social unit. Several generations of one family often live together, and if you are asked to a meal in a private home, you can expect to be introduced to babies and senior citizens. The eldest family members are always served first when you are not there. As a guest, you may be offered the first serving; however, as a sign of respect for the family elders you should say, "No, thank you; I'll wait until Mr. X has tried some." This will endear you to your hosts (not to mention Mr. X!).

Albania, Bulgaria, Turkey, and Greece share many of the same customs and manners, not simply because of their geographical proximity, but because of the geographical similarities. The rocky terrain and sparse vegetation make daily life a challenge, and blood ties are cherished—and that is reflected in their dining etiquette.

This also means that when a guest is present, sometimes too much food is prepared or ordered, so as to keep up appearances in front of the family. (Anyone who has seen the movie

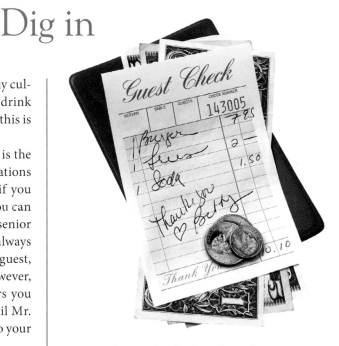

Picking up the check can be an honor.

My Big Fat Greek Wedding might recall the mountain of potatoes that the main character's mother peels in preparation for a visit from her daughter's fiancé's parents.) Sometimes this food goes to waste, but the upside is that everyone gets plenty to eat of the most popular dishes that the family or the restaurant prepares. There's another good side, too—as a guest you will never be allowed to split or foot the bill. That's a pretty good incentive for remembering to honor the elders.

OBJECTS OF ETIQUETTE: Two-tined Forks Forks were originally used for spearing rather than lifting or scooping, and for this reason usually had just two tines, set widely apart. The third, middle tine caught on quickly for lifting food to one's mouth, but two-tined forks persist in carving sets, where they are used to spear roasted meats.

No man is lonely eating spaghetti,
for it requires so much attention.
—CHRISTOPHER MORLEY, AMERICAN JOURNALIST, 1890-1957

A Little Overheated

NO ONE WANTS OVERCOOKED PASTA, which is why Italian cooks usually throw a piece or two at the wall to make sure it sticks and is "al dente," or pleasing "to the tooth." Same goes for dinnertime conversation—everyone wants to be sure it's pleasing to as many as possible.

Every culture also has certain subjects that are taboo or discouraged. If you're in Chicago, don't praise the Green Bay Packers; if you're in China, you might want to think before launching into a discussion about Mao's Little Red Book. In some places, it's just one topic, while in others it's many.

That's the case with the pasta-loving Italians. Due to politics, history, and temperament, there are several subjects visitors might want to

Pasta goes with lots, but not politics.

avoid, especially when invited out for a meal or (less likely) to a private home. The first, which you might have guessed, is the Roman Catholic Church. Even if you're a devout Roman Catholic, unless you know your host's views on religion, skirt any issues of newsmaking priests. Even for the many modern Italians who are agnostic or atheist, the Catholic Church is a strong cultural institution.

Second, slightly less obvious, is World War II. Of course, Italy was an Axis power and against the Allies—but the real reason to avoid this topic of conversation is obvious to anyone who has studied history. There's no sense in dredging up a painful past, especially among those who are too young to have played any role in it. But there's no reason to fall into either of these conversational pitfalls given the multitude of things you can talk about in Italy—including the delicious pasta you're likely to be served any minute now . . .

Someone said that life is a party.
You join in after it's started and leave before it's finished.
—ELSA MAXWELL, AMERICAN COLUMNIST, 1883–1963

May I Be Excused?

EVERYONE KNOWS WHEN to arrive for a dinner party, even if some choose to appear "fashionably late" (word to the wise: "fashionably late" is up to 30 minutes; after that, you're just rude). Getting people to leave is a different matter. French hostesses offer fruit juice and mineral water to those who won't move towards the door; Americans put cups of strong black coffee in revelers' hands. But there are always guests who don't take the hint.

In China, nearly every aspect of social life has its protocol, and leading guests to depart is no exception. In a private home, most Chinese guests know it is their duty to rise after a round or two of postprandial drinks; no one leaves before the guest of honor does.

However, when a Chinese meal is hosted at a restaurant, several steps help an event come to an end. First the waitstaff will bring fresh fruit

Bubbly water when the party's gone flat

(the only type of dessert ethnic Chinese serve unless they are hosting a party of Westerners). After that, hot towels are passed around for cleaning hands and mouths.

Of course, even the fresh towels don't always do the trick, so Chinese restaurateurs have one last trick: When all else fails, they simply don't refill the teapot. For the tea-loving Chinese, this is like turning off the lights and shouting "Last call!" Before the host can say "Thank you so much for coming," everyone has left and is en route home.

UTENSILS

OUR FIRST FOOD TOOL IS OUR MOUTH; our second, our hands. Between these two parts of our human bodies, we first managed to take in water, fruit, and nuts. But as our societies and bodies evolved, other types of food became desirable, and these foods required cutting. The earliest knives, made of flint, shell, and bone, were fashioned by repeated rubbing on harder stones and allowed humans to divide carcasses. Not so different, really, from your uncle's prized carving set.

Actually, there was a big difference: Your uncle's prized carving set includes some sort of fork, and of the three implements common on most tables today, the fork was the last to be invented and come into usage. Spoons are known from 5000 B.C.; metal knives, from about 2000 B.C.; but forks aren't commonly seen until A.D. 800. (They were known in ancient Greece and are mentioned in the Hebrew Scriptures, but very few people had or used them.) Even once forks were used by individuals, they only had two tines—fantastic for spearing pickles, but not particularly helpful for scooping up peas or casserole. People used their hands and spoons and pieces of bread for moving food from table to mouth. In Ethiopia, it's still common to use bread instead of utensils.

> *If people take the trouble to cook, you should take the trouble to eat.*
>
> —ROBERT MORLEY

The most important thing to remember is that the utensils we use for eating are just tools and not objects of mystery. Elaborate place settings are less about good manners and more about etiquette. If a knife can't cut or a spoon can't ladle, it's not worth anything, especially intimidation. Think about that the next time you're worried about using the right fork.

*Do carry food to your mouth with an inward,
not an outward, curve of the fork or spoon.*
—DOROTHEA JOHNSON, *THE LITTLE BOOK OF ETIQUETTE*, 1997

Know When to Hold 'Em

FOR CENTURIES AFTER INDIVIDUAL use of knives and forks became common, people carried their own from place to place; the wealthy even owned telescoping forks that stayed clean and would not damage their garments. This wasn't merely a matter of being finicky; in the Renaissance and even afterward, hygiene was decidedly iffy. The person who looked after her own utensils ensured that they weren't covered with bacteria and grime.

When everyone carried their own different styles and sizes of knives and forks, there weren't standard rules about how and when to use them. However, slowly households began to accumulate collections of flatware: spoons, forks, and knives, along with plates used at mealtimes (as opposed to hollowware: bowls, glasses, and other objects of depth). Eventually manufacturers began to make and sell sets of all three that were approximately the same style and size, and at that point, people started to notice what their tablemates were doing with their utensils.

Ever wondered why your steak knives end in a point and your regular knife has a blunt tip? That's because France's King Louis XIV, apparently fearing mealtime violence, ordered in 1669 that all dining knives have a ground-down point. Well into the 19th century, men used their own pocketknives if and when they wished to, and as a result Europeans ate by cutting their food, then putting their knives down (safer!) and using their fork with their dominant hand.

You're thinking: "But Europeans eat with the fork in the left hand and the knife in the right!" You're correct: Once the dratted colonials (i.e., Americans) began aping the Old Country's table manners, Continental types switched their forks from the right hand to the left.

However, it's not just the use of opposite hands that distinguishes the European style; the fork and knife are held in different grips, too. In the Continental style, the fork is used to spear already-cut food and is rarely employed as a scoop (proper use in the States), which certainly slows down the dining process.

The world was my oyster but I used the wrong fork.
—OSCAR WILDE

Fork Tender

SOMETIMES HOW YOU USE your fork indicates whether you're from the United States of America or from Europe; sometimes it indicates something about the state of the food; and sometimes it can be a compliment to the chef.

This goes back thousands of years, to the days long before humans used any utensils other

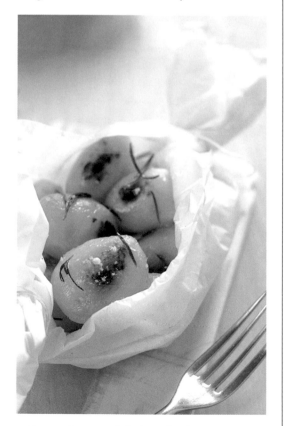

German hosts and chefs prefer that you spear, not slice, your spuds.

than their hands. Food served communally had to be easy to divide communally, too; the best candidates were stews, tender meats, and soft vegetables and starches. There was also the matter of human taste, which changed over the centuries as cooking methods became more standard and people could reliably differentiate between a roasted meat versus a fried or baked one, for example.

In Germany, people became quite accustomed to soft starches. Even today, German *Brat Kartoffeln* (fried potatoes) and *Semmelknödeln* (semolina dumplings) are very popular dishes in that country and many others. These long-cooked tubers and steamed grains contrast well with the strongly flavored sausages and braised roasts that German cooks and diners favor (often, other vegetables are served cold, as marinated salads, for a crunchy counterpoint).

It is a point of some pride for those German cooks that their potatoes and dumplings be tender enough for a fork to glide right through. Even if you're dining with your knife and fork poised in the "Continental" style, stop before you take a knife to a dish of potatoes when you're dining in a German home. Indicating that those steamed potatoes are "fork tender" by using only your fork to cut and eat them is considered quite correct and extremely polite. The general rule in Germany is anything that does not require a knife should not be touched with a knife—but that goes double for the humble potato.

*Marriage is like twirling a baton, turning hand springs,
or eating with chopsticks. It looks easy until you try it.*
—HELEN ROWLAND, AMERICAN JOURNALIST, 1875-1950

Pick Up the Sticks

WHILE WESTERNERS ARGUE about where to put dessert forks, billions of people on the other side of the world never use forks. Chopsticks are used in China, Japan, Korea, Vietnam, Laos, Thailand, and Burma, and have a long history that might surprise those who have only seen the splintery wooden kind at North American Chinese restaurants.

Although the "chop" in chopsticks comes from the Chinese Pidgin English phrase "chop chop," meaning "to hurry," the Mandarin Chinese compound for the sticks, *kuazi*, also includes the idea of "quick." The Asian concept of quick in chopsticks isn't about fast food, but rather about fast eating; chopsticks allow a rapid delivery from bowl to mouth.

We know chopsticks were used in China about 1200 B.C. and quickly spread to nearby lands. They can be used like tongs (very young children are given "teaching chopsticks" that are hinged at the top to make the tong-like action easier).

Simple chopsticks can have complex rules.

Very long chopsticks, called *saibashi* in Japan, are used for cooking. Chopsticks can have blunt ends (most usual) or pointed ends (for picking bones out of fish and spearing larger pieces of food). Some have ridged ends for slippery foods.

Few Asians keep disposable bamboo chopsticks at home; most have plenty of nondisposables made from wood, metal, bone, jade, and even porcelain. There are many rules governing their use. One tip: It's very rude in any Asian restaurant to rub wooden or bamboo chopsticks together (Americans often believe this eliminates splinters) because that indicates that you think the utensils (and establishment) are cheap. And never, ever, jam your chopsticks vertically into your food unless you're ready for an aggressive and hostile challenge.

OBJECTS OF ETIQUETTE: Grape Scissors When 19th-century dinners included a fruit course as part of the gastronomic ritual, small, easily handled scissors to snip clusters of grapes from bunches were essential. Today, grape scissors seem fussy—but whenever someone uses kitchen shears to cut up grapes, they're following an old custom.

A loaf of bread, a jug of wine, and thou.
—OMAR KHAYYÁM, PERSIAN SCHOLAR AND PHILOSOPHER, 1048-1131

Very Well Bread

DINING WARE VARIES: Fine bone china, rough pottery, paper plates, straw mats, and even banana leaves are all potential options, depending on your location. However, one of the early and long-popular individual serving surfaces was what the English called a "trencher," a thick slice of dense, often stale, bread that could be placed on a table to hold one person's portion of a meal.

Often these sauce-soaked slices were given to the hounds or to the poor, but sometimes (depending, no doubt, on how stale the original loaf was), diners would break pieces of their trenchers off to sop up a bit of rich gravy that otherwise would go to waste. This practice continues in many bread-loving cultures, although its frequency and technique vary widely. In some communal-plate cuisines, thin and/or spongy bread like the Mediterranean lavash can be the main utensil.

However, in Western European traditions, bits of the "trencher" came into their own. Sometimes known as "sops" or "sippets," these bits of bread would be left to soften in broth or wine or a sauce, then eaten with gusto. Today "soppin' bread" (a colloquial American expression from the South) is common in many European countries, including France, Italy, and Spain where pieces of bread or rolls are used to soak up bits of sauces. The Spanish found even more utilitarian duties for their bread—the country's small dishes called tapas are said to have begun when people started putting bread atop their wine to keep the flies away.

In Great Britain and the United States, wiping a plate or bowl clean with a piece of bread was for many decades considered a sign of being ill-bred (pun very much intended). Eventually the bread trencher evolved into an indented wooden slab, but the bread as food-holder tradition has never quite died. In recent years, the practice has picked up as new appreciation for dense bread—perhaps very similar to what once appeared on our tables as trenchers—has increased.

FOODS

OODS PLAY AN IMPORTANT ROLE in manners and customs everywhere in the world, from the "milk and honey" mentioned in holy books to the elaborately planned menus for state dinners to the preservation of regional ingredients and recipes.

Food can be considered from many different aspects, including where it comes from, how it is prepared, the manner in which it is served, and how it is meant to be eaten. Whoever first said "One man's meat is another man's poison" must have been thinking of a situation that involved some display of good *and* bad manners—of course, the proper way to deal with the offer of a food you think you won't like is to at least taste it. Regardless of whether you confirm your first impression or discover a new favorite dish, if you are socially skilled you will express gratitude for the food and never complain even if you'd rather eat rotten eggs than the item you've just tasted. Graciously sampling food offered by others is good manners almost anywhere.

> *Before eating, always take a little time to thank the food.*
> AMERICAN INDIAN PROVERB

The trouble is, when it comes to food, manners and customs do vary a great deal around the world, and people who travel are bound to make a mistake or two as they cross borders. The best way to minimize these errors is to watch the locals carefully. How do they hold this particular snack, or order that kind of beverage? Which serving implement do they use? Do they eat while walking down the street, or only when sitting? And so on. Since everybody eats, people are almost always willing to at least try to explain about local foods and customs. But remember: Trying a food somewhere else means you're a guest of a sort. Even if you swallow a yummy-looking snack and realize it's made of fried crickets, try not to express distaste. It's just plain good manners.

If a man has no tea in him, he is incapable
of understanding truth and beauty.
—JAPANESE PROVERB

Loud and Proud

Different kinds of tea, or tea-like infusions, are brewed, sipped, and enjoyed in almost every part of the world—but just as the styles of preparing those teas can be quite different from place to place, they can taste extremely different, too. The Asian *matcha* green tea has a bitter, grassy flavor, while some kinds of Indian and Chinese black teas are smoky. The main characteristic of Moroccan mint tea (which is really a green tea with mint leaves mixed in it) is its intense sweetness. It is always brewed with sugar, sometimes so much that Western palates wince on the first sips.

While Westerners wince, Moroccans (and other residents of Arabic countries) are busy slurping, and slurping very audibly, in a sort of "sip, sip, SLURP" rhythm. Since mint tea is usually served three times in succession, sitting in a Casablanca café can be a noisy experience. Servers stir tea leaves in pots to clean them, then pour the brewed tea from a height so that foam will form atop each glass tumbler of tea. The clanging, hissing, and slurping is all part of a culture in which noisy ingestion of food and drink indicates true enjoyment and satisfaction.

Of course, slurping any liquid is the height of bad manners in Western countries, so visitors to Morocco may wince at more than the sugar content of "Tuareg tea," as it is sometimes called in honor of the local indigenous peoples. The irony is, when Europeans first began to drink tea, they considered it proper to slop from cup to saucer, then slurp loudly to make the hot liquid easier to drink, proving that manners aren't really about right or wrong—but they are some combination of common sense and general consensus.

Moroccan mint tea served in glasses

Condiments are like old friends—highly thought of,
but often taken for granted.

—MARILYN KAYTOR, AMERICAN JOURNALIST, 1929-2007

Cast of Condiments

NOT EVERY DINNER party table includes a central dish with bread-and-butter plate to its upper left, an array of crystal goblets on the right, and fine silver arranged in decreasing sizes on either side of the plate. In some regions of India, a guest at a dinner is just as likely to be seated in front of a *thali,* which is a rimmed tray filled with smaller dishes of several different sizes meant to accommodate a few main courses and a number of condiments, garnishes, and salads. Essentially, it's meant to accommodate every whim that the diner might have.

Indian thali *can hold lots of "dishy" treats.*

Properly arrayed, an Indian thali meal not only allows guests to tailor dishes to their own particular taste—it is also a nutritional bonanza. A vegetarian thali is as robust as the "non-veg" version and includes protein (in *dals,* or legume stews, as well as dairy products). In addition, both veg and non-veg thalis include starch in the form of rice and sometimes breads, vegetables, healthy oils, and spices. (Are you feeling healthier yet?) The contents of a thali, whether served in a restaurant or a private home, vary from region to region and chef to chef. In the various dishes on the platter you might be tempted by smooth yogurts, spicy curries, pickled vegetables, sour chutneys, and seasoned lentils. The style of presentation might vary, too—some hosts in the Indian state of Kerala, for example, might display the meal on a thick, green banana leaf the size of a place mat.

The most important thing to remember is that the thali refers to the serving pieces and the way of eating, not the foods that are actually served; thali does not mean only vegetarian foods, for example. It's simply a type of cuisine etiquette that allows a host or cook (who are sometimes, but not always, the same person) to make decisions about what to serve, yet also allows guests to make decisions about how they would like to consume their food.

Considering the cast of characters that populate the Hindu Upanishads, it's amusing to think of the cast of little dishes that populates the average thali—but both of these things have the same purpose, really: to remind us that for Hindus, all humans are divine, and worthy of eating food they find so, too.

*Civilization has taught us to eat with a fork,
but even now if nobody is around we use our fingers.*

—WILL ROGERS, AMERICAN COMEDIAN, 1879-1935

Finger Foods

THE ETIQUETTE DOYENNES, from Emily Post to Miss Manners, have long told us that it is inoffensive to eat certain foods with our fingers—vegetables on a crudités platter, for example, and fried chicken if served at an informal meal. But in some cultures eating with the fingers is the norm—and offers ways of connecting to other people, as well. Ethiopia and Eritrea have cuisines based on thick, spicy stews known as

Rolls of injera *bread await Ethiopian stews.*

wats that are intended to be eaten using the fingers along with strips of flat, spongy *injera* bread made from a fermented form of the grain called teff.

Different wats, some including meat, such as lamb, chicken, or beef, and others made with yogurt, cottage cheese, or vegetables only, are usually arranged on a large round tray on top of several large, flat round injera breads. The meal often takes place atop an hourglass-shaped wicker table. Diners tear off pieces of the spongy bread with their right hands and use the bread to pick up the stew, perhaps by rolling it up in the bread, and bring it to their mouths. Honey wine called *tej* and *buna* (coffee) are the beverages traditionally served with the meal. The entire meal is a communal experience, but its most symbolic moment is the *goorsha*.

A goorsha (or *gursha*) occurs when a person rolls a strip of injera in the wat sauce and puts the finished roll in a friend's mouth, usually smiling as broadly and warmly as possible while doing so. It's considered an act of friendship, and the larger the roll is, the stronger that friendship must be. There is an Ethiopian saying: "Those who eat from the same plate will not betray each other"; the goorsha is a way of making stronger relationships even stronger.

OBJECTS OF ETIQUETTE: Finger Bowls Today people see finger bowls—small, hand-sized vessels—as pretentious, but these shallow containers of warmed, scented water helped when people ate multiple courses and ladies donned gloves again after dinner. If presented with a finger bowl, simply swirl your fingers and dry them on your napkin.

The only way to keep your health is to eat what you don't want, drink what you don't like, and do what you'd rather not.
—MARK TWAIN

Just for Me?

ONE TRADITION OBSERVED in almost every global culture is the practice of serving guests first. Those who come to our homes to dine are considered honored, and are offered favored status for the hours they share with us.

Because guests are honored, hosts want to give them the best: the juiciest steak, the most perfectly mixed drink, the . . . liveliest octopus? Yes, in Korea, *sannakji* is live, partially dismembered octopus, garnished with herbs and sesame oil (unfortunately, since the tentacled creature is still alive, its suction cups pose a health risk, so please warn any guests in advance).

In some places, politely refusing a proffered foodstuff is all right. A guest can say "No, thank you; I can't eat live octopus." But when you are the honored guest at a goat roast, it's probably best to say you're a vegetarian before accepting the invitation.

Guests receive the finest garnishes.

Refusing snacks like these can be rude.

Unfortunately, the most awkward situations are the most difficult to wiggle out of, as when you've been invited to, say, a Syrian home for dinner and simply don't have a big appetite. In Syria, refusing food is considered rude, as it's the host's job to make sure guests are completely sated—perhaps a holdover from days when life was more nomadic and people didn't always know when they'd be able to eat again. Take heart: If you start politely saying you're nearly full early and often, and make sure to at least sample each dish that you can, your hosts will view your light appetite with good humor and not outrage.

MANNERED LIVES

Jonathan Swift

Sometimes manners seem arbitrary and off-putting, but how we treat people is an important part of any culture. Jonathan Swift, the renowned author, cleric, and political activist, wrote his essay "A Treatise on Good Manners and Good Breeding" late in life, after observing the effects of injustice, poverty, and ignorance on people in both his native Ireland and in England.

Cleric Jonathan Swift used biting words to convey the need for kindness.

Best known as the author of *Gulliver's Travels* and still considered one of the greatest literary satirists in the English language, Swift was ordained in the Church of Ireland. Perhaps the irony of being an Anglican priest in a largely Roman Catholic country contributed to his acerbic and conflicted views of Ireland.

One of Swift's most famous essays, "A Modest Proposal," seems to urge the people of Dublin to bear and raise children to be slaughtered for food. The cleric was actually suggesting that things were so unbearable for Dublin's poor that the most lunatic ideas seemed sane when compared to the conditions these people endured. Swift truly believed that charity and the Golden Rule ("Do unto others as you would have others do unto you.") were the foundation of Christianity, and that the way we treat other people—our manners, our everyday dealings with them—was more important than debating fine points of theology.

Swift's satire was meant to make his readers think long and hard about their own behavior, as well as that of their government. However, he was naturally funny, and people began and continue to read his work because of its humor long after the problems he wrestled with were old news.

DRINKS

W HILE WATER HAS ALWAYS BEEN the obvious beverage for human beings, sources of potable water haven't always been reliably available. Thousands and thousands of years ago people discovered that adding foodstuff to water and allowing it to ferment could provide long-term, disease-free sources of liquid to quench thirst and replenish fluids.

Most historians are unsure of which came first: beer or wine. One thing is sure: As civilizations began to settle in one place and plant crops, the fruits of those crops were found to help make beverages that helped people feel, shall we say, a little bit better about life. Different civilizations had different crops: Rice made sake. Potatoes made vodka. Juniper berries (with various other ingredients) resulted in gin. Rich soil was good for grapes and the wine that they produced.

A good apprentice cook must be as polite with the dishwasher as with the chef.

—FERNAND POINT

Just as each civilization has its tipple, each civilization has some kind of ritual for imbibing that tipple. Of course, not every liquid refreshment involves an alcoholic buzz. Some involve a caffeinated buzz! Coffee, tea, drinking chocolate, and some soft drinks provide pep. Still other drinks, from the Latin American *horchata* to the Egyptian hibiscus cooler to Indian *lassis,* are designed to satisfy the senses without stimulation. Still, none of those would be possible without the earliest forebears who began both gathering and cultivating the crops (seeds, blossoms, fruits) that make those drinks possible. With all the work that goes into making a keg of beer, a bottle of wine, or a pot of coffee, it makes sense that tradition-loving humans would forge rituals about serving and consuming these potables. Drink up!

If you're going to steal, steal a heart. If you're going to cheat, cheat death.
And if you're going to drink, drink with me.
—ANONYMOUS TOAST

To Your Health

YOU MIGHT BUY FILTERED WATER or filter water through your refrigerator or faucet—we all want tasty water that's free as of many "off" flavors and unnecessary chemicals as possible. What's in those devices? Often, charcoal—because this burnt substance traps odors and toxins.

You might consider this an odd introduction to the idea of toasting. Isn't a toast what you do at a wedding? Well, yes; you lift your champagne flute and say "Cheers!" But the reason we call that a toast has a lot to do with your water pitcher. Hundreds of years ago, people found that a heavily burnt slice of bread placed in the bottom of a goblet made home-brewed

A toast to good Champagne!

Real bubbly comes from one region.

alcoholic substances taste better. You guessed it—the charcoal in the "toast" acted as a filter. Sometimes people even put different kinds of flavorings on the toast, but that is not why some bridal toasts are spicy.

No one knows when and how this practice turned into an English idiom. Perhaps it was because drinkers would call for a toast when they wanted wine to be particularly flavorful, or because toast in wine meant people were celebrating. Today, toasts can be funny, bawdy, loving, and sometimes even insulting. There is even a specific occasion for the latter, known as a "roast"—but that is not because people put meat in their goblets. It's all about subjecting the guest of honor to high heat!

Get up and dance, get up and smile, get up and drink
to the days that are gone in the shortest while.
—SIMON FOWLER, ENGLISH MUSICIAN

I'll Drink to That

ONCE HUMANS BEGAN creating alcoholic beverages, they wanted to thank supernatural beings for existence of these magically delicious drinks. The ancient Greeks and Romans had a specific god, named Dionysius (Greek) or Bacchus (Latin), who "ruled" over alcoholic spirits. However, people saluted the deities Hermes, the Three Graces, and Zeus when they lifted their cups. The Roman rulers eventually decreed their own primacy over the gods and ordered their subjects to salute them with their raised cups instead. When drinking wine with potential rivals, to make it clear that no one had secretly slipped poison into anyone else's wine they would each pour a bit of wine into one another's goblets, and only then would the drinking begin. How jolly!

Even jollier was the Nordic practice of drinking spirits out of the skulls of (dead) conquered enemies. The Scottish word was *skiel* and the Scandinavian *skoal,* but both words derived

Whether Dionysus or Bacchus, here's to him!

from the Germanic *skelo,* meaning both "to cut" and "skull." Eventually, skoal came to mean "bowl," which is appropriate, considering the human skull's natural shape.

The first recorded use of a drink along with a salute in peacetime was in A.D 450, between British King Vortigen and the very attractive Rowena, daughter of the Saxon leader Hengist. At what was technically their "rehearsal dinner," Rowena raised her glass (really, more likely an urn or drinking horn) and cried, "Louerd King, waes hael!" ("My Lord, to your health!"), and drank to the king. Vortigen supposedly responded "Drink, hael!" and that led to both the terms "To your health!" and "wassail," as well as the Yuletide practice of drinking from a loving cup, just like these two wacky Anglo-Saxon lovebirds. According to the story, the pair, after some negotiations and an exchange of land between Rowena's father and the king, were married that very evening.

OBJECTS OF ETIQUETTE: Ainu Mustache Holders The men of Japan's Ainu people, the indigenous inhabitants of the wintry island of Hokkaido, traditionally grew their hair, beards, and mustaches as long as possible. To manage these tresses, they used individually carved wooden "lifters" to hold their facial hair out of the way when eating and drinking.

The pub was a revolutionary invention [and] immediately
began to erode the whole traditional image of the hotel as a house.
—MARK GIROUARD, BRITISH WRITER

Cheers, Mate!

IN CASE YOU DIDN'T KNOW (and if you never thought about it, you wouldn't), the British term "pub" comes from "public house," meaning an establishment where the general public could obtain alcoholic drinks. This was in contrast to the stuffy gentlemen's clubs where only members (usually possessing only the qualification of proper birth) could order a pint of beer or glass of port.

Today pubs can be found on nearly every corner of most British cities, and that includes cities in the British Commonwealth nation and continent of Australia. Just as in England, pubs in Australia often included rooms to let—and because early Australian laws allowed pubs to serve alcohol only to travelers, these pubs called themselves "hotels" so anyone could know that alcohol was available. A few bedrooms above the bar? Voilà, a hotel!

Although the laws have changed, hundreds of Australian bars are still known as "hotels,"

A symbol of Australian swagger

and their rowdy culture is still going strong, popularized in movies like *Crocodile Dundee* and *Priscilla, Queen of the Desert*. However, the most remarkable characteristic of Australian pubs, hotels, and bars is their conviviality. Australians do not consider it good form to drink alone, and this often leads to sharing a pint whenever you run into a friend. The person who says "Come have a drink" handles the bill.

Whether Australian communal drinking culture evolved from a society of misfits whose lone drinking often got out of hand or (more likely) it came about due to the loneliness of a large, empty countryside, today it's definitely the lay of the land.

I have measured out my life with coffee spoons.
—T. S. ELIOT

To a Tea

PEOPLE DRINK COFFEE and tea around the world, but one type of plant-based stimulating beverage is popular only in Latin American countries: *yerba mate.* Stress the first syllable of mate ("MAH-tay")—to avoid saying "I killed" in Spanish ("mah-TAY"). This tealike drink is brewed from the dried leaves and stemlets of the perennial tree *Ilex paraguarensis* (yerba mate). The name mate derives from the Quichua word *matí* that names the gourd *(Lagenaria vulgaris)* traditionally used to drink the infusion.

Mate is drunk for its stimulating properties (the U.S. Food and Drug Administration deems it as safe as coffee and tea), but many people who drink it add different kinds of herbs to give it medicinal properties (e.g., diuretic). However, the ritual and social aspects of yerba mate drinking are prominent and continue to grow in popularity.

Many kinds of yerba mate at market

Sterling gourd holder and bombilla

Yerba mate is traditionally made and served in a hollowed-out calabash gourd and drunk through a special kind of straw called a *bombilla.* Originally made of silver, today these straws are often other types of metal, but they usually share a special, spatulate sieve at the bottom so that the person drinking gets just the liquid and not the leafy, twiggy bits that remain in the hot brew.

The etiquette surrounding *yerba mate* is all about drinking the stuff at the best temperature—since it is cold-brewed first, then heated with more water, the first sip can be too cold or too strong, and is referred to as the *mate del zonzo* ("mate of the fool"). Great lengths are taken to create and preserve a perfectly hot mate, from special thermal gourds to different kinds of straws.

RANK'S PRIVILEGES

We poor humans can only keep so many ideas in our brains at once, so we sometimes have to make decisions: Left, or right? Hot, or cold? Cat, or dog? In order to make those decisions, we sometimes have to decide which is better at the time—and "better" can depend on so many circumstances. Hot is better than cold when you've just walked a mile in snow, but cold is what we crave on steamy summer days. If we live in a place that has more of those steamy days than wintry ones, we'll probably decide that being cool is more important than being hot. While debating switching on a fan may seem trivial, many of our decisions set the courses of our lives. Where do we go to college? Whom do we marry? Our personal hierarchies define us.

Same goes for our various societies, institutions, and governing bodies. Hierarchies develop around the things people find most important. In some times and places, that's military prowess. For others, it's mental acuity, and for still others, religious conviction. Sometimes it's all of the above and more. The point is that we decide what matters most to us and put it in order of importance—a hierarchy. We then decide how the different levels of that hierarchy will be treated—the matters of decorum and protocol.

King Victor Emmanuel III and Queen Elena of Italy receive welcome gift of flowers.

MATTERS OF STATE

DIPLOMACY IS THE ART AND PRACTICE of conducting negotiations between separately governed states. Part of diplomacy's practice is called "protocol," which basically means a sort of officially sanctioned etiquette. The word "protocol" is derived from the Greek words *proto* (first) and *collon* (glued or attached), meaning that the first page of a manuscript, often serving as a summary of a treaty or diplomatic dispatch, must be glued to the outside of the document or volume.

> *Anyone who considers protocol unimportant has never dealt with a cat.*
>
> —ROBERT A. HEINLEIN

One interesting modern legacy of this type of dispatch is the British Queen's "red boxes," which are the repositories for official papers that require Her Majesty's attention. These deep-red Morocco leather containers are locked, lined with lead (formerly done to make sure they would sink if lost at sea) and are constructed to be bombproof. They are one of the longest-running tangible expressions of protocol in active use in modern times.

Another way to define protocol is as the set of rules, procedures, conventions, and ceremonies governing relations between states. Much of protocol is written down, but it is also a fluid thing that changes as times and societies do. Some countries, especially those like Great Britain and China that have been engaged in formal diplomatic endeavors for centuries, still adhere to complicated protocols, while other, newer nations conduct their business on a more relaxed, pragmatic basis. Trust, but verify is a good rule of thumb to use in situations calling for diplomatic protocol. Protocol involves much more than the language of treaties. It can be established for the largest event—the Armistice—and the smallest gesture—a wave to the people.

Do not let that trouble Your Excellency;
perhaps the greetings are intended for me.
—LUDWIG VAN BEETHOVEN

Royally Speaking

IN THE 2010 FILM *The King's Speech,* King George VI and Queen Mary visit the home of commoner Lionel Logue, a speech therapist, and his wife. Left alone with the queen, Mrs. Logue becomes tongue-tied (in a humorous echo of the king's stammer, which brought him to their home). The queen says, "Oh, it's 'Your Majesty' first, then afterwards just call me 'ma'am,' which rhymes with 'ham.' "

That rule still stands, and is codified in the Royal Navy handbook for service aboard the royal yacht the H.M.S. *Britannia.* No one is sure why "ma'am" must rhyme with "ham," but it may be because uttering a soft "a" would sound too close to "mum," what English children call their mothers—certainly not dignified enough for the monarch.

The reigning monarch and her consort (or his, as the case may be) are the only members of the British Royal Family who can be addressed as "Your Majesty." "Lesser" royals, from Prince Charles on down, are called "Your Highness" at first address, then "sir" or "ma'am" ("miss" or "master" when below the age of majority). Since more than 2,000 men and women are in line for the English throne, from Prince Charles to the last, a German countess, one never knows who might wear the crown jewels next. Practice that "ma'am" with a hard "a" now and be ready for the next coronation!

Queen and consort: Elizabeth II and Philip

FAMOUS GAFFES: Michelle Obama puts her arm on the Queen's waist. If you've ever taken a photograph with someone you don't know particularly well, you'll know about the hesitation involved in whether or not to put arms in back of each other's waists—so you can sympathize with First Lady Michelle Obama, who chose to do so with Queen Elizabeth II in a 2008 official meeting, and incurred the censure of those who hold that no one touches the monarch's person.

It's not a flag that I look at with anything favorable.
That's for sure...I can't tell people what flag to fly.
—LESLEY STAHL, AMERICAN JOURNALIST

Flag Waving

THE OLYMPIC FLAG consists of a white background and five interlocking rings that symbolize each of the five continents. The colors of red, yellow, blue, green, and black were selected by Pierre de Coubertin in 1914 because at least one of those colors appears in the flag of every country in the world. Although many people know that a white flag symbolizes surrender, fewer realize that red stands for revolution, courage, and power; yellow for caution and valuable gold; blue for fidelity and trust; green for safety, youth, and hope; and black for loss and mourning.

Just as the bright colors of the Olympic rings have special meaning, the use of flags during the Olympic Games has its own special etiquette. Flags of every country that participates in the Olympics are proudly displayed during the opening ceremony of each Games. Each procession is led by the Greek team, because the Olympic Games were founded and first conducted in ancient Greece. All of the other nations march in alphabetical order, except the current host country, which marches last and then has the additional honor of introducing its country's presentation and festivities.

A country's choice of flag bearer is seen as a great honor and is always interesting—it might be a relatively famous athlete, or the youngest competitor, or even one who has overcome some kind of personal challenge to get to the Olympics. During the Winter 2010 games, the host country, Canada, selected Clara Hughes, who had won medals in previous Olympics in both speed skating and cycling. "This is without a doubt the greatest honor of my sporting life," she said, according to the Associated Press. At the 2008 Summer Games, the United States selected runner Lopez Lomong, who had survived a harrowing childhood in Africa. Lomong, who was kidnapped at a young age in Sudan and managed to escape from a prison camp, had been a citizen for just over a year when he paraded with the flag during the opening ceremonies. Yet one of the most fascinating aspects of the opening ceremony is that so many nations are there together, flying their flags peacefully and in mutual admiration, and celebrating their talented athletes together. Considering that the flags derive from battle standards, this is a demonstration that cannot vex vexillologists. Instead, it should make us all proud.

Cuban stamp honors the Olympic flag's rings, circa 1988.

*To say nothing, especially when speaking,
is half the art of diplomacy.*
—WILL DURANT, AMERICAN WRITER, HISTORIAN, AND PHILOSOPHER

Let's Shake on It

U.S. PRESIDENT WILLIAM JEFFERSON Clinton was so worried it might not happen that he paced the halls of the White House at 3 a.m. the night before. "It" was the chance of a simple gesture between two men. On September 13, 1993, Clinton was effecting a meeting between then-Prime Minister Yitzhak Rabin of Israel and PLO Chairman Yasser Arafat, at that time sworn adversaries. People around the world wondered if the two opposing leaders would clasp hands and signal an end to overt hostilities and at least begin steps toward peace in the Middle East.

Although handshakes have been around for thousands of years, the "diplomatic handshake" is a relatively recent phenomenon. Some of its negative instances are most telling, such as Britain's Prince Charles ignoring Idi Amin's proffered hand at Jomo Kenyatta's 1978 funeral, or Romanian dictator Nicolae Ceauşescu refraining from handshakes altogether because he feared poisoning. France's President Charles de Gaulle was a master at snubbing people with outstretched arms.

But other diplomatic handshakes have happier outcomes, such as the famous but private shake between British Prime Minister Tony Blair and Sinn Féin leader Gerry Adams on October 13, 1997. There was such an outcry over the two men meeting that although they knew they wanted to shake hands and begin working together on peace in Northern Ireland, they chose to do so behind closed doors.

Idi Amin was denied a handshake.

Fortunately for President Clinton's insomnia, in 1993, Arafat reached out to Rabin. It must have seemed like a long time to those waiting with bated breath, but after a number of seconds, Rabin responded, clasping his former enemy's hand. Later these two would exchange public embraces—but this brief moment was unforgettable in terms of international relations.

Presidential success can hinge on a handshake.

We should give as we would receive, cheerfully, quickly, and without hesitation; for there is no grace in a benefit that sticks to the fingers.
—SENECA THE YOUNGER, ROMAN PHILOSOPHER

Truly Gifted

AFFAIRS OF STATE ARE ceremonial and can be showy; the same goes for gifts of state. The tradition of leaders exchanging presents is as old as the human practice of gifting. No doubt some of the earliest gifts were, in fact, between leaders who were either attempting to join forces or to keep their warring factions at peace. Egyptian pharaohs gave stone jars engraved with cartouches to the Hittites, and rival Vikings and Visigoths exchanged heads of livestock. For centuries, jewels, foodstuffs, weapons, exotic animals, and much more were given and received across diplomatic lines, with the display of these items being as much a diplomatic exercise as anything else—just think of how carefully King Henry VIII in the television series *The Tudors* decides which neck chain to wear each day.

Statesman John Jay received a live gift horse from Spain.

Things changed significantly for the United States of America in 1785, when gifts to two statesmen, minister to France Benjamin Franklin and Secretary of Foreign Affairs John Jay, threatened to disrupt diplomatic relations for the young nation. King Louis XVI presented Franklin with a diamond-encrusted snuffbox, and King Charles III of Spain gave Jay a horse. Both men accepted those lavish gifts, but ever after American heads of state were supposed to immediately disclose items received and donate all but the most inexpensive of them to the National Archives. Thomas Jefferson, for example, would accept books; today, U.S. Presidents are allowed to choose to keep gifts worth less than $335. In practice, this was not truly regulated until after the Nixon Administration—that President received and kept expensive gifts, and Jacqueline Bouvier Kennedy received many gifts of jewelry that she did not surrender to the Archives, for example.

U.S. gifts to foreign dignitaries are legislated by Congress but handed out by the State Department, where a "gift vault" holds shelf after metal shelf of metallic-gold–wrapped gifts of appropriate type and value for various occasions and levels. The treasures inside that shiny paper have ranged from sparkling jewelry appropriate for princesses to basketball shoes personally autographed by Shaquille O'Neal and Derek Jeter baseball bats.

DOWN TO BUSINESS

RULES AND CEREMONIES APPLY TO MORE THAN affairs of state. As anyone who has worked in an office will tell you, there's a pecking order in the lunchroom, let alone the boardroom. Employees guard their patches more zealously than the most embattled outpost dictator, but just as intra-national matters are less governed by protocol than inter-national affairs, intra-office struggles have nothing on inter-office protocol. Each company wants to keep its place in the pecking order, so all sorts of rules, official and unofficial, are put in place. Woe be unto the hapless officer or administrator who fails to put out the correct number of pens, pads of paper, and glasses of water—or forgets someone's agenda item. Even the numbers of doughnuts or bagels are scrutinized. This is not, of course, because anyone is actually hungry, or really needs a pen—it's about territory.

Things get even more complicated when the businesses are from different countries. Adhering to the simplest, basic good manners (e.g., saying hello, saying please) helps, but can't possibly prepare a guest for the cultural norms that keep Germans punctual and South Africans eager to organize cookout business dinners, but there are also factual things to learn: titles, for example. An entire industry has sprung up around keeping executives apprised of good manners and proper etiquette around the world, including publications, seminars, and online resources, so that no one—regardless of her status—ever has to feel like a foreigner when attempting to conduct good business.

> *It is better to have a lion at the head of an army of sheep, than a sheep at the head of an army of lions.*
>
> —DANIEL DEFOE

Doing business without advertising is like winking at a girl in the dark:
you know what you are doing, but nobody else does.
—EDGAR WATSON HOWE, AMERICAN JOURNALIST AND AUTHOR

Getting Carded

ANY NUMBER OF DESK DRAWERS in the United States are littered with wrinkled and smudged business cards that have never been properly filed, and countless of those were wrinkled and smudged before they were even handed to a recipient—fished out of tote bags, wallets, and trouser pockets during lunches and networking events.

Such cavalier and careless treatment of the cards that represent our names, titles, corporations, and how to reach us would appall

A formal exchange of business cards in Japan

Japanese people, whose etiquette surrounding these cards is quite specific and requires a great deal of attention and care—and no folding or wrinkling. Everyone has a card, although individual titles and contact information are always subordinate to corporate identifying marks such as logos. Everyone makes the extra effort to keep their business cards *(meishi)* in a separate case. They do this because presenting a card that has been warmed by contact with one's body or worn out from lazy, careless storage is considered a sign of great disrespect.

Meishi kokan (business card etiquette) calls for cards to presented with two hands, the text facing the recipient, who should accept it with both hands then thank you for the card and take a few seconds to read it carefully before placing it on the meeting table, face up (for referral, if needed). Writing on the card, folding it, or placing it in a pocket or briefcase is considered very bad manners. When you are presenting your own card, you should also handle it by the top two corners—never push it across the table, or flick it in a thumb-and-forefinger hold that is common at American offices and business lunches.

While a business-card exchange may seem like a very small moment in an ongoing deal, especially in a time when email and digital address books seem to trump paper, this ceremony is important to the Japanese and is a first impression that can affect further negotiation. Taking a few moments to learn this protocol can be a card in your favor.

I can't sit around and wait for the telephone to ring.
—TONY CURTIS

Party Lines

IMAGINE A TYPICAL American business meeting: Five to seven men and women are gathered around a conference table in a room with a closed door. While there may be someone "conferenced in" by phone, everyone is expected to focus on the agenda and save other calls, messages, and appointments for later. (In reality, today, some of those people may be surreptitiously checking their mobile devices . . . but that's another story.)

Nothing could be further from the typical Egyptian business meeting, which will usually include at least one phone call, if not several—not to mention colleagues stopping by with questions and paperwork, and even calls from a relative with questions about family matters. If an American boss or colleague did this, it might be disrespectful, or reflect poorly on her time management, but for an Egyptian, it's a sign that you are very welcome.

1789 merchant's office is orderly compared with some.

Egyptian people place a high emphasis on networking. The more connections a person has, the more his organization values him. Keeping up with those contacts requires a great deal of communication, but showing that a person has many connections and also welcomes contact is very important. Remember that no matter how many people interrupt the business you're trying to conduct, it is not meant as a slight to you, and it is definitely business as usual. If you betray frustration or anger, your Egyptian contacts may think less of you and your intentions. Calm and patience are the keys to this game of telephone.

Telephone etiquette sometimes requires a script.

OBJECTS OF ETIQUETTE: Cubicles, Pods, and Office Dividers Modern office space can be crowded and noisy and even worse, completely public. One solution that provides at least the illusion of privacy and cuts down a bit on noise is the employee cubicle, often referred to as a "pod," constructed of two or three freestanding office dividers.

Avoid having your ego so close to your position
that when your position falls, your ego goes with it.
—COLIN POWELL

Such Modesty

BRITISH AVERSION to boasting is the stuff of many a silly Monty Python moment, but the most famous may be an early sketch called "Four Yorkshiremen" in which a quartet of men in dinner jackets try to outdo each other in tales of how tough they had it while growing up. When one of them finally brags that in his family they worked "29 and a half hours a day," the others give up, saying, "Tell that to the young people today."

Of course, the funniest part of the bit wasn't the tall tales—it was that an Englishman would brag about anything at all. The famous "British reserve" may be dissipating a bit with modern celebrities like soccer stars and musicians boasting about their achievements, but most people in England still try not to talk too much about themselves and what they've accomplished. Children are taught that boasting is bad manners. Consider what British director Stephen Daldry told a *New York Times* blogger

about his 2009 Academy Award nomination for *The Reader*: "I sincerely don't expect to win this year," he said, joking that he wanted to vote for his competition. (He was right—*Slumdog Millionaire* got the Oscar.)

Part of this attitude is to prevent people from feeling badly because they haven't "won," and also to keep grades, awards, possessions, physical beauty, and connections firmly in their places. What was really important, after all, was supposed to be character.

However, there are a couple of other interesting factors at play. The first is that for the English, especially the upper-class English, everything is supposed to come effortlessly. To claim a win smacks of "trying," and that would never do. The second factor is tied to the first—part of English culture is a deep sense of shame and wish to avoid embarrassment whenever possible. They're terribly, terribly sorry, but . . .

OBJECTS OF ETIQUETTE: The "High Table" at English Universities   If you've watched a banquet scene in a Harry Potter movie, you've seen a "high table"—the large, heavy, and usually dark table placed at the end of a dining hall at which dignitaries (usually professors and visiting academics) are seated to set them apart from the larger mass of students.

I think all business practices would improve immeasurably if they were guided by "feminine" principles—qualities like love and care and intuition.
—ANITA RODDICK, BRITISH BUSINESSWOMAN

Draw a Veil

BUSINESS PROTOCOL DEPENDS ON both era and location. While the protocol proffered by medieval Christendom is irrelevant in a time when the Christian church no longer permeates society, almost the reverse is true for the modern Arab world.

In Arab countries, Islam affects everything: Government, the military, social structures, entertainment, and family. While not everyone living in that world is devout and observant, due to a number of modern regime changes, quite a few nations where Islam dominates have adopted protocol that adheres to Islamic principles.

One of the most enduring principles is the status of women. There are many ideas about what women can and cannot do, depending on the country and its interpretation of Islamic law (sharia), but in Saudi Arabia, the United Arab Emirates (UAE), Iran, Iraq, and Turkey, a few rules hold when it comes to business and women.

Strict Islamic law requires a separation of men and women. The men's sphere includes all dealings with the outside world, including business and politics. In some countries and regions, women will never be part of a conference. The separation extends to the most innocuous of inquiries: You've just greeted your hosts and are making polite chitchat. You know that one man is married and has three daughters, and you want to ask after them. Instead of saying "How is your wife? How are your daughters?" you should ask "How is your family?"

In Dubai, business meetings are often conducted with male colleagues only.

ALL IN THE TIMING

FOR MOST OF US, TRACKING THE TIME is difficult enough; presented with daily, weekly, monthly, and annual commitments, we do our best to keep up with our responsibilities. For most U.S. citizens, that means arriving on time for meetings, doctors' appointments, and dinner reservations. We believe that keeping others waiting is bad manners and shows a lack of respect.

A diplomat's life is made up of three ingredients: protocol, Geritol and alcohol.

—ADLAI STEVENSON

But time zones aren't the only things that change as you travel the world—habits about punctuality, waiting, and even regular business hours change from place to place. Numerous factors play into time manners: For example, mechanical clocks did not arrive in Japan until the mid-19th century, and while this doesn't necessarily change modern Westernized business habits, it certainly had an effect on the development and pace of some Japanese business rituals.

For that matter, all sorts of technology, from clocks to electric lights, and on to the DVR, affect how we conduct ourselves in relation to time. We no longer need to confine activities to daylight hours, and we no longer need to wait to receive most communications—if the telephone didn't guarantee instant access, online chatting services do. Time may be the thing that has been most affected by human progress—yet it's also the thing that cannot be changed by human progress. We may speed up our ability to do things, but we still have exactly the same span between sunrise and sunset as any humans ever did. The best advice regarding how to learn about another culture's approach to punctuality? Take your time.

I've been on a calendar,
but I've never been on time.
—MARILYN MONROE

Timely Tactics

RUSSIA HAS HERITAGE AND CULTURE in spades, from masterpieces of literature to the Bolshoi Ballet to elaborate Fabergé eggs, but it has also had its fair share of hard knocks from history, including invasions, famines, and political turmoil (to use understatement). While there's no way to summarize Russian history easily, it is also fair to say that the difficulties this country has experienced have shaped its behavior and manners. Russians view compromise as a sign of weakness; they are generally less interested in proposing solutions than in identifying problems.

These factors influence any kind of Russian business matter. While punctuality is expected from visitors, the "home team" in an office may come to the meeting table as much as two hours late. This delay tactic might be designed to test the other party's patience, to make a statement about how little they value the meeting, or to rattle the waiting visitors and push them toward making concessions out of sheer fatigue. Once they've finally arrived, the Russians might continue to test your patience. They could prolong negotiations and refuse to back down, sometimes even engaging in walkouts, threats, and outbursts. If you're able to involve a Russian intermediary in negotiations—do! That can only help smooth your interactions with the company you hope to do business with.

However, Russian tardiness isn't just about being aggressive; it's also a sort of tone for the society as a whole. Russians do not like to be . . . rushed, or hectored, overscheduled or overly busy. They like to be deliberate in their decisions. Russians also have a markedly different approach toward work life than people from the United States and other Western countries do. To someone in Moscow, having a comfortable, low-pressure, and moderately well-compensated position at work can be much more important than making the effort to rise on the corporate ladder. That gives Russians a distinct advantage in business meetings: They want to win for winning's sake, and aren't afraid that they'll lose an opportunity by delaying things. But as for you? You should show up on time. After all, in our culture, the early bird gets the worm.

This clock at the Kremlin doesn't necessarily keep Russians on time.

FAMOUS GAFFES: Political foot-in-mouth The trouble with being in public office is that you're often in the public eye, even when you aren't sure of the facts. Such was the case with Tennessee's Lieutenant Governor Ron Ramsey, who in July 2010 referred to Islam as "a cult or whatever you want to call it" in a speech in his state's Hamilton County.

He was always late on principle,
his principle being that punctuality is the thief of time.
—OSCAR WILDE

Tardy by Nurture

ASK A FRIEND IN MEXICO CITY to meet for café con leche at three o'clock, and it isn't unusual for one or both of you to show up at the coffee shop closer to four o'clock. This isn't because Mexicans can't tell time or don't understand punctuality; it's due to a cultural difference.

The idea of being on time is less fixed in Latin American countries than it is in North American and many Western nations. Spanish-speaking countries even have a term for being on time: *la hora inglesa,* or "English time," and often invoke their country to say it isn't necessary to show up on time. Even Brazilians say, in their native Portuguese, *hora brasileira,* for example.

These relaxed notions may be due to another time-honored Latin American custom, the post-lunch siesta. In many warm regions, the hours after what is typically the day's heaviest meal are set aside for rest. Two to five hours will be business-free (for example, stores in Spain generally close from lunchtime until late afternoon). Of course, the actual naps during a siesta may be as brief as ten minutes, even if the afternoon closures go on longer. People aren't expected to know how long a friend is napping, so why not allow for tardiness?

Now that people in chillier climes are learning the benefits of daytime sleeping, and "power naps" are gaining popularity, maybe *la hora inglesa* will change meanings once again. After all, time is a fluid concept.

Streets are empty during afternoon siesta in Guanajuato, Mexico.

You may delay, but time will not.
—BENJAMIN FRANKLIN

Delayed Gratification

In China, who you know makes a big difference.

IN CHINA, THE CONCEPT OF "FACE," or maintaining honor, is so important to manners that it has its own word: *guanxi*. But guanxi doesn't mean saving one's own face. Properly translated, the word means "relationships," and refers to the idea that each person in a society supports and is supported by others. Many people doing business in China find that it helps to have a Chinese "go-between" to facilitate contact with Chinese companies, because these professional negotiators know whom to approach.

While *guanxi* might sound similar to the Western "old boys network," it isn't confined to the upper classes. Guanxi certainly can apply to families and to groups of peers. A laborer can provide a favor to a high-ranking executive, and vice versa. *Guanxi* crosses familial, class, and professional strata.

Of course, this system comes into play in business dealings, and it may be very difficult for Westerners to understand how crucial relationships are to Chinese culture while they're trying to get a contract signed. To the Chinese, relationships and the trust embodied in them matter a great deal more than any signed piece of paper—which is why Chinese businesspeople often ask for concessions after a contract is inked.

It's also why Chinese business negotiations can take such a long time. Depending on any number of factors, the Chinese team may take its time conducting meetings, banquets, and other activities so that they can feel they have learned enough about and formed relationships with the Western team. Considering their long history it's not surprising that Chinese businesspeople are cautious and take the long view regarding business negotiations.

OBJECTS OF ETIQUETTE: Scepters or Gavels   A gavel is a small ceremonial mallet (never meant to actually smash anything!) used by a person in authority to signal the opening of a meeting or ceremony and also struck against a wooden block when things become noisy as a reminder to keep order.

Ukrainian ceremonial mace commands attention.

*The only reason for time is so
that everything doesn't happen at once.*
—ALBERT EINSTEIN

Time Zones

SOMEWHERE THERE MIGHT EXIST a person who loves to stand in line—and many of us would like to find her and hire her to take our place when we're rushed and stuck in back of the guy with a bursting cart of groceries at the supermarket checkout.

The truth is, standing and waiting is especially hard on modern bodies and minds. We're less accustomed to long stretches on our feet and we're often on very tight schedules.

But things are different when busy Westerners really want something: Look at the long lines that form for new technology gadgets and concerts by major musical stars. Many people don't

*Punch clock and time card:
essential to hourly wage earners*

even mind bringing pup tents so they can wait overnight.

It's interesting to contrast those lines, with their plastic coolers full of drinks (hard and soft) and people anxiously checking their mobile phones and laptop computers, with the long lines that can form for more basic needs. In some countries, like Nigeria in the spring of 2011, people wait in line for hours to cast their votes for forms of government that provide them with better lives. After the devastating Japanese earthquakes during the same time period, residents of seaside towns had to wait patiently in line to get water for drinking, cooking, and washing.

However, frazzled Americans don't have to look outside of our borders to see that real need begets truly stoic patience when it comes to time spent waiting in lines. Every year a group called Remote Area Medical brings medical, dental, and optometry services to needy rural areas such as Appalachia. Hundreds of people who have no medical insurance and/or no access to doctors or other health services show up and wait for days and nights to have tests run, teeth filled, and shots administered.

MANNERED LIVES

Benjamin Franklin

Founding Father Franklin's reputations as a political activist, diplomat, scientist, and civic leader are all secure—but we shouldn't forget that alongside all of these facets of his career he was also quite committed to good manners. Benjamin Franklin believed that living out the virtues through polite behavior helped individuals to develop into intelligent, useful, engaged citizens.

A naturally curious and perceptive writer, the man behind *Poor Richard's Almanack* filled page after page with letters, diary entries, newspaper articles, and books, including a well-regarded autobiography. In that work he outlines the 13 virtues of Temperance, Silence, Order, Resolution, Frugality, Industry, Sincerity, Justice, Moderation, Cleanliness, Tranquility, Chastity, and Humility.

Franklin writes,

In this Piece it was my Design to explain and enforce this doctrine, that vicious Actions are not hurtful because they are forbidden, but forbidden because they are hurtful, the Nature of Man alone consider'd: That it was therefore every one's Interest to be virtuous, who wish'd to be happy even in this World.

Keenly aware of how individual behavior affects society, Franklin encouraged his fellow citizens to integrate virtue-based actions into their daily lives. He was also mindful that because manners should spring from virtues and not the other way around, that there were different ways to do things. "Savages we call them because our manners differ from ours," Franklin famously said of Native Americans, "which we think the perfection of civility. They think the same of theirs. Perhaps, if we could examine the manners of different nations with impartiality, we should find no people so rude, as to be without any rules of politeness; nor any so polite, as not to have some remains of rudeness."

Statesman Benjamin Franklin wrote pithy manners lists as "Poor Richard."

BETTER LEFT UNSAID

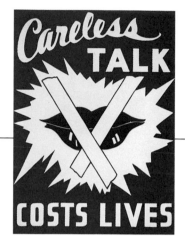

T HE TITLE OF THIS BOOK CONCERNS the things we are supposed to say, but there are plenty of things that aren't polite to discuss. Good manners, like good editing, often consist of what isn't included.

Members of hierarchical organizations learn what topics are best for official discussion, and which are best for private conversations. Politics and sex are generally "off the table" around the world, although there are some specific political topics that have to be doubly censored from time to time (for instance, you might not want to praise the loser of a presidential race when you have dinner at the White House). Many people would add religion and money to that list, while others would say "No pets and children!" These "forbidden" subjects aren't always censored because they might offend or be too revealing; they can also be subjects that can get boring quickly. Nothing brings an intimate dinner party to a crashing halt faster than a long-winded monologue about Fluffy's veterinary distress, or a hot-aired boast about Junior's prowess on the soccer field.

Once a list of topics that shouldn't be shared is finished, it might seem as if the only safe one is the weather. However, the truly observant will find that part of good manners is taking cues from present company. Unlike etiquette, which prescribes certain conduct for certain situations, manners allow for adaptation. If your adventure group decides to chat about kayak prices, there's no reason for you to let your end of the conversation sink.

> *Something as curious as the monarchy won't survive unless you take account of people's attitudes. After all, if people don't want it, they won't have it.*
>
> —PRINCE CHARLES

A "No" uttered from the deepest conviction is better than
a "Yes" merely uttered to please, or worse, to avoid trouble.
—PYTHAGORAS

Yes and No

ASK ANY FRIEND who hails from India about the "Indian head bobble" and you'll probably get a laugh of recognition, and maybe even a bit of an impromptu bobble. This bobble is well known to people inside and outside of that nation. Ask an Indian person a yes-or-no question, and you'll see her jut her head forward a bit and then waggle back and forth—no matter which answer she's giving. Yes, no, or maybe so, can all come with a bobble.

Does that mean all Indians are indecisive? Not at all. What it does mean is that India has a culture in which disappointing another person means not measuring up in that person's eyes, a definite no-no (which would probably be indicated by another head bobble or two). While Westerners often find this lack of ability to simply say "No" frustrating and confusing,

Sometimes there's not a simple "yes" or "no."

for Indians the gesture's ambiguity is quite useful. For example, instead of telling a parent or a senior person at work "No," a younger Indian might bobble his head, which is a wordless way of communicating "Yes, I'll do what you asked me, but I'm not particularly happy about it."

Because it is nearly impossible to get past the ubiquitous head bobble, outsiders conducting business in a city like Mumbai or Bangalore might consider trying out the Indian way, which is to keep wiggling until a compromise has been reached. In the West this might be considered passive-aggressive; in India, it's considered a polite thing to do.

It's also considered peaceful. One blogger points out a passage in the novel *Shantaram* by Gregory David Roberts about what Roberts calls "the head-wiggle":

"Gradually, I realised that the wiggle of the head was a signal to others that carried an amiable and disarming message: I'm a peaceful man, I don't mean any harm."

No need to consult a psychic to gain clarity

I think to be oversensitive about clichés
is like being oversensitive about table manners.
—EVELYN WAUGH, ENGLISH WRITER, 1903-1966

Keep It Down

FRANCE MAY NOT BE the official birthplace of "etiquette," but French royal courts certainly refined systems of social rules. Though French culture and population have changed significantly over the last few decades, the society still retains a degree of formality in everything from dress to table manners.

Both men and women in France are carefully turned out, even for minor errands, with stylish accessories and precise grooming (no unkempt ponytails or stray nostril hairs). At dining tables, French hands are always in sight, never in a person's lap—a mannerly relic of days when a concealed hand might hold a concealed weapon.

Some French manners are harder to discern, because they can't be seen—or heard. While dining, especially in public, the French keep noise low. Braying laughter will earn you a withering glance.

The French don't have delicate ears—they just value civilized dining conversation. Speaking demonstrates education (extremely important in France) and respect for others. In business, hierarchy is strict, so a meal might be an employee's only chance to talk directly and informally with her boss.

Louis XIV grants an audience to the Persian ambassador at Versailles.

The dinner table is the center for the teaching and practicing not just of table manners but of conversation, consideration, tolerance family feeling...
—JUDITH MARTIN, AMERICAN AUTHOR AND JOURNALIST

No Funny Stuff

THE UNITED STATES has Emily Post; Great Britain has Debrett's; and Germany has *Der Knigge*. Yes, it sounds funny to say it—the "k" is pronounced—but this phrase, which is shorthand for manners in Germany, is taken quite seriously.

Der Knigge takes its name from 18th-century nobleman and Freemason Adolph Freiherr Knigge (Baron Adolph Knigge), who wrote a treatise called *On Human Relations* that outlined his philosophy of human rights. While Knigge didn't actually establish any rules or social customs, the German system of etiquette that evolved based on his work came to be known as *Der Knigge*. In fact, *Der Knigge* has become the German shorthand for "etiquette," and there are now books with titles like *Der Klein Gastro-Knigge (The Little Book of Table Manners)* and *Der Knigge fürs Bett* (yes, that does mean *Manners in Bed*).

We can only hope that the Germans are slightly less serious as regards the latter than they are when it comes to business etiquette, where they are very earnest indeed. Hierarchy and credentials matter more than anything else at first, and are used to establish trustworthiness. Unlike other cultures, where personal relationships precede business negotiations, in Germany meetings require no prior friendship or other type of relationship. With no personal relationship to cushion your negotiation, be sure to come prepared with lots of facts and examples to support your case—the analytic German mind will appreciate these details. At the start of the meeting, rules like punctuality, allowing higher-ranking people to enter rooms first, and sticking to an agenda are highly valued in this European nation. They are what the Germans believe make things run smoothly.

That said, if you're unsure about something before a meeting, it's perfectly all right to clarify beforehand; your German host will appreciate your directness and your efforts toward making the meeting itself go efficiently—and, after all, directness and efficiency are very German traits.

Since meetings are carefully organized and run, anything that upsets the apple cart is a bad idea, and humor is something that rarely translates well. Telling jokes, even at one's own expense, is not done in German business meetings or at any sort of public occasion.

Der Knigge is the father of German etiquette.

MANNERED LIVES

Peter Parley

Modern authors might be dazzled by Samuel Griswold Goodrich's sales numbers: By the time the 19th-century American was about 60 years old, his works had sold over eight million copies around the world.

The single highest-selling book Goodrich wrote was *Peter Parley's Geography for Children*, representing a persona the author adopted that helped him to become famous. As Parley, an elderly man, Goodrich wrote books for children about history, science, art, and more. However, while geography may have sold widely, it was Peter Parley's lessons in manners that became most famous. A sample of his style: "Perseverance gives power to weakness, and opens to poverty the world's wealth. It spreads fertility over the barren landscape, and buds the choicest flowers and fruits spring up and flourish in the desert abode of thorns and briars."

Ironically, it wasn't just because of Goodrich's writing (We can allow literary critics to judge it on its own merits.) that these lessons gained so many readers, but because of the 19th-century American trend toward teaching young people manners in school and through books. Part of this trend involved a movement toward cozy domesticity, in the mode of the Transcendentalists; another part was due to the contemporary distaste for what Goodrich and others saw as the British biases of 19th-century schoolrooms, as well as the questionable morals of British and European nursery rhymes. A nascent society was trying to find its own way of both forming and teaching good manners, and "Peter Parley" was a sort of Emily Post of his age to the juvenile set.

As manners maven Peter Parley,
Samuel Goodrich was a best-selling author.

CLOTHES CALL

TODAY EVERYONE FROM ROCK STARS to railroad workers wears blue jeans, but look at the price of some denim: While a ranch hand in Oklahoma might pay $15 for a pair of stiff Wranglers, a celebrity happily plops down hundreds of dollars for "pre-stressed" jeans full of holes.

Clothing affects how people see us. Consider how attorneys transform clients with wild hairstyles and unconventional clothing into clean-shaven, conventionally coiffed and neatly dressed defendants. Long ago, only high-ranking people got the "royal purple" fabric dye. So-called "sumptuary laws" once dictated who could wear certain garments and accessories. In China, before the 20th-century Republic, only the emperor wore yellow. In ancient Rome, men could not don the *toga viriliis* until they could vote. Some cultures have religious bases for sumptuary laws, like the Islamic ban on men wearing silk and gold jewelry. (Women can don both, but also often must wear full-body coverings.)

> *What spirit is so empty and blind, that it cannot recognize the fact that the foot is more noble than the shoe, and skin more beautiful than the garment with which it is clothed?*
>
> —MICHELANGELO, 1475-1564

Modern nations are less interested in what people wear—purple for everyone!—but these laws survive in military garb, where insignia can indicate rank, skills, and bravery. Symbols on clothing of occupation (e.g., a nurse's caduceus) or power (e.g., a barrister's wig) help identify people; many of these conventions were set before mass literacy.

If honor be your clothing, the suit will last a lifetime;
but if clothing be your honor, it will soon be worn threadbare.

—WILLIAM ARNOT, PREACHER AND THEOLOGICAL WRITER, 1808–1875

Sky Blue Ideals

FEW SOLDIERS HAVE their heads in the clouds, but if you meet a member of the UN Peacekeeping Force (UNPKF), who "wage peace" on behalf of the global institution, you might think about the skies above: These soldiers wear helmets and berets tinted a bright, intense blue.

The hue helps both civilians and combatants in troubled regions immediately distinguish UN peacekeepers from other troops, and it speaks to the peacekeepers' ideals. The Force formed in 1948 to be "dispatched by the Security Council to help implement peace agreements, monitor cease-fires, patrol demilitarized zones, create buffer zones between opposing forces, and put fighting on hold while negotiators seek peaceful solutions to disputes.

But, ultimately, the success of peacekeeping depends on the consent and cooperation of the opposing parties." The Force's troops are provided by UN member nations.

Aside from their cerulean headgear, troops in the Department of Peacekeeping Operations, or DPKO, wear the battle-dress uniform or fatigues and combat boots that lace up the calf. This isn't to make them look like warriors; this uniform is simply the most practical for their duties. Ultimately, the most successful tool the UNPKF carries is the one on their heads, the blue beret signifying their impartiality.

UN peacekeeping forces at attention in their distinctive sky-blue berets

Love has a hem to her garment that reaches the very dust.
It sweeps the stains from the streets and the lanes, and because it can, it must.
—MOTHER TERESA

Torn Asunder

IF A COLLEAGUE HAS A BIT of ragged, torn black ribbon on his jacket, don't try to brush it away: You're probably seeing the modern, Reform Jewish version of an ancient Torah law, *keriyah*. Also known as *keriah* and *kria*, this ribbon symbolizes the rending of garments that follows the death of any "first degree" relatives (mother, father, brother, sister, husband, wife, son, daughter).

An ancient Hebrew scribe amid Torah scrolls

Orthodox Jews rip actual pieces of clothing, with the stipulation that the torn article be one that covers the heart, like a shirt, vest, or jacket, and that it be worn over something else (e.g., an undershirt) for modesty's sake. According to halacha (Jewish law), the piece of clothing cannot be new, cannot be mended, and cannot be simply thrown away once the mandated seven-day shivah mourning period is finished.

While it might seem that the *keriyah* symbolizes a broken heart, its prescribed meaning is that once dead, a person cannot return to life and will always be missed (hence the prohibition on mending the tear). Today, families sitting shivah together usually have resources in the outside world, but hundreds of years ago a torn garment would signal to other members of the community that a person was a mourner who was not allowed to do certain things for herself or her family (for example, people sitting shivah are not supposed to cook for themselves). The *keriyah*—whether garment or ribbon—gives people advance notice that the person before them may be in a most fragile emotional state.

OBJECTS OF ETIQUETTE: "Within the Ribbon" Cards/Markers   Large formal weddings often require a separate seating section, traditionally marked off with ribbons or swags. "Pew cards" or "within the ribbon" cards are enclosed with invitations so that guests may give these to ushers and be quietly and properly seated in this area.

Is there anything worn under the kilt?
No, it's all in perfect working order.
—SPIKE MILLIGAN, COMEDIAN, 1918-2002

Pinched Pleats

HUMANS LOVE PATTERNS, and they also love messages, which goes a long way toward explaining the prevalence of Burberry's distinctive red, black, and tan checked accessories, which are charmingly patterned and quickly send a message of "luxury."

Now, Burberry refers to that pattern as a "tartan," but many people call it "Burberry plaid." Which is correct? If you look at some sources, they'll tell you both are—that "plaid" is simply "American" for tartan. In terms of colloquial speech, that might be true, but etymologically speaking, it's completely false.

Long ago, when the Sassenachs roamed the Scottish Highlands with blue paint on their faces like Mel Gibson in the 1995 film *Braveheart,* a "plaid" was the Gaelic word for a blanket-sized garment that could be draped in a number of useful ways and used as a cloak or even a sort of sleeping bag in a pinch (there were a lot of "pinches" in those days, which is probably why they invented Scotch). Today, Scottish people who wear the traditional dress for ceremonial occasions still call a draped shoulder shawl that is cinched at the waist a "belted plaid."

"Tartan" is the proper word for the pattern of different colored threads that cross and mingle in the dress typical of the Scottish Highlands. The Gaelic word for tartan is *breacan,* which means "speckled," and probably referred to the shadings that those threads made when they met in the fabric. According to experts, the word "tartan" is (shockingly) not Gaelic, but

actually comes from a French word *tiretain.* Tiretain was a thin, "linsey-woolsey" (linen and wool) cloth that was regularly imported from France in the 1500s.

Now you know: A kilt is a skirt made from tartan cloth, and you can also have that cloth made into a plaid. Simple, isn't it?

Any garment which is cut to fit you is much more becoming, even if it is not so splendid as a garment which has been cut to fit somebody not of your stature.
—EDNA FERBER, AMERICAN NOVELIST, 1887-1968

History in Its Folds

SARI FABRIC IS RECYCLED into pretty women's accessories, and stitched into evening clutches and hair bands and even blue jeans. As it happens, the original designers of saris for women and dhotis/lungis for men would strongly disapprove—not because they would dislike the nice adornments, but because they were made with needle and thread.

The early and most devout Hindus believed that fabric should not be pierced by any sort of tool, so wrapping the body with long lengths of cloth was the most effective way to clothe it. The Sanskrit word *sari* means "band of cloth." However, another Hindu belief was the Great Being emanated from everyone's navel, and so leaving the navel and often the breasts exposed was important. So women's saris were usually two pieces until the 20th century. Then British notions of propriety led to the choli, a cropped blouse, worn beneath a one-piece sari draped

Traditional two-piece saris expose the navel.

across the belly and covering the navel. (The choli had been around for centuries, but wasn't worn with the sari until British rule.)

It took centuries for saris to achieve their present iconic form, and to shed the prohibition against piercing the fabric. For a while, decorations could only be woven into the sari's silk, but today, elaborate embroidery, especially on wedding saris (often red), is common.

Saris are now worn in India, Pakistan, Bangladesh, Sri Lanka, and Nepal. There are dozens of regional styles of decoration and folding, with some saris made of coarsely spun cotton, and others of silk so fine the entire sari can be pulled through a wedding ring.

Richly embroidered and dyed modern saris

*The only man who really needs a tail coat
is a man with a hole in his trousers.*
—JOHN TAYLOR, ENGLISH MUSICIAN IN POP BAND DURAN DURAN

Penguin Suits

ANY MAN WHO has ever buttoned himself into formal evening attire probably calls it his "penguin suit," because the possibly tight trousers and stiffly starched shirt remind him of that bird's awkward gait.

However, the real "penguin suit" in men's haberdashery is the so-called "morning suit," consisting of a cropped, double-breasted jacket with peaked lapels and a long divided "tail," giving a gentleman wearing it the look of a penguin—black from the back and white in the front. The coat is worn over a double-breasted waistcoat and baggy, chalk-striped trousers along with jodhpur boots or shoes covered with spats. Yes, it's a costume of many pieces, with all sorts of strict etiquette about each one, from color of the waistcoat (buff, gray, or in the most solemn cases, black), to the style of the trousers (double pleated and cuffed).

Prince Philip in full proper morning dress

But the morning suit did not spring from a fashion designer's drafting table. The ensemble comes from what well-bred men wore in the morning—and in the morning, well-bred British men of the 19th century were either heading out or coming from riding horses. The coat of the morning suit was short, with tails, because it developed out of the riding jacket. Meant to give men a dignified, daytime formal option, in the 20th century it was eclipsed by what would once have been called a "lounge suit" and is now the globally accepted business suit.

Morning dress survives in wedding parties (especially British ones), at certain sporting events (Ascot), and at the English preparatory school Eton. Acceptable alternatives include Scottish full Highland dress, military "dress mess" (which has a short jacket without tails), and the West African London suit.

ARCHAIC MANNERS: Top Hats Unmistakable in shape and style, "top hats" were once made of beaver fur or silk and even sometimes constructed so that they could collapse for cloakrooms (known as "opera hats"). Although U.S. President John F. Kennedy donned a top hat for his 1961 inauguration, he removed it before the inaugural address: His informal style led to his being named "Hatless Jack." Today, top hats are seen at weddings and a few sporting events, like the Kentucky Derby and Royal Ascot.

NO RULES

SOMETIMES RULES ABOUT PROPER DRESS aren't written down or legislated, but they're still so carefully adhered to that they're noteworthy. And no, we are not talking about nude beaches. All you need to think about to confirm this statement is any trend among teenagers (and we are still not talking about nude beaches): Human beings observe and imitate each other in all sorts of ways, so it's natural that sometimes they will ape each other's clothing habits.

Some of those habits are so rooted in ancient times that we no longer remember that they probably came about because of imitation, but others are either so recent or so widely understood that there are no official decrees about them. In African-American churches, women don't just wear hats;

In a hierarchy, every employee tends to rise to his level of incompetence.
—LAURENCE J. PETER

they usually carefully coordinate their hats to their suits and dresses and almost vie with each other over styles and sizes of headwear—but while these ladies know that a baseball cap would never be acceptable, there aren't any rules about hats. Most of us would never wear a bathing suit anywhere except in a pool or on a beach, but during warm weather in waterfront communities it's understood that a partially covered bathing suit is acceptable while shopping or dining.

Other clothing styles and decorum involve a strict etiquette, but because they are not well-known to the industrialized world, they are not much written about or considered. Fortunately, the world is changing and so are methods of disseminating information, so learning about the way other cultures dress will be better documented than a few photos of anthropologist Margaret Mead wearing a palm-leaf hood somewhere in Samoa.

As to matters of dress, I would recommend one
never to be the first in the fashion nor the last out of it.
—JOHN WESLEY, CHURCH OF ENGLAND CLERIC, 1703-1791

Quietly Formal

IF THE WORDS "BUSINESS CASUAL" make you weep for the state of haberdashery, board the next flight to Lisbon. Portugal is small but proud of its heritage, language, and culture, all of which remain quite traditional and conservative in the 21st century, including its suit-and-tie-clad men.

Portuguese gentlemen wear suits everywhere—even to a casual evening at the movies. Both men and women can usually be seen in quiet but very fine clothing, with fabrics, labels, and tailoring important and often even remarked on in daily chitchat.

This attention to sartorial detail stems not from the top of society, the way it might have in the days of royal Versailles, but from the bottom: Until recently, most of Portugal's population were hardworking peasants. There was very little opportunity for social mobility upward into the small-size middle and upper classes. Anytime a person or family was able to make a change in status, it was hard-won and expected to be appreciated.

Part of living in a higher class included dressing the part—not simply to show that one could afford better things, but also to maintain a sense of public decorum. But Portuguese formality is less about money and rank than about setting a certain tone; while suits are ubiquitous, dinner jackets and white tie are almost unknown—there are few occasions in which a plain, dark business suit will not suffice.

Another factor is the nation's strong ties with the Roman Catholic Church, which has a long history of exhorting members to modesty—and also maintains a tradition of formality.

Women wearing Portuguese native costumes

When a woman is wearing shorts her
charms are enlarged without being enhanced.
—BEVERLEY NICHOLS, ENGLISH JOURNALIST AND WRITER, 1898-1983

She Wears Short Shorts

IN 2010 SOME EYEBROWS were raised in dismay when U.S. First Lady Michelle Obama exited Air Force One wearing "short shorts." The Obama family was returning from a casual vacation to the Grand Canyon, and the First Lady wore her gray hiking shorts with athletic shoes and a long-sleeve sweater; hardly a titillating ensemble.

But to some protocol police, the outfit was shocking. Was that because we don't expect to see the actual flesh of our First Family? Maybe, or maybe not; it's worth noting that when photos of a bare-chested Barack Obama on holiday surfaced, no one was similarly shocked. It's because we expect our rulers and their spouses to maintain business-class standards of dress and behavior when they are taking part in official occasions. Unfortunately for Michelle Obama, who probably felt like just another mom back from a family getaway, walking off of Air Force One is considered an "official" act.

However, government officials aren't the only people who generally don't wear shorts. Anyone who has ever traveled to a cosmopolitan region during a warm season knows that adults in other countries rarely wear "shorts" in public (a notable and historic exception is on Bermuda, where even the police officers wear knee-length "Bermuda shorts"). "Short trousers" are seen in most places as something for children and not dignified enough for grown-ups to wear unless they are on an athletic field. Since so many casual, "American" styles have grown popular overseas, this will

The First Family goes comfy, but were the First Lady's shorts too casual?

probably change drastically in the next decade or two. For now, unless you're putting on a pair of lederhosen for Oktoberfest, save the shorts for stateside.

As for our American shorts protocol, it could be changing. After the First Lady's "misstep," the *Huffington Post* polled 13,000 of its readers—nearly 60 percent of them said they had no problem with the First Lady showing a little leg.

Any man may be in good spirits and good temper when he's well dressed. There ain't much credit in that.
—CHARLES DICKENS

Suits Everyone

EVEN IF YOU'VE NEVER heard the term "dashiki," you've probably seen photos of South African President Nelson Mandela in a colorful dashiki suit made from the distinctively patterned African cloth. Although the dashiki ("shirt" in Yoruba) originated in West Africa, during the 1960s civil rights struggles in many Western

The brimless kufi is often worn with dashikis.

nations, the garment became popular and is now proudly worn outside the region as well.

The most common dashiki style is a short-sleeve shirt with drawstring pants *(sokoto)* and cap *(kufi)*. Depending on the length of the overshirt, it may be known as a Senegalese kaftan. The dashiki suit worn only by tribal chieftains and officials includes a special open-sleeve robe, called *le Grand BouBou* or an *agbada* overall.

The "London Suit" is a dignified blend of tradition and compromise that was developed by West Africans living in England. While they adopted the dark trousers, laced-up shoes, and white shirt with dark tie of their new home, for many formal occasions, especially those that concern the family, they wished to wear family robes. Thus, the "London Suit" is a dark trousers-to-tie combo covered by an agbada, which is often passed down for generations. Sometimes men who want to wear an all-African costume but not trespass on a chief's right to the formal dashiki suit will wear an heirloom *agbada* over an all-white cotton shirt and pants.

Dashiki suits are made for women, too.

Clothes make the man.
Naked people have little or no influence on society.
—MARK TWAIN

Covered Heads

THE ROMAN CATHOLIC CHURCH prohibits divorce, which is technically why King Henry VIII had his bishops break from Rome and form The Church of England—he wanted to divorce Catherine of Aragon and marry Anne Boleyn.

So it was a tad ironic when Charles, Prince of Wales, and his second wife, the divorced Camilla Parker-Bowles, with whom the Prince had conducted a famous affair throughout his first marriage to Diana Spencer, were presented to Pope Benedict XVI in a 2009 "private audience." Perhaps even more ironic was seeing Camilla, now the Duchess of Cornwall, in a black lace mantilla head covering.

Many religious traditions have closely followed rules when it comes to head coverings. Christians of both sexes also covered their heads for centuries, but for most Western Christians of any denomination, by the 20th century this meant a traditional "business" hat for men (e.g., a fedora) and a simple hat or even just a small square of lace pinned on for women. Since the Prince of Wales and his wife are not Roman Catholic, why would she don a mantilla? Papal etiquette requires that men wear suits and women modest day clothing in the Pontiff's presence, but does not specify head coverings.

The answer is simply that many women, from a divorced British aristocrat to the First Ladies of the United States to countless celebrities, feel that a complete costume for meeting the Pope and conveying respect for his office includes a lace mantilla as a nod to pre-Vatican II Roman Catholic tradition.

The Duchess of Cornwall donned a black mantilla to meet Pope Benedict XVI.

ALL IN THE FAMILY

I f charity begins at home, then so must good manners, since charity (from the Greek *caritas*) means treating other people with kindness. Children learn their earliest lessons about giving and taking from the people who care for them, and as they grow older and use these lessons, they affect other people outside of their circle. Perhaps that's why there are careful ceremonies centered around a child's arrival, and equally careful rituals designed to help that child learn when she can and can't do certain things.

The ties to home are strong, and influence family events for decades into the future of a person's life. They certainly affect how a person behaves towards relatives. Depending on many factors, these ties may also influence religious and spiritual observances. Those occasions, of course, are all about living in community. One of the ironies of being human is that we have to start with training the individual in order to make things civil for the group. Each baby's birth is a chance to start fresh and make things right for a family and a community. The American poet William Ross Wallace wrote in 1865, "The hand that rocks the cradle is the hand that rules the world." That makes this chapter as much about international relations as anything else.

Domestic scene from The Real Mother Goose

BIRTH

BIRTHING A BABY MAY NOT make one think of etiquette, but there are a host of social interactions that surround pregnancy and the birth itself.

While women probably preferred to give birth surrounded by other women, who knew the challenges involved, at some point (no doubt after the Judeo-Christian scriptures dictated that "in sorrow shall ye bring forth children") men were officially banned from the proceedings. So strict was this ban that when a German man, one Dr. Wertt, attempted to attend a birth dressed in drag, his punishment when caught was to be burned at the stake.

If there is anything we wish to change in the child, we should first examine it and see whether it is not something that could better be changed in ourselves.

—CARL GUSTAV JUNG

Men had a long revenge after this, because once the all-male profession of medical doctor managed to make midwives less important, those doctors also began arranging labor and childbirth in ways that made their own calling more important. Instead of sitting up for labor, which is helpful (gravity!), women were told to lie back because it made examination and use of forceps easier for the attending physician. Going to the hospital to give birth became common in the 20th-century Western world, and births scheduled as cesarean sections for the convenience of the delivering doctor. Only somewhat recently did the pendulum swing a bit back toward home births, doulas, midwives, and other options of the solely female experience once governed solely by women.

Let your father and your mother be glad,
And let her rejoice who gave birth to you.
—PROVERBS 23:25

Lying in Bed

Japanese woodcut of a newborn and parents

SOME CULTURAL customs die out while others remain firmly entrenched. While there are usually reasons for the ones that disappear, like inequality or superstition, it isn't always as easy to pinpoint why those that remain do so. However, in the case of the traditional Japanese post-childbirth confinement, many women would say it simply makes sense to stay quiet and at home during the first few weeks of caring for a newborn baby.

Even today, new moms in Japan spend the first two to four weeks (usually 21 days) at home, and most often at the home of the maternal grandparents. Customarily a new mother is not allowed to touch water for dishwashing or laundry, so the baby's grandmother takes on all chores for the postpartum confinement period. For new mothers, this "lying-in" period is a relief from having to observe social customs of receiving visitors. They are given a complete break from

courtesy and obligation.

The lying-in for new mothers is still observed in other countries and cultures, too. For example, a 40-day confinement used to be common in Mexico, but is now observed only in quite rural, countrified areas. As recently as the 1960s in the United States, new mothers remained in the hospital for two weeks after giving birth; today, health insurance providers allow more than a day or two only in cases of other medical issues, like cesarean section recovery (even then, the entire stay will be less than a week).

One place where confinement has found a 21st-century foothold is in China. There, the age-old practice of *cho yuet* (sitting through the month) is practiced by modern moms who hire "confinement ladies" and even sometimes go to stay in "postpartum hotels" so that their bodies as well as their babies will be well cared for after the exertions of labor and delivery.

OBJECTS OF ETIQUETTE: Dutch "Birth Biscuits" One of the quaintest traditions surrounding an infant's arrival is from the Netherlands, where new parents eat a breakfast of *beschuit met muisjes*, or "biscuits with mice." The "mice" are sprinkles—pink and white for girls, blue and white for boys.

You know you're getting old when you get that one candle on the cake. It's like "See if you can blow this out."

—JERRY SEINFELD, AMERICAN COMEDIAN

Lit With Joy

ALMOST ANYONE WHO PICKS UP this book will have some kind of image in mind at the words "birthday cake." Many of those images will have candles of some sort in them, too; we're used to the anniversary of our birth being feted with a sweet baked concoction topped with lit wax tapers. It's actually strange, if you consider it, presenting someone with a gorgeous iced dessert and then lighting it on fire. Who thought of candles, anyway? It may be that it was just a way to treat someone as very special on their special day.

We know that the ancient Greeks placed candles on round cakes that were given to Artemis, goddess of the hunt and of the moon, so that the "baked offerings" would glow like that orb. Early humans, who relied so heavily on fire yet understood its properties so little, superstitiously believed that flames from candles on offerings might send messages to the gods about good intentions.

Early cakes didn't look at all like today's many-layered and frosted concoctions. The Romans celebrated with flat, yeasty cakes sweetened with honey and filled with dried fruit and nuts. It wasn't until well into the 19th century that cakes for celebrations started to look and taste the way they do today. While we don't know precisely when birthdays started to be celebrated with cake, we do know when they started to be topped with candles. Eighteenth-century Germans celebrated children's birthdays with *Kinderfest,* and part of the festivities included a cake topped with candles that were lit just before the birthday boy or girl was allowed into the room.

This is also where the American and British custom of placing the same number of candles on the cake as years in the child's life comes from. (Remember, this was for children; no wonder it gets tough to put enough candles on the cake after college!)

FAMOUS GAFFES: VP Dan Quayle misspells "potato" On June 15, 1992, Vice President Dan Quayle visited a Trenton, New Jersey, sixth-grade class and participated in one of the middle-schoolers' regular activities: a spelling bee. When 12-year-old William Figueroa wrote "potato" on the blackboard, Quayle told him he'd left something off and should add an "e" to the end. Figueroa, demonstrating a mature sensitivity to protocol, complied "because it was the vice president," but the press had a field day at the Veep's mistake.

People's fates are simplified by their names.
—ELIAS CANETTI, BULGARIAN NOVELIST, 1905-1994

Name Day

DIFFERENT CULTURES HAVE different ideas about when a baby's name should be bestowed and how it should be chosen, but eventually almost most human infants receive their own names.

However, while each individual receives a name, that doesn't mean the name itself is unique (although a few bestowed on children of rock stars can be rather unusual). In many European and Latin American countries, certain names come with the legacy of an old Christian church

tradition of giving children saints' names. This tradition led to that of "name days," which are the days on which those saints are feasted, so that each person has a chronological birthday as well as a name day. Some of these are associated with the Roman Catholic Church, others with the Greek Orthodox Church, the Eastern Orthodox Church, and still others with the Scandinavian Lutheran Church.

In many places, the more universal birthday celebration has replaced name days, but in other countries, like Sweden, Poland, France, Finland, Hungary, and Argentina, the practice is still very common. Ways to celebrate vary greatly, but often include greetings from friends and relatives along with small gifts. In Hungary, for example, you'd want to bring bouquets of flowers to women and bottles of liquor to men on their name days. In countries where churchgoing is still common, name days are often a time to attend Mass with family and then have a quiet but festive meal, when gifts are presented.

For those of us who might not share our names with saints—but still want an excuse for another party and gifts—an organization in the United States has the answer. The folks at Mynameday.com took the 2,000 most popular names in the country and assigned each to a day on the calendar. Start celebrating!

Mother-and-child images abound globally.

Babies are such a nice way to start people.
—DON HEROLD, U.S. CARTOONIST, 1889–1966

A Cleansing Ritual

COMMUNITY CONNECTIONS IN TIBET are best understood through the ancient system of *gyido* ties, a complex network that is not unlike the "seal brothers" relationships among Inuit peoples. Those in one's *gyido* are meant to offer support in many ways, including sharing in special celebrations like the birth of a child.

Tibetan Buddhists believe that when a child is born, foul spirits are, too—and they must be flushed out in order that the baby grow properly both mentally and physically. Part of this belief comes from Bön, the indigenous spiritual system of the Himalaya; this has been done for at least 1,500 years. Immediately following the birth, other people in the community traditionally avoid the home of the newborn, considering it "polluted" and fearing that their presence could harm the child. On the third day after a baby boy's birth or the fourth day after a girl is born, members of that family's *gyido* visit to participate in the *pang sai* ceremony (*pang* meaning foulness, *sai* meaning cleansing). They bring barley, butter tea, meat, salt, clothing, and other gifts to provide for the new child and his or her family. Notably, tradition dictates that married women without children avoid these festivities and do not interact with newborns. (Note: *Pangsai* means "waste" or "defecation" in Mandarin Chinese; here it is meant to convey "elimination.")

On entering the baby's home, members of the *gyido* present white *hada* scarves to all as a symbol of purity and shelter for life to be given by the community. The family often burns purifying incense and prepares a feast of pancakes for all, after which a senior monk, designated as a Living Buddha, is present to oversee the cleansing and to name the baby. In some cases, however, the parents do the naming themselves.

Astrologers are often consulted for another early-life ritual for the baby: leaving the house for the first time. The family might head to the monastery where the child would be blessed and the Buddha worshipped. They might also visit a friend who might, in celebration, rub a little butter on the baby's head.

Sichuan villagers wear garb like Tibetans.

CHILDHOOD

C HILDREN NEED TO LEARN good manners because habits formed early stick the best. It's possible (though not advisable) to learn by careful observation and trial and error, which might be the only option for an adult outsider. Think about it: When was the last time you saw a *basic* etiquette course for adults? Though there is plenty of training for diplomats, high-level corporate leaders, and military officers, there is little training for the regular employees who often really need it.

Children need to be told how to treat others; no toddler has a pre-imprinted word for "thank you" in his head. However, when children are simply instructed in but not shown manners, these rules become hollow, superficial, automatic responses, rather than true demonstrations of responsibility and respect. One society may call for constant use of the knife and fork at the table and another allow hands in communal dishes, but the purpose is the same: to provide a foundation for smooth social interaction that doesn't require thought or negotiation when people gather.

> *The best training any parent can give a child is to train the child to train himself.*
>
> —A. P. GOUTHEY

Children learn from repetition, from the earliest mechanics of nursing to the late-childhood skills of bicycle riding and whistling, but with manners, there's an additional challenge: Sometimes even if a child knows how to say "please" and "thank you," more fundamental urges can result in distinctly uncourteous behavior. Because of their supercharged egos, children and teens can be the worst violators of manners or even basic civility. Parents, caregivers, and the rest of "the village" have, throughout time, had to continuously reinforce the lessons required for children to live in society. After all, the future of civilization rests on their shoulders.

In every family home there's a word which people find it really hard to say to each other. It ends in "y."
—LYNNE TRUSS, AUTHOR OF *EATS, SHOOTS AND LEAVES*

No Sir, Sir

NOT TO CAUSE FRICTION, but there is still a divide in the United States between the North and the South: the sir/ma'am division. In the South, people of all ages use those terms. In the North, they rarely, if ever, do.

"Sir" and "ma'am" derive from the French *monsieur* and *madame,* titles of respect for men and women. However, in English both have some baggage. "Sir" connotes the slangy Elizabethan "sirrah," a 16th-century term for a fool, and "ma'am" can make women feel like instant grandmothers.

But consider the geographical chasm in the U.S. Southerners believe teaching children to address adults with honorifics (e.g., "Miss Justine") and to answer saying "No, sir" and "Yes, ma'am" demonstrates their innate courtesy. For northerners or southerners, it certainly helps to mitigate any qualms adults may have about the trend for children to refer to them by first name.

But there are still complicated feelings about the terms. Some believe, although there isn't necessarily evidence, that repeating "sir" and "ma'am" is a holdover from when slaves worked Southern plantations. Others think that it smacks of a disingenuous attitude—that if you say "Yes'm" and "Nossir" you can do so with a smirk and no real respect.

On the other hand, the military-minded know that "sir" and "ma'am" can be used instead of an official title when addressing a fellow enlisted person. In the military or nonmilitary world, they get a stranger's attention quickly. "Hey, you" doesn't dispose a person to respond.

1840s advertisement: hats for "madame petit"

ARCHAIC MANNERS: Children Should Be Seen and Not Heard Often attributed to the etiquette-conscious Victorians, this "old saw" was first recorded in the 15th century. Not surprisingly, given the history of women's rights in the Western world, its original composition was that "a mayde" should be seen and not heard. The quiet and obedient young of both sexes were preferred by adults for centuries, but in today's parenting atmosphere, at least, children are seen, heard, and catered to with a vengeance.

Education is an ornament in prosperity and a refuge in adversity.
—ARISTOTLE

Separate Doors

OLD-TIME SCHOOLHOUSES that still exist in many parts of the United States often have doors marked "Boys" and "Girls," harkening back to an era when the sexes—if allowed to attend the same school at all— were firmly corralled during classroom hours. There were many reasons for this, some of which never made any sense at all, and some of which still make sense today—but even though in U.S. public schools these separate doors no longer exist, the debate about single-sex education still hasn't been won.

Some people still feel that boys and girls are less easily distracted from their work and more likely to speak freely when classrooms are segregated by gender. Old-fashioned, perhaps, but then it's an old idea: The sexes were separately educated for hundreds of years, and sometimes girls weren't educated at all outside of the domestic arts.

But single-sex education hasn't gone the way of the one-room (perhaps we should say two-room?) schoolhouse. It's still hotly debated. In 2006, the United States changed federal regulations to give public schools more flexibility in allowing boys and girls to be educated in

Gender markers for separate restrooms

separate classrooms, and more schools started giving families single-sex education options. The National Association for Single-Sex Public Education was thrilled—the group claims that girls are more self-critical and need more encouragement, while boys often think they're quite smart and need teachers to give them regular reality checks. In the other camp are groups like the American Civil Liberties Union, which says separating the sexes is based on antiquated gender stereotypes.

However, in some countries, separating girls from boys isn't a matter of distraction, but a matter of getting those girls educated in the first place. As UNESCO reports, girls in African and South Asian countries may spend three years less in school than boys of the same age, and in rural areas, dropout rates are even higher. In many areas, there is no provision made for girls' education, and even if they do manage to attend, no guarantee of their safety.

So if you see an African school, for example, that retains separate entrances or lines for boys and girls, keep in mind that some girls and women have fought hard for the protocol of having two doors instead of just one for boys only.

Oh! There is an organ playing in the street—a waltz too!
I must leave off to listen.
—LORD BYRON

The Well-Mannered Waltz

SOME CUSTOMS AND MANNERS are undeniably based on socioeconomic status. Upper-class Americans of a certain age will recall the excruciating ordeal of cotillion classes, in which boys and girls were instructed in matters and manners ranging from proper place-setting etiquette to polite conversation to writing thank-you notes.

Usually run by women in positions of authority, cotillion classes are meant to prepare young ladies and gentlemen to take their eventual places in society. The first time they do so is supposed to be at a "cotillion," or gala ball introducing debutantes (girls, usually aged 18) to their elders and community, an event that once formally signaled that those debutantes were ready to begin considering courtship, engagement, and marriage.

A gala ball means lots of ballroom dancing, so cotillion classes always included formal dance lessons in which boys, sometimes inches shorter than their partners, and girls marched (and perhaps tripped) stiffly over a plywood floor learning the patterns and rhythms of the foxtrot, the box step, and, of course, the waltz. As if the close-quarters contact weren't difficult enough for young teens (sweaty hands, anyone?), their instructors and parents insisted that for every lesson they dress in party frocks, stiff shoes, and jacket-and-tie combinations.

The funny thing is, those very fancy clothes are actually the inspiration behind the name of this custom. In 17th-century France, the *cotillon* was a patterned "social dance" or *contredanse* in which four couples stepped with and around each other. Cotillon meant petticoat, and the dance took its name from the quick flash of women's petticoats that could be witnessed when a couple turned to switch partners. Since today's boys and girls in cotillion classes are being prepared for a figurative social dance, the name is rather apt.

Not marble, nor the gilded monuments
Of princes shall outlive this pow'rful rhyme.
—WILLIAM SHAKESPEARE, SONNET 55

Stuff and Nonsense Rhymes

WHEN YOU HEAR "Ring around the rosey/A pocket full of posies/Ashes, ashes/We all fall down!" do you think of a benign childhood game, or the bubonic plague? Probably the former—but there are some people who believe that a great many common English "nursery rhymes" or "Mother Goose rhymes" have political and social meaning. Likewise, some historians have argued that "Three Blind Mice" was about Queen Mary I of England and that "Humpty Dumpty" refers to King Richard III.

Nursery rhymes, as English speakers began calling them in the 19th century, have their origins deep in human parenting and infancy. Mothers around the world, in every language, make certain sounds to soothe their babies to sleep. In the Western world, the sounds were often "lu, lu" or "la, la," and "by, by" (indicating both "bye-bye" and "by the by"), and historians

A popular edition of the iconic Mother Goose

think that the word "lullaby" came from the three sounds together. People often took these simple tunes and created poems that fit with them to amuse children once they woke up, as well.

These rhymes are certainly calming to young children, who enjoy their repetition and melodic sounds, and the most interesting point about nursery rhymes is actually not any historical or political clues they might hold, but how easy they make it for children to retain information. It's not just that rhymes make it easy to remember things; it seems that learning them actually increases brainpower for other skills, too. Not the stuff of nonsense, after all.

RELATIVES

ONE OF THE MOST COMMON COMPLAINTS that parents around the world have about their offspring is that children who are ill-mannered at home, in every way from quarreling with their siblings to leaving laundry on the floor to insulting their parents, will be paragons of etiquette virtue when visiting with a friend's family.

Yes, we always hurt the ones we love, and it starts early. Because our relatives are often (certainly not always) the people closest to us who also care about us the most, we humans seem to believe that we can take that closeness and care for granted. How many mothers still beam with pride at their middle-aged sons who wear ball caps at the table and talk with their mouths full? However, there's another side to our relative rudeness, which is that we can't choose our blood kin. When an aunt won't stop giving you unsolicited advice about your love life or a cousin makes a snobby remark about your neighborhood every time she visits, you might be able to convince yourself to overlook those actions. But if you want to stay in contact with your family, you probably have to overlook them again and again. (This is, naturally, where good manners like "Two negatives don't make a positive" and "If you don't have anything nice to say, don't say anything at all" come in handy.)

If you want children to keep their feet on the ground, put some responsibility on their shoulders.

—ABIGAIL VAN BUREN

Strangers are easier. If we don't like their manners, we can ignore them. We can choose our friends, and keep choosing them, if we like, until we've formed a community that conforms to the manners and attitudes of our own choosing. Eventually, we may select one person we like the most, and even live with or marry that person. Guess what? Then we have to deal with . . . that person's relatives.

If you bow at all, bow low.
—CHINESE PROVERB

Bowing to Age

EVERY NASCENT YOGA BUNNY has bowed and said *"Namaste"* after receiving a skinny decaf soy latte, but that doesn't mean the posture itself is superficial. In fact, it's more complicated than any barista's menu.

The *namaskaram,* or ritual bow in Hindi, is thousands of years old. Yoga practitioners perform its original form, the "sun salutation," at the beginning of class. Saying *"Namaste"* means "I bow to the god within you," and ancient yogis saw the sun as a source of divine power. The full namaskaram prostration is a surrender to a deity, and while modern Westerners make much of "the mysterious East" and its exotic ways, the Hindu namaskaram is quite similar

Hands together symbolize greeting in India.

An Indian in traditional dress does namaskaram

to early Christian postures which survive today in old-fashioned and extreme orders.

Since the namaskaram is meant to rid the self of ego and to signal respect for inner divinity, it is not surprising that Indians began to use it when saluting family elders. As recently as the 1960s, boys and girls performed namaskaram before their grandparents (who would have been accustomed to the practice) to receive a blessing for, say, success at school.

The full namaskaram before relatives is no longer common, but it's worth noting an interesting divide between the sexes; the women's *panchanga namaskaram* is designed so that the female womb and breasts, which are vital for gestating and nourishing new life, will never touch the ground.

Behind every successful man stands a surprised mother-in-law.
—VOLTAIRE, FRENCH ENLIGHTENMENT WRITER, 1694–1778

Second Parents

THERE IS NO MARRIED PERSON anywhere on this earth who has not had some kind of miscommunication at some point with his or her spouse's family. Think of Endora in *Bewitched*, the perennially popular 1960s television sitcom: She and her son-in-law Darrin couldn't understand each other because he was a mortal and she was a witch. Those of us with no magical powers can often have a pretty tough time understanding our in-laws as well, even if they are mortals (we think!).

Around the world, there are different ways to address one's in-laws. In France, parents-in-law are known as *les beaux parents,* which, in typical French elegance, means "refined parents." The lengthy mouthful of a word *Schwiegereltern* is how Germans refer to their in-laws, and this phrase derives etymologically from the Middle High German word for "sister/mother." So, really, the connotation is that a *Schwiegermutter* is a sort of mother and sister all wrapped up into one package.

One of the most interesting compromises on how to address in-laws comes from Italy, where

In-laws even cause etymological stress.

grammar offers a kind of middle path. Many men and women address their mothers-in-law as "Mamma," which is fairly intimate and familial. However, rather than use the truly intimate *tu* with her or the standoffishly formal *lei,* Italian spouses can address their most important legal relative with the cordial *voi.*

In the United States, we don't seem to have completely made up our minds about what to call our in-laws. Some people call them by their first names. Other couples may call them simply "Mom" and "Dad." And still others may not feel comfortable doing either.

OBJECTS OF ETIQUETTE: Footstools "A cricket on the hearth" actually had nothing to do with an insect: A "cricket" was a low, three- or four-legged stool for whoever turned the roasting spit. Eventually people discovered this low stool was perfect for raising tired feet while sitting, too, and helped people to make others comfortable.

Have a heart that never hardens, and a temper that never tires,
and a touch that never hurts.
—CHARLES DICKENS

Touchy Subject

ONE OF THE REASONS the world waited breathlessly for "the kiss" during the Royal Wedding of April 2011 was that Britain's Prince William has often told the press that he shies away from "PDA"—"public displays of affection." When he and his new wife, the former Catherine Middleton (the couple are now known as the Duke and Duchess of Cambridge) finally engaged in a modest buss on the balcony of Buckingham Palace, the cheer was as much for overcoming a mannerly stricture as for the moment. Nonetheless, the newlyweds' first public kiss was indeed quite brief, provoking some disappointment, groans, and discussion from broadcasters narrating the day on television. But with the whole world watching, the prince overcame his PDA-shyness for one more instant and, before the couple retreated from the balcony they leaned toward each other once more and exchanged one more kiss.

Prince William, who attended the British military academy at Sandhurst and is currently an active-duty Royal Air Force officer, follows a long line of military traditions in eschewing PDA. However, many cultures frown on too much personal contact, for reasons of discretion and honor.

One such culture is that of Korea. Web sites catering to diplomats and businesspeople caution them not to backslap, pat, or otherwise touch a Korean counterpart, as deliberate bodily contact is generally restricted to close friends and family members. This is in stark contrast to the traditional Korean bathhouse, where complete strangers may scrub and massage every nook and cranny of a person's body—but that is considered completely different and perfectly acceptable, the ministrations of a professional as opposed to the casual contact of an acquaintance.

While it's doubtful we'll ever see a video of the Duke and Duchess getting exfoliated (although given some British royals' behavior, never say never . . .), we can probably state with some degree of certainty that they would approve of the Korean PDA disapproval.

In Africa think big.
—CECIL RHODES

It Takes a Village

WHEN A YOUNG WOMAN (or heck, any woman) decides to get married, she and her friends will celebrate, and usually more than once. They may have drinks to toast her engagement, a lunch when that engagement is officially announced, a bridal shower, a bachelorette party before the big day, and so on, and so on . . .

One specific tradition in which a bride gets both friends and relatives together before she

is wed is the Indian *mehndi* party. Sometimes known in the West as "henna tattoos," the art of mehndi is quite old and can be quite complicated, too—but it's temporary and is not actually tattooing, which is the act of inserting pigment beneath the dermis. Mehndi is decorative dying in patterns, done on the palms of hands and soles of feet because the henna binds with the higher levels of keratin on those surfaces. Eventually the rich brown swirls, lines, and dots that stain the skin fade away.

Women in India get mehndi done before many different types of festivals, like Diwali and Eid. In urban areas, the mehndi dye comes in an easily transported cone, but in some rural areas women still mix the henna and oil together using a mortar and pestle.

The pre-wedding mehndi ceremony is usually held for the bride's family and friends, but the groom usually comes to this event, too. Sometimes brides-to-be make their grooms wear purple, the better to fit in with all of the other bright colors worn by celebrating attendees. A professional mehndi artist might be hired, or a female relative of the bride may apply her henna patterns. The designs are intricate, and often include the groom's initials hidden somewhere among scrolls and flowers.

Of course, these days, you need not be an Indian bride to be painted with henna swirls. The Indian custom has become a staple at American festivals, where the designs are, admittedly, often less traditional.

CELEBRATIONS

I f we're very well mannered, we'll be rewarded with social invitations. Courteous behavior leads to positive reinforcement: It makes one more socially skilled, which makes one's company more desirable, which puts the person into the company of others more often, which provides more opportunities—such as special events with members of our community—to practice courteous behavior.

The best celebrations don't take place before a community; the best celebrations actually involve a community, including people of all ages, stages, levels, genders, and talents. In her book *The Gift of Thanks: The Roots and Rituals of Gratitude,* British social historian Margaret Visser details a local French festival, a celebration whose regional participation is a measure of its success. The contributions of people make the celebrations in this section so joyous.

There was never a child so lovely but his mother was glad to get him to sleep.

—RALPH WALDO EMERSON

Celebrations are also joyous because community members are following the manners that they've been taught—often, but not always, from early childhood. Celebrations in which participants follow their own whims—think Woodstock—happen much less frequently than those involving some prescribed roles and rules. Because we're human, those rules often wind up ensconced in their own etiquette systems. "But we've always done it this way! It's a tradition!" someone will cry. Before you know it, last year's banners are being dragged out of mothballs and last century's recipes are on the stove. If everything goes right, regardless of the ritual's precision, the same good feelings will be center stage—and that means we'll be back next year.

Our birthdays are feathers in the broad wing of time.
—JEAN PAUL RICHTER, GERMAN ROMANTIC WRITER, 1763-1825

Princess for a Day

IN AREAS OF THE UNITED STATES with large Hispanic populations, like South Texas, it's quite common to see groups of beautifully dressed men and women escorting girls in fancy gowns to a church or restaurant. The gowned girl will be a *quince*—a teenager celebrating her 15th birthday—and her *damas*—other 15-year-old girls who are serving as members of the quince's retinue on her special day.

The *quince* celebration, or *quinceañera*—literally, "15th year"—is a milestone for young Hispanic women. Today most quinceañeras include a full Mass or at least a nod to the Roman Catholic Church, but the tradition is actually much older, dating to the Aztec civilization in 500 B.C. At 15, girls were deemed ready for womanhood and its attendant responsibilities of marriage and childbirth, and this induction not only initiated them as adults into society but also instructed them in the culture's ideals.

Today this coming-of-age rite has spread from Mexico to Puerto Rica, Cuba, Central and South America, and has become a combination of religious confirmation, birthday celebration, debutante ball, and family party. Families begin to plan for the quinceañera as much as a year in advance: choosing venues, picking out a gown, buying special jewelry (most of which has ritual significance), and selecting friends and relatives to play special roles during the proceedings. Usually the girl's mother presents her with her first pair of high-heeled shoes, after which she has the first dance of the evening with her father.

A young quinceañera *in all her party regalia*

ARCHAIC MANNERS: Asking Permission of a Father to Marry His Daughter   Just as women were once their husband's possessions, children were once their parents' possessions. Any man who wished to marry a young woman was legally required to ask her father for permission to do so because otherwise the groom-to-be would be literally stealing someone else's property. Sentimental, traditionally minded couples today may follow this old-fashioned tradition, but it is thankfully no longer a legal necessity.

Share our similarities, celebrate our differences.
—M. SCOTT PECK, AMERICAN PSYCHIATRIST AND AUTHOR, 1936-2005

Two Peoples

*A Maori wood carving
from New Zealand*

MANY COUNTRIES have celebrations of nationhood that commemorate revolutions, separations, and conflict—think of Bastille Day in France or the Fourth of July in the United States or Yom Ha'atzmaut, Israel's Independence Day. New Zealand is one of the few countries affected by colonialism to have struck an early balance between indigenous independence and European interference, as its Treaty of Waitangi with the British was signed in 1840. The treaty, eventually signed by more than 500 Maori chiefs, is considered New Zealand's founding document.

That doesn't mean New Zealand's native Maori people have had an easy road with those they call *pahekas* (European whites). Under the terms of the Waitangi Treaty, the Maori people agreed to accept British sovereignty and they in turn were granted citizenship and land rights. However, the Treaty of Waitangi has never been officially ratified, and despite a 1975 act seeking to honor its terms, the Treaty remains a source of trouble, especially when it comes to land and seabed rights. The treaty has been particularly problematic because it is written in both English and Maori, and the translations are not an even match. The English version, for example, promises the Maori control over their forests and fisheries, while the Maori version also suggests protection of language and culture. And rather than embrace a full transference of power, as the English version does, the Maori translation implies that there would be more sharing.

But the controversial historic document's effects on New Zealand's nationhood and its spirit of honoring the Maori people are celebrated each year in February. Near the Treaty House and its Maori-built Whare Runanga ("Meeting Place") is the world's largest *waka,* or war canoe, the Ngatokimatawhaorua, named after the great canoe of Kupe, traditional Polynesian ancestor of the Maori people. While tensions between Maori and paheka have and may continue to mark the Waitangi Day celebrations, in recent years an increased effort has been made to honor and showcase the country's native culture while at the same time celebrating all of this nation's history.

You are the music while the music lasts.
—T. S. ELIOT

Torch Songs

CELEBRATED BY SEVERAL ETHNIC groups in southwestern China, the Chinese tribal Torch Festival or Torch Day, sometimes called "the Carnival of China," shows how festivals can celebrate something elemental to several groups.

It's a practical celebration, inspired by legendary wrestler Atilaba, who drove away a plague of locusts using torches made from pine trees. Nowadays, torches burn for three days, driving away pests that would otherwise devour newly growing crops. Standing around with burning torches isn't so exciting, so for hundreds of years the Yi, Bai, Hani, Lisu, Naxi, Pumi, and other peoples have added singing, dancing,

horse racing, bullfighting, wrestling and more to keep people awake during the three-day chore. Things get especially interesting when fire is built into the activities; the Yi of Yunnan Province have horses leap over torches during races, while the Sichuan Lisu form a parade to look like a fire-breathing dragon.

The Torch Days are tied to ancient fire worship, but also to the veneration of elders, who share their farming experience with the younger people.

Traditional Yi women of China's Yunnan Province around a fire pit

MANNERED LIVES

Frederick Douglass

A one-time slave who purchased his freedom decades before the Civil War, Frederick Douglass was ahead of his time in many ways. He was the first black person to run for Vice President of the United States, on the Equal Rights Party ticket with Victoria Waddell. After his beloved wife Anna Murray-Douglass's 1882 death, he married progressive feminist Helen Pitts, attracting scandal because she was not only white, but 20 years his junior.

Douglass, one of the greatest Americans in history, cared very little about convention—after all, convention had done very little for him, especially during his years as a slave: He was born to a slave mother (and an unknown white father) on Maryland's Eastern Shore. He was separated from his mother, denied a real education, and brutally beaten as a teenager.

However, one of Douglass's owners had a wife who secretly taught Douglass the alphabet. She took some risk in doing so, because teaching a slave to read was against the law at that time. After her husband put a stop to the lessons, Douglass continued to learn to read on his own. In 1838, two years after promising himself he would be free, he escaped from Baltimore to New York in a single day.

Douglass could not get enough of newspapers and books, and eventually published his autobiography and a weekly newsletter. "Once you learn to read, you will be forever free," said Douglass. He became convinced

Frederick Douglass: American abolitionist, author, and statesman

that education was the most important route to equal rights, and despite his championing of many other causes including abolition and suffrage, education remained his most important.

Part of education, Douglass felt, was maintaining good manners between teachers and students so that good communication resulted.

*If you can't get rid of the skeleton in your closet,
you'd best teach it to dance.*

—GEORGE BERNARD SHAW, IRISH PLAYWRIGHT, 1856–1950

Skeleton Dance

LIKE THE QUINCEAÑERA, which is aligned with the Roman Catholic Church but has its origins in Aztec beliefs, the annual "Day of the Dead" celebrations in Mexico and many other Spanish-speaking countries are now linked to early-November All Saints liturgy—but began with ancient tribal customs.

When it was held during the Aztec calendar period that would now correspond to August, the "Day of the Dead" was an entire month, dedicated to the "Lady of the Dead." The Aztecs and other Meso-American civilizations displayed skulls as trophies that symbolized death and rebirth. The skulls honored the dead, whom the Aztecs believed visited during the month-long ritual. Unlike the Spaniards, who viewed death as the end of life, the natives saw it as the continuation of life. To them, life was a dream and only in death did they become truly awake.

Skull-costumed Mexicans on Day of the Dead

Family members still gather in cemeteries, although fewer of them now believe that the souls of their loved ones remain there and can communicate with them.

However, even if modern Mexicans don't literally believe in the spirits, they still celebrate them by constructing small elaborate altars known as *ofrendas* at home and in graveyards, including various sweets and other foods to tempt them, writing short poems in their honor, and picnicking in cemeteries on all manner of skull- and death-themed snacks, like sweet *pan de muerto* ("corpse bread") and elaborate candy skulls. As they clean and decorate tomb stones, families tell stories and reminisce about their absent ones.

FAMOUS GAFFES: Diana Spencer spoke her fiancé's names wrong during 1981 wedding ceremony
The bride's blue eyes gazed up as the world waited for Lady Diana Spencer to say her vows to the Prince of Wales on July 21, 1981. "I take thee, Phillip Charles Arthur George," she said. Unfortunately, her fiancé's name was "Charles Phillip Arthur George." The Archbishop of Canterbury proceeded anyway.

OBSERVANCES

CERTAIN TYPES OF CELEBRATIONS CAN BE more properly defined as "observances," because they're linked to a religious or spiritual practice and have particular social behaviors. Unlike purely secular celebrations, these observances have an obligatory nature beyond the immediate community that recognizes ties to a much larger group, many of whose members may never meet. You can learn a great deal about a culture from its observances because these are the rites that are "in between": They do not determine salvation or reincarnation, they do not exist just for fun, but are instead about the things a society chooses to take seriously.

The end product of child raising is not the child but the parent.

—FRANK PITTMAN

Unlike secular celebrations, observances are more highly circumscribed. Only certain people are allowed to participate, or if large groups are permitted, then there will be certain figures who are in charge of the ritual performed. Generally, because they are somewhat spiritual in nature, observances are less likely to have commercial objects associated with them. However, as anyone who has ever attended a wedding featuring personalized matchbooks, napkins, and party favors will attest, this is not a hard and fast rule.

Some observances are a little more than secular and a little less than spiritual, like memorials for war dead or victims of genocide or disaster. Most of these have a solemn tone and are recognized as occasions for reflection. Participants may not have prescribed roles to play, but there is a tacit agreement to behave in a way that allows the group to come together. Really, that's what observances are and what "observance" means: a time for reflection. These are special types of celebrations that integrate joy with serious meaning and allow connection not just with other people, but with other parts of history.

*Ceremonies are different in every country,
but true politeness is everywhere the same.*
—OLIVER GOLDSMITH, IRISH WRITER, 1730-1774

Taking Part

POPULAR IMAGES OF MODERN bar and bat mitzvahs include souvenir satin yarmulkes (beanie-like head coverings) and lavish parties complete with buffets, bands, and gifts, all for 13-year-old boys and girls who are barely comfortable in their own skins yet, let alone being the center of attention for hours on end. As a courtesy towards guests, each attendee receives a small gift—perhaps a T-shirt printed with the name

A bar mitzvah wearing a kippah *reads from Torah scrolls at temple.*

of the new "adult"— chosen by the 13-year-old and his or her parents.

But the ancient Hebrew rite of welcoming adolescents into adulthood has a serious purpose that belies its current frivolity. For thousands of years, upon physical puberty (which is why some congregations allow girls to make their bat mitzvah at age 12), boys and girls became men and women responsible for their own actions. That meant both actions in their faith and in their community; the terms *bar mitzvah* and *bat mitzvah* literally mean "good boy" and "good girl," but the terms connote moral and legal ownership, too. A Jewish boy automatically becomes a bar mitzvah upon reaching the age of 13 years, and a girl upon reaching the age of 12 years. No ceremony is needed to confer these rights and obligations.

Nonetheless, ceremonies are held to publically mark this transition. Often, the most anxious moment for the youth comes when he or she is called up to the bima to read, in Hebrew, from the Torah. More than anything, however, the bar mitzvah ceremony formally, publicly marks that a person now has a social responsibility toward others: The youth is obligated to observe the commandments, and also has the right to take part in leading religious services, to count in a minyan (the minimum number of people needed to perform certain parts of religious services), to form binding contracts, to testify before religious courts, and to marry. In its earliest and most basic form, a bar mitzvah is the celebrant's first aliyah, or ceremonial honor.

Faith is the ticket to the feast, not the feast.
—EDWIN LOUIS COLE

A Happy Witch

TECHNICALLY THE "Feast of the Three Kings," also called "Epiphany," is observed in any place with a substantial Christian population—but some countries celebrate more than others.

The church holy day of Epiphany commemorates the first physical manifestation of God as Christ to human beings. According to the Christian New Testament gospel books, the Magi (three kings of the East) were guided by a star shining over the city of Bethlehem to the lowly stable where the infant Jesus lay in a feeding trough, or manger. While Western Christians observe this "epiphany," or appearance, the Eastern Church chooses instead to emphasize Christ's baptism in the River Jordan.

The church may call January 6 Epiphany, but the English call it "Twelfth Night," referring to it as the 12th day after Christmas, the Dutch call it *Dreikoningengedag,* and in Portuguese Goa it's known as the *Festa des Reis.*

Old Befana brings treats to children at Epiphany.

However, the Italian "translation" of Epiphany is most creative. According to some historical sources, speakers of that language garbled *Epiphania* into *Befana,* and humanized this concept as an old witch. The legend claims that Befana, who lived near Bethlehem, heard a knock at the door one night. It was the Three Wise Men asking about the Christ child. Befana scoffed and closed the door—but as time went on, she too believed. She gives bread and cakes to children in perpetual hope that she may find the "king."

Unlike children in other countries who get small gifts from the Magi or Three Wise Men on this feast day, those in Italy are treated to candy and other presents by Old Befana. If children are naughty, Old Befana, just like Santa Claus, leaves them coal. Good behavior, you see, always garners more rewards than bad.

A typical Christian Nativity scene

As the innocent moon, that nothing does but shine,
Moves all the labouring surges of the world.
—FRANCIS THOMPSON, *SISTER SONGS*, 1895

Moon Dance

EARLY EACH YEAR, Koreans honor the moon in a special festival called Daeboreum. The first full moon of the lunar calendar takes place at this time, and its appearance is a reminder of the annual change of seasons.

But there was an older and more superstitious element to the Moon Festivals around Korea, which was that people once believed the light of a full moon actually prevented illness and disease. The first person to see the moon rise is said to be assured of good luck all year; therefore, on the evening of the first full moon, some people still climb mountains to catch the moon as it begins to rise, while others crack nuts with their teeth in a practice *(bureom)* that was believed would keep teeth and skin healthy for the year and would drive away evil spirits. Cracking nuts, such as walnuts, chestnuts, pine nuts, and peanuts, was supposed to be done in a single bite before uttering one's first words of

Daeboreum at Han River in Seoul, South Korea

the day. Farmers used to predict their harvest by examining the moon on Daeboreum. Pale moonlight was said to bring frequent rain, red moonlight indicated a drought, dim moonlight forecasted a good harvest year, and hazy moonlight predicted a bad harvest.

Jwilbinori was another tradition practiced on the night of the first full moon of the year. Jisinbapgi was mainly done by farmers, who would burn dry grass on top of the mounded dirt ridges in their fields of rice. At the same time, the farmer's children would wave pierced cans of burning charcoal so that the smoke would destroy insects. Another important tradition associated with Daeboreum is the *dalijip-tae,* or "moon house," which was the ritual construction and burning of a straw house in hopes of a trouble-free 12 months. Interestingly enough, given the emphasis on heat and fires during Daeboreum, one of the most common things to say to others is *"Nae deowi sara,"* or "Take my heat," a cheeky "wish" for a mild summer.

To me rites of passage through life,
that's a wonderful, beautiful thing.
—LANCE HENRIKSEN, AMERICAN ACTOR

Welcoming Spring

FOR MORE THAN A MILLENNIUM, Bulgarians have celebrated a national holiday on March 1, which is known as Baba Marta, or "Grandmother March" (in other words, a moody old lady). However, this particular holiday is also part of an ancient rite of spring.

The symbol of this rite is called the *Martenitsa,* and it takes the form of a small red-and-white ornament made of yarn. You won't see or hear any instruction telling you it's time to don your tasseled Martenitsa, but traditional Bulgarians know it is worn around the wrist from March 1 through March 22. You may also get away with tying it to a tree or flowering shrub. Some Bulgarians wear it until they see a tree's first buds or a stork or swallow fly. Just as Americans look to Punxsutawney Phil on Groundhog Day (February 2), Bulgarians believe that if you wear a Martenitsa that spring will come more quickly. Apparently, the United Kingdom's Prince Charles is a fan of the woven ornaments. In 2003, the *Times* of London reported that he had been wearing a Martenitsa, a gift from a Bulgarian. The article questioned why the prince hadn't removed the charm after two months, but speculated that he forgot or he simply hadn't seen a swallow yet.

The national story behind Baba Marta involves the first Bulgarian king, his captured sister Huba, her escape on horseback, and a falcon whose white tether became stained red with blood when he was shot before flying back to Huba. Despite the falcon's death, Huba found her way to her brother and his new kingdom, where they lived in prosperity.

The Martenitsa became a symbol of peace and love, health, and happiness. The white color symbolizes purity and honesty, and the red color means life, passion, friendship, and love. Sometimes the Martenitsa tassels are fashioned to look like little male and female dolls, *Pizho* and *Penda*. Pizho is the male doll, usually white. Penda is the female doll, usually red and distinguished by her skirt.

The figures remind wearers that like the seasons, life has a cycle.

Tasseled Bulgarian Pizho and Penda dolls

OBLIGATIONS

ALMOST EVERY CULTURE HAS A RELIGION ATTACHED TO IT—a means of explaining and relating to the forces humans cannot understand. Today we make much of explaining some belief systems as "mythological," but while the ancient Egyptians and Greeks were busy worshipping gods of the sea, gods of the sky, and gods of nearly everything else, they certainly believed in them every bit as strongly as a devout confessor of one of today's "major" religions does in her creed.

"Religion" is not the same as faith, or belief. The word comes from the Latin *religare*, which means "to bind," and most modern theologians believe this has to do with choosing to tie oneself to certain practices.

> *What's done to children, they will do to society.*
> —KARL MENNINGER

The thing about religion is that there always exists a complicated etiquette about everything from one's status as an infant to one's final resting place, not to mention the endless matters of who can be a celebrant, who can receive different kinds of rites, and what is worn and given and eaten and sacrificed when. Complicating matters is the fact that, in some cases, even within a religion

there can be dozens of interpretations of the proper way to live and the proper way to acknowledge a higher power in our everyday lives. While any of us can learn about another religion, it's no wonder that most of us practice only one or two religions in our lifetimes. It's exhausting trying to remember all of the ins and outs, not to mention the standing ups and standing downs, of most religions.

One thing that is less taxing is how to behave toward a religion that isn't your own: with the same good manners you always use. Even if you're invited to attend some kind of worship that is in a different language and uses symbols you don't understand, you can be respectful.

Don't get up from the feast of life
without paying for your share of it.
—DEAN INGE, ANGLICAN PRIEST, 1860-1954

Fast or Feast

MANY RELIGIOUS OBLIGATIONS involve fasting, meaning taking in no food or drink for certain periods of time. One of the most extreme and also most globally known examples of fasting is the Islamic feast of Ramadan, which takes place in the ninth month of the Islamic lunar calendar (meaning that it happens at a different time in the Western calendar each year). During daylight hours, all able-bodied adult Muslims of both sexes are supposed to abstain from all food and water, breaking their fast each evening at sundown.

Breaking Ramadan's fasting with tea and dates

Ramadan commemorates the time in A.D. 610 when Muhammad was wandering in the desert where Allah (God) chose to reveal his holy word, the Koran, to the Prophet. Just as Christians during the time of Lent use fasts to refocus their minds on their faith, so Muslims during Ramadan use *sawm* (fasts) to purify their thoughts as well as their bodies. In the evening, a prayer is said and the daily fast is broken, often by eating a date, which Muhammad is said to have done. Then a meal known as *iftar* is eaten before any other activities are pursued. The iftar itself is often a reason to invite guests over—it becomes both a community and a culinary event. In some places,

corporations host iftars, transforming them into lavish events meant to impress. Typically, however, after a round of visits and contemplation, people sleep, then rise early before the sun for a meal called *suhoor* that is meant to sustain them until sundown.

Not everyone is obliged to fast. Babies, young children, the elderly, the pregnant, and the infirm are excused from the practice. At the month's close, the festival of Eid al-Fitr ("Breaking the Fast") is held, which involves not just sumptuous meals, but also new clothes and shoes, toys and gifts, and household decorations.

OBJECTS OF ETIQUETTE: Covered Dish   People once asked guests to "bring a covered dish" when communities weren't sure how many guests were expected—or when the hosts didn't have enough food to go around. Bringing a covered dish (covered to keep the food fresh and at the right temperature) was also a gesture of care and concern, done for wakes, baby and wedding showers, and more.

MANNERED LIVES

Mrs. Beeton

Her name is synonymous with "cookery books," as they were once called, but English-woman Isabella Mary Mayson Beeton was neither precisely an author nor a cook. She might more accurately be called an etiquette doyenne, and here's why:

In the 19th century, as farm life grew less common and jobs "in town" became more so, gender roles were redefined, too. If men's role was to take the train to London and desk jobs, women's role was to remain at home and organize daily life. After marrying an older, successful publisher, the woman born as Isabella Mayson realized that her peers did not have the knowledge they needed to put their new households together. And so, she took it upon herself to publish books and articles to instruct everyone from a housekeeper to a coachman to a nursemaid in the ways of running a household in Victorian Britain.

Mrs. Beeton decided to start commuting to work with her husband—something that was shocking in the Victorian era and annoyed the male passengers on their route, who felt they had to refrain from smoking and bad language in the presence of a lady. She had the time to devote to her work because she had no children. She bore a son who died in infancy and suffered three miscarriages; she would eventually die of "childbed fever" at the age of just 28.

But her years in publishing books and magazines helped her to build a brand so famous that after she was gone, the publishing firm kept her death quiet so that they could continue to publish books with her imprimatur. While recipes were part of those books, they weren't Beeton's own—she actually merely gathered them from other sources. The real value of her *Mrs. Beeton's Book of Household Management* lay in its teaching middle-class women the manners they needed to deal with tradespeople and staff in putting together their households.

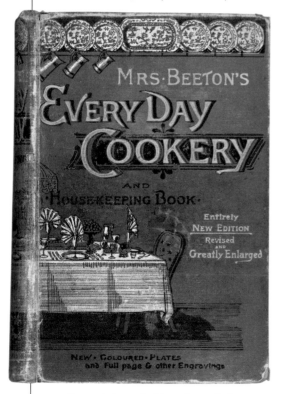

Beeton's household guides aided generations of middle-class British women.

*Those have a short Lent,
who owe money to be paid at Easter.*
—BENJAMIN FRANKLIN

A Real Fry-up

MANY CULTURES MARK THE beginning of spring, and many religions have a set of holy days in which believers are supposed to repent of their bad actions. When Christianity came to what is now Western Europe, the church fathers wisely recognized that their holy days might be better observed if they corresponded to rites that the native people already followed. For example, why not tie a "holiday" marking the birth of Jesus Christ to a midwinter festival called Yule?

That's what happened with the early-spring pagan (pre-Christian) observance called "Lent," which is a Teutonic word meaning "dawn of spring." During Lent, people paid homage to the goddess Eostre, a minor Anglo-Saxon deity whose chief cultural significance is the lending of her name to the Christian holiday that follows Lent: Easter.

Masterfully decorated Polish Easter eggs

Hot cross bun, a sweet treat for Easter

Lent was an easier word for the non-Latinate peoples of Germanic, Norse, Celtic, and Anglo-Saxon heritage to adopt, since the church term for the period leading up to Jesus Christ's resurrection was *quadragesima,* or "40 days." For centuries, the Roman Catholic Church imposed a strict fast during the weeks of Lent, calling for people to give up all rich foods, from meat to fats. Observing an imposed fast on tempting items reminded everyone that resources aren't limitless.

In many places, this led to a special holiday the day before Lent began, known as Shrove Tuesday in England and Mardi Gras (Fat Tuesday) in France. People would make all kinds of fried foods in an effort to use up perishable fats and meats in their larders—it is still typical in many English towns to find pancake feasts held on Shrove Tuesday, while Mardi Gras carnivals are notorious around the world for deep-fried treats, alcoholic beverages, and licentious behavior—hardly the stuff of penitence! There's always tomorrow . . .

Great men are they who see that spiritual is stronger than material force, that thoughts rule the world.
—RALPH WALDO EMERSON

Daily Devotions

MUSLIMS ARE MEANT TO MAKE a hajj (pilgrimage) to Mecca at least one time in their lives if at all possible; millions of Roman Catholic Christians make pilgrimages to holy sites like Lourdes and Częstochowa; Jews visit the Wailing Wall in Jerusalem. Believers in the Hindu faith have *puja*.

All of the other major religions have prayers and devotions that can be performed every day, but the difference between the Hindu *puja* and these others is that *puja* can refer to many different types of religious observation. Puja (also *pooja*) is the act of showing reverence to an aspect of the divine through prayers, songs,

A veiled Hindu performs a puja *by candlelight.*

Elephant-headed Hindu god Ganesh removes obstacles.

and rituals; making a spiritual connection is paramount. Often, an object serves as the way for the devotee to make that connection, and it can be a painting, a branch, or even a beautiful vase. Believers feel that the object becomes filled with the deity's cosmic energy.

Puja is something that can be performed daily, after washing and dressing but before eating or drinking. However, puja can be much more elaborate, and made in a temple—in which case the temple may be visited several times in a single day. The full "temple puja" includes a 16-step list of actions that involve the deity's feet being washed, scented oil anointing the deity's likeness, and various foods and beverages being offered as well.

Hindus may also apply pujas to guests in the home, which is one reason why a visitor to an Indian household may find herself seated and having her feet carefully bathed. There are also any number of large, public pujas like the Diwali Festival.

Do not dwell in the past, do not dream of the future,
concentrate the mind on the present moment.
—BUDDHA

Flying Free

EVERY SPRING, Christians have Easter, Jews have Passover, and Buddhists have Wesak. This spring holiday has different spellings and names in all the countries it's celebrated in, but the easiest translation is simply "Buddha Day."

Not all Buddhist traditions celebrate Wesak, but in Thailand it is a major spiritual holiday that venerates the birth, life, and death of Siddhartha Gautama, the spiritual teacher who founded the religion in ancient India and is known as "the Buddha."

On Buddha Day, formalized only in 1950 by the World Buddhist Congress, believers gather in temples before dawn, offering hymns and prayers to the Buddha, the Dharma (his teachings), and the Sangha (his disciples). Flowers, candles, and burning incense or "joss sticks" are placed around altars. Many Buddhists don simple white robes to mark the purity of right thinking.

Vegetarian meals are standard on Buddha Day, but the most interesting custom may be the release of birds, animals, and insects to represent mankind's liberation from bondage by the Buddha's enlightened wisdom.

Devout Buddhists march with a statue of their divinity during Wesak.

THE GAME OF LIFE

Upon the fields of friendly strife, are sown the seeds that, upon other fields, on other days, will bear the fruits of victory." General Douglas MacArthur was comparing athletic competition at the U.S. Military Academy to battlefield action when he said this in 1962, and while few modern people would want to use this analogy given what we know of modern weaponry, the quote shows how serious games are to human beings. The ideas and customs featured in this chapter aren't child's play, even when actual children are the ones playing games. Sports, games, education, and rites of passage reflect bigger issues of survival and competition.

Still, sports and education have rules of etiquette all their own, especially when they come together, as anyone who has ever watched kickoffs and touchdowns at an Army-Navy football game will tell you. From the team mascots (a mule and a goat) to the cadet uniforms to the "fight songs," these schools transferred customs to many other American colleges and universities. One of the most important, of course, has very old human roots: After each year's Army-Navy game, the teams shake hands, regardless of which side has triumphed. After all, nobody likes a sore loser.

1940s WPA poster touts swimming for fitness.

EQUIPMENT

TODAY URBAN SUBWAY RIDERS AND PEDESTRIANS often tote special elongated bags for their yoga mats, zippered cases for tennis and squash racquets, or bulky duffels stuffed with shower essentials and running shoes. While sometimes unwieldy, these carry-ons show how convenient exercise can be compared to some other activities, like hockey, skiing, or riding to hounds, which involve special kinds of equipment not easily carried. For example, riding to hounds requires tight-fitting boots and clothing; special, carefully fitted saddlery; and well-trained horses. While equipment-intensive sports have definite appeal, most people find that they can more faithfully adhere to daily exercise routines when the required equipment is not too cumbersome.

I always turn to the sports section first. The sports page records people's accomplishments; the front page has nothing but man's failures.

—EARL WARREN

Of course, modern Western plenitude means that people can practice an ancient discipline like yoga with lots of accessories. A true yogini requires little more than a loincloth and a patch of earth, but today's yoga devotees buy special mats, organic aromatherapeutic mat spray, bamboo-fiber yoga pants, special "pose straps," and mango-flavored coconut water for after class.

But equipment needs don't come from advertising-fed desire alone; they can also be based on religious dictates, practical concerns, and even social convention. One of the most equipment-burdened sports, golf, includes a rigorous etiquette for using "caddies," people (mainly young men or boys) whose job it is to carry heavy bags of clubs from one hole on the course to the next. Over the centuries, the exhausting position was carefully cultivated as a prestigious one to ensure the perpetuation of the golfing culture.

*Water, air, and cleanliness are the
chief articles in my pharmacopoeia.*
—NAPOLEON I

Keep It Clean

YOU, YOUR SPOUSE, your best friend, and your postal carrier all talk about "going to the gym," by which you all mean "heading to a facility with lots of exercise equipment and machines, and hopefully a place to shower after working out." But the earliest "gyms," or "gymnasia," were simply spaces—sometimes even outdoors—in which groups of people could gather and perform "gymnastics," or rhythmic exercises.

The modern "gymnasia" date back to the mid-19th century and Germany, where a man named Friedrich Jahn promoted the *Turnplatz* public gymnasia and inspired the "Turner Movement." Various *Turnverein* (Turner Associations) were formed during the most active period of German immigration to the United States, and were important in forming communities in places like Cincinnati and Louisville, among others, and even influenced politics: Several Turner groups were highly influential in getting Abraham Lincoln elected to the presidency.

Naturally, the two 20th-century world wars had a negative effect on membership in Turner Associations, but as time went on the members focused less and less on matters of politics and education and more and more on physical fitness and health. The Turner philosophy for both was based on the Latin epigram *"Mens sana in corpore sano"* ("Sound mind in sound body"), and the Turners practiced exercises both outside and inside. The indoor Turnplatz is one of the precursors of our modern "gyms," a place where both men and women can go to use space and equipment to work their muscles and get their heart rates up. The American *Turnvereins* also emphasized cleanliness as essential for health, hygiene, and preventing the spread of illness, which may be part of the reason why so many modern health clubs insist that each individual attend to cleanliness, wiping down machines like treadmills and bikes after use.

*Friedrich Jahn's stern mien belies
modern fitness ideas.*

*Fencing is a game of subtlety,
and bluff can be met with counter-bluff.*
—CHARLES L. DE BEAUMONT

Point and Thrust

YOU'VE PROBABLY HEARD reference to someone's "rapier wit," and knew that it meant cutting humor—but do you know what a "rapier" is? How about an "épée"? A "foil"? A "saber"?

Each of those is a particular piece of equipage in modern fencing (so called to distinguish it from historical sword fighting), one of the four sports that has been part of every modern Olympics since the first in 1896—and originally the only combat sport included in the Olympics. With the advent of electronic equipment, the 750-gram weight test—the amount of pressure required to score—is based on the amount of tension required to break the skin. In a duel, honor was done when blood was first drawn—even if it merely trickled from a minor wound such as a blister.

A modern fencer lunges with her épée.

Because it is a combat sport that involves an armory of weapons, fencing equipment and uniforms have a relationship that's rare in the athletic world. Once the sport became established and participants were not aiming to draw blood, it was necessary for officials and coaches to be able to determine whether a "hit" had been made— because, of course, the "aim" of scoring a hit in fencing is to be able to draw blood, even if you're genteelly no longer doing so. That may be why 19th-century aficionados of the sport insisted on white garb that quickly and easily displayed stains and blots from ink, soot, or chalk that many competitors applied to the ends of their foils.

Today, fencing enthusiasts have a new, highly technical method of scoring hits—through electric weapons and wired (but still all-white) fencing suits. Regardless of form and style, a fencer must manage to connect her weapon with her opponent's uniform in order to score a point. Fencing has gone from being a bloody and fatal sport to one no less competitive—but far more gentle in its conduct and scoring.

OBJECTS OF ETIQUETTE: Spittoons   Once a common site in saloons, courtrooms, and doctor's offices (for the tubercular), spittoons or "cuspidors" (from the Portuguese *cuspir,* or "to spit") are rarer these days, but still used by plug-tobacco fans and professional wine tasters, who spit out mouthfuls after swilling for flavor in order to stay sober.

On matters of style, swim with the current,
on matters of principle, stand like a rock.
—THOMAS JEFFERSON

The Great Swimsuit Cover-up

MAUREEN DOWD, COLUMNIST FOR the *New York Times,* indulged in a little swimsuit modeling for a *Vanity Fair* feature about her trip to Saudi Arabia in 2009. The feisty redhead appeared in a full-frontal photo clad in radical bathing attire: a "burkini." Yes, the preferred (in fact, the only) swimming togs for Saudi Arabian women are full-body ensembles that come with attached head wraps. Face, hands, and feet are the only body parts left uncovered.

While contemporary devout Muslim women abide by modesty laws that make wearing a "burkini" (a word that mashes together "burka" with "bikini") a necessity, these suits aren't history's first to cover women from head to toe. In ancient Rome, we see skimpy women's bathing costumes in wall paintings, and then women's bathing suits disappear until around the 18th century when they show up again as long "bathing dresses," sometimes with small weights sewn into the hem to keep the diaphanous gowns from floating up around the waterbound wearers. It wasn't until over a century later that women began wearing tunics over bloomers to swim, sometimes even revealing an inch or two of shockingly bare leg between those bloomers and their stockings.

Stockings, to swim? That's what sounds shocking to most of us today—yet the "burkini" still has its adherents, even in an age in which most swimsuits almost seem to need adhesive to get them to stay in place and cover the bare (pun intended) essentials. The contrast between the average Western two-piece bathing suit and

Pablo Picasso's 1918 painting "The Bathers"

the average burkini is about more than yards of polyester fabric; it's also about religious decorum, society's norms, and individual choice. Of course, most women around the world will choose something from the middle to cover their own middles—hence the popularity of the tankini. But even for those who agonize over figure flaws, the burkini is too much fabric to wear on a hot day.

*The game of golf would lose a great deal if croquet
mallets and billiard cues were allowed on the putting green.*
—ERNEST HEMINGWAY

Easy Being Green

OLD MEN IN THE FRENCH and Italian countryside have been playing boules and bocce for hundreds of years, rolling small, hard wooden balls over strips of grass or dirt toward goal markings. Their game developed from one in ancient Greece that involved stone balls called "spheristics," and early wooden balls used in what is now modern Europe were often studded with nails to give them more heft. Various ground-based ball sports evolved into croquet during the 18th and 19th centuries, a game that added wooden mallets and U-shaped "wickets," targets through which players struck the ball.

All of these games evidently derive from a more ancient game known as "ground billiards." We don't know much about that pastime. What we know for sure is that at some time during the reign of France's King Louis XIV, the monarch decided to take croquet from humble ground to tabletop, surrounding an expanse of sod with rudimentary sandbag "bumpers."

Et voila! The "billiards table" was born, and now comprises a wooden base with legs, covered with green felt or baize, and with rubber bumpers on all four sides of the baize, along with pockets in which to shoot the heavy billiard balls. Today we see billiards or pool tables in bars, restaurants, and private homes, the latter often elaborate heirloom pieces made of carved wood settled beneath faux-Tiffany lamps in rec rooms. However, their green felt playing surfaces still reflect the grass upon which the older games were once played.

Set of wooden croquet balls and mallets for playing on well-manicured lawns

TRAINING

R EMEMBER THAT OLD JOKE ABOUT HOW YOU get to Carnegie Hall? The answer is "Practice, practice, practice . . ." Athletes of every type and at every level know that natural gifts will get you to a certain point—and sometimes that point is pretty impressive—but that to truly know your limits and maximize your potential, you have to train well and regularly. Going out for a single jog won't get even the most natural runner ready to tackle a marathon any more than playing one scale will help a violinist prepare for a recital.

Training in athletics involves plenty of good manners, because even individual sports like running and cycling can take place on shared tracks, but it also involves a great deal of etiquette. Most sports involve hierarchies. Some-

> *Games lubricate the body and the mind.*
> —BENJAMIN FRANKLIN

one is stronger, faster, more flexible, more coordinated, or all of the above—and those who are better at a specific skill receive priority during training. It isn't necessarily a fair system, but then, this isn't about being picked last for the school kickball team. Serious training is a serious business at any age, whether the athlete involved is a wizened jockey or a fresh-faced 14-year-old gymnast.

Since those young gymnasts are female, a note about training and women: Until Title IX was passed in the United States in 1972, federally funded schools were not required to spend any money at all on activities for girls and women. Once the law was in effect, it had a great impact on physical education programs, increasing numbers of teams—and their training facilities. For many American women, this was the first time that they had equal access to the kind of training necessary for mastery of a sport.

Self-respect is the fruit of discipline.
—ABRAHAM J. HESCHEL

Clean Sweep

To MARTIAL-ARTS AFICIONADOS, the dojo is a training ground, where they practice kicks and thrusts—but to Zen Buddhist monks, a dojo is sacred ground, where they practice meditation and *zasen*. In reality, a dojo, which means "place of the way" in Japanese, can be any physical training facility.

But no matter how it is used, a dojo is never considered just another messy gym. In both martial-arts and spiritual dojos, a strict decorum is observed. Shoes are never worn beyond

Karate, one of many martial arts practiced at dojos

the door and it is deemed a special place with special rules.

One rule enforced by all members is cleaning the dojo, which is done at the beginning of the day's classes as well as at the end. Each member is generally assigned a specific task on par with his age and skills, from floor sweeping to toilet scrubbing to mat stacking. It might sound simple, but it has deeper purposes in harmony with the goals of training.

First, when dojo members clean together they remind themselves and each other that they share responsibility for the space. Traditional dojos are supposed to be managed and supported by students, not instructors. Second, during cleaning, members can think while doing a mundane task. Someone who is having trouble with breathing or balance will pay attention to breaths while scrubbing or, for example, balance on one foot while dusting. Third, by cleaning together, dojo members reinforce unity over individuality, an essential facet of Japanese culture.

The only real power comes out of a long rifle.
—JOSEPH STALIN

Steady Shot

YOU MIGHT ALREADY HAVE an image of a British shooting party: Gentlemen dressed in stout leather boots and heathered tweeds traverse romantic hills with well-polished mahogany rifles slung casually over their arms, on the hunt for partridge, quail, or grouse, which will be dressed and cooked for dinner.

Modern sport shooters are more likely to wear Gore-Tex and Kevlar than waxed cotton and wool. They'd more likely aim at clay targets than birds or mammals; their rifles are made of high-tech materials and never placed casually anywhere—safety first!

One longtime safety measure in British shooting sport is that no one can go on the hunt or on a target range who has not shot a weapon.

This makes good common sense, but there is also a historical reason: When the all-volunteer British Army faced crippling defeat in the late-19th century Anglo-Boer War, a movement toward training civilians in riflery sprang up.

Learning target shooting became less about class than patriotism. The National Rifle Associations in both Great Britain and the U.S. were founded to encourage good marksmanship when that skill was crucial on the battlefield. Today, though still nostalgically carried out in some areas, shooting parties are more common on the silver screen than the grassy moor.

Skeet shooters take aim at "clay pigeons" on a rifle range.

The best horse doesn't always win the race.
—IRISH PROVERB

Lucky Charms

ANYTHING CAN HAPPEN in a horse race. A complete unknown might gallop up from behind to sneak across the finish line, while a "sure bet" could stumble and suffer a devastating leg injury. Even though most races take mere minutes to run, the combination of terrain, weather, training, hurdles, and thousands of pounds of horseflesh packed tightly together around turns is a recipe for uncertainty.

That's why the people in the racing community are well known for their abundant superstitions. Jockeys have long been famous for their good-luck charms, talismans, tics, and gestures. One contemporary jockey changes whips when he's in a slump. Another insists on having his left boot polished first before a race, and another never dons her silks without first tying on an evil-eye amulet.

However, good-luck superstitions aren't just for jockeys, and they also aren't just for race days either. Owners, trainers, and attendees (especially the betting kind) all have their own rituals and charms to capture good luck. One racing fan never parks in the same area where he did after losing a chunk of money. In 1935 one English horse owner drove past a funeral procession. That day his horse won—and he spent hours driving around Liverpool the following year, looking for another funeral procession. He found one—and once again his horse triumphed.

That's the trouble with superstitions: At most 50 percent of the time, and usually much less often, they manage to "work." The horse world is far from the only sector of society affected: One historian estimates that businesses lose an estimated $800 million to $900 million when the 13th falls on a Friday because people won't fly or go about other normal business. Hmmmm. Maybe if they tried carrying a lucky horseshoe . . .

ARCHAIC MANNERS: A Lady's Favor in a Joust Our ideas of gallant knights tucking scented lady's hankies into their armor has more to do with late-Victorian imaginings about the Middle Ages than real life, but we do know that some rowdy late-medieval jousters sometimes wound ladies' sleeves (detachable from their bodices, usually with laces) around their visor hinges.

What other people may find in poetry or art museums,
I find in the flight of a good drive.
—ARNOLD PALMER

Course, Corrected

GOLF IS RIFE WITH ETIQUETTE, but that isn't because of snobbery—the real reason behind golf's insistence on rules is that it's an unsupervised team sport. Groups of golfers in different numbers and combinations (men with women, beginners and experts, adults and children) roam the same courses together without penalty flags, red cards, or a penalty box.

Good golf manners have nothing to do with wearing pink-and-green plaid or belonging to a country club with a good bar—they're about showing fellow athletes that you're aware of their presence and rights. No polite golfer will consciously step on another's "putting line," the path from a golf ball to the hole being played. The very attentive will even walk around the back of the ball so that the other player doesn't worry about a change in the surface of the turf.

One famous golf custom is called "playing through," and it has become a catchphrase for fair behavior in the boardroom as well as on a golf course. Since golfers play at different rates, depending on factors from skill to schedule, sometimes a foursome will reach hole five, say, and find another group of golfers there. At that time, it is perfectly appropriate for the foursome to ask "Do you mind if we play through?" meaning "Since we appear to be moving more quickly through the course, may we play this hole and continue our way?" What's never cricket—to mix sporting metaphors—is to simply stand and swing in the middle of someone else's game.

Golfers observe course etiquette as well as each other's swings.

COMPETITION

URING THE 1980S ENGLAND EXPERIENCED a spate of "football hooliganism"—fans behaving very badly indeed during soccer matches both at and away from stadiums. The brawls often got very violent, but the most remarkable thing about them is that they usually didn't involve the football players themselves. Over centuries of human competition, for everything from food, water, and shelter to money, natural resources, and real estate, perhaps one of the most well-mannered arenas is that of professional competitive sports.

The "rules of the game," regardless of which game it is—football, rugby, basketball, baseball, jai alai, cricket, and more—are strictly codified and enforced by players, their coaches, and neutral referees. Infractions carry penalties, which can range from setbacks in scoring to paycheck cuts. Of course, just because professional sports competitions have well-defined rules doesn't mean that they follow what are considered good manners in other areas: Athletes and coaches bark instructions at each other, chew gum with their mouths

The trouble with referees is that they just don't care which side wins.

—TOM CANTERBURY

open, and perform bodily adjustments in front of television cameras that most "civilians" do only behind closed doors, in the dark.

However, when you consider what they don't do—tear each other limb from limb, attack fans in the stands (almost never, anyway), or send the losing team into an alligator pit—these competitors are really quite civilized. They should be—they're not fighting for their lives, they're raking in very comfortable annual salaries. Modern athletic competition is quite tame compared with the gory struggles of the Colosseum or Maya ball courts. Perhaps that explains the football hooligans. They still have those primitive urges for blood lust with their sports.

Faintly as tolls the evening chime,
Our voices keep tune and our oars keep time.
—THOMAS MOORE

Row, Row, Row Your Boat

THERE AREN'T MANY THINGS in the world that can claim use of a definite article and be instantly understood by everyone, but a few of those things are British: The Queen. The Tower. And . . . The Boat Race—no other descriptor needed.

Everyone knows (well, at least The Queen does) that The Boat Race takes place each year between the Oxford and Cambridge rowing crews. Historically, the original Cambridge team wore pink sashes and the original Oxford team wore dark blue jerseys, leading to the phrase "Oxford blue" for a student who won a coveted spot on the crew team. Today Oxford still claims dark blue, and Cambridge wears light blue for the event.

These two venerable English universities first competed on the Thames in 1829, when Oxford triumphed—and Cambridge instituted a tradition that continues to this day, that of challenging the winners to a rematch. Each March or April since 1829, whichever side loses in The Boat Race officially issues an invitation to the winner. The formal challenge, made by the losing side's captain, applies only to the "heavyweight eights"—the eight-person crews without weight limits. Previously these crews comprised only men; women have been included since Oxford coxswain Christina Paul in 1975. (The coxswain is the person who steers the boat.) Some consider the race to be among London's top 10 annual events, and it regularly attracts television audiences in the millions and about 250,000 people who crowd the riverbanks to watch the race in person.

The Boat Race is not a brief athletic event like the seven-minute Henley Regatta; the four-mile, U-shaped course from Putney to Mortlake is an upstream one that tests rowers' strength and endurance so severely that one year an Oxford captain collapsed from exhaustion before his team's craft reached the finish line. The "loser's challenge" is no mere bagatelle; teams begin training in September for the spring event, and since they are required to be enrolled, degree-earning students, they also have course work to navigate.

FAMOUS GAFFES: Ilie Nastase temper tantrum at the U.S. Open In 1979 at the normally staid U.S. Open tennis tournament, Romanian tennis legend Ilie Nastase caused 18 minutes of chaos during his match with American John McEnroe, himself known to throw a tantrum or three on the court. When an umpire's controversial call went against him, Nastase refused to accept the decision and was disqualified from the match. The crowd backed him, and Nastase fumed and raged until a referee's opinion reinstated him and the match continued. McEnroe, 19, defeated the 33-year-old Nastase 6-4, 4-6, 6-3, 6-2.

Excellence is not a singular act but a habit.
You are what you do repeatedly.
—SHAQUILLE O'NEAL

No Apologies

THE U.S. MARINES BELIEVE IN leaving no man or woman behind, but in sports, when you're down, you're out. An athlete who falters, whether because of injury, illness, or sheer accident, will be quickly overtaken by her competitors.

Unfortunately, sometimes an athlete falters because of one of those competitors. Such was the case of Mary Decker Slaney, a U.S. track-and-field star who had become famous as

Track's Zola Budd and Mary Decker compete.

"Little Mary Decker" when the pigtailed runner broke records at age 14. Her career was sidelined, however, when she was diagnosed with a condition known as "compartment syndrome" that affected her leg muscles and left her unable to compete in what would have been her first Olympics in 1976. She recovered and broke the world record for the women's mile in 1980.

By 1984, "Little Mary Decker" had swapped her pigtails for a trendy mop of curls—and was a favored contender for the Olympic gold medal in 3,000 meters. In the final, South African runner Zola Budd (famous for running races barefoot) was half a stride ahead of Decker, moved to the inside lane, and thus crowded Decker. Decker fell and injured her hip. Although Budd was initially disqualified, she was reinstated after officials viewed a videotape of the incident at the Los Angeles games.

Decker, however, in pain and in tears, was carried off the track by her then-boyfriend (now husband) Richard Slaney. She refused to accept any apology or overture from Budd, who was distraught and considered Decker one of her heroes. Sometimes in sports, when a referee's or official's ruling seems unfair, the behaviors of good sportsmanship are difficult to summon. The two didn't speak following the games, but in 1985, Decker wrote a friendly letter to Budd, and in a quite mannerly gesture, asked a marathon running friend to hand-deliver it to Budd at an upcoming race. The two women would come to a deeper understanding of what happened.

Chess for me is not a game, but an art. Yes, and I take upon myself all those responsibilities which an art imposes on its adherents.

—ALEXANDER ALEKHINE, FOURTH WORLD CHESS CHAMPION, 1892-1946

Board Silent

THERE ARE SOME SPORTS that demand silence from audience and participants: Snooker, for instance. Curling. Diving. Gymnastics. The tension involved is excruciating, and can last for different amounts of time: A dive is finished in seconds, while a snooker match might go on for hours.

Chess is a board game that is now recognized as a sport by the International Olympic Committee (IOC)—but not as a competitive sport for the Olympic Games. What makes an Olympic sport? The choices can be bewildering: ice dancing is considered a competitive Olympic sport, but ballroom dancing is not. Handball and badminton, yes; rugby and squash, no .

For decades, modern Olympics officials have dismissed chess and its archrival, bridge, as activities that require mental stamina but have no physical component. Lobbyists for the

American chess prodigy Bobby Fischer in 1957

board and card games counter that endurance and strength do play a role in their "sports," but the IOC contends with an organization that has grown large over the century-plus that the modern Olympic Games have been played.

Chess advocates also point out that during the ancient Olympic Games, many nonsporting events, from music to theater, represented mental stamina—as did some of the events included in the modern Games through World War II. For example, croquet was once an Olympic sport.

While chess—and bridge—still have a long way to go in their battle towards Olympic acceptance, during the 2008 Beijing Olympic games the first-ever "World Mind Sports Games" was held in the same city, and included both of those "sports" along with some other cerebral challenges, including checkers, draughts, Go, and Chinese *xiang qi*.

Granite curling iron, ready for its slow slide

Boxing is the ultimate challenge. There's nothing that can compare to testing yourself the way you do every time you step into the ring.
—SUGAR RAY LEONARD, PROFESSIONAL BOXER

Touch Gloves

MODERN PARENTS ARE WELL accustomed to the sight of their pint-size soccer or baseball players solemnly filing past one another at the end of matches and games and shaking hands with their opponents in a show of "good sportsmanship." For teams, especially in friendly competition, post-play bonhomie makes sense.

But combat sports, from martial arts to shooting, are different. Two people facing off in a duel, whether the weapons are hands, swords, or pistols, weren't always sure what the outcome would be (think of Alexander Hamilton, may

he rest in peace). Bowing to or saluting one's opponent was the honorable way to acknowledge both his prowess (or at least its possibility) and the solemn result of the proceedings.

Today martial arts and fencing with swords still have followings, but duels with pistols are no longer considered "sporting," perhaps because increasing sophisticated firearms became not just the main weaponry used in actual combat, but also became capable of killing so many people in such a short amount of time. In any case, the most common U.S. form of hand-to-hand combat sport is boxing. Since boxing has ancient roots, some of them in the Asian martial arts, it is a sport with its own forms of etiquette and one in which humility and respect for the more skilled are important. Nonetheless, while it may not seem to bear mentioning, proper "manners" in the boxing ring include keeping your teeth out of your opponent's flesh. Mike Tyson apparently wasn't aware of this when he bit Evander Holyfield's ear in 1997, but not everyone in the boxing world learned from his mistake. At the 2008 Olympics, a boxer from Tajikistan was disqualified after chomping on his opponent's shoulder.

One of the most iconic images of boxing is that of two opponents touching their padded, laced gloves together before the bell is rung to begin a match (in some arenas, the gloves are tapped together after the bell; this varies). Although modern boxers rarely fight to maim or kill, this gesture reminds them of the element of luck that follows all athletes.

MANNERED LIVES

Fannie Farmer

Most 19th-century girls who suffered the kind of paralytic stroke Fannie Merritt Farmer did in 1877 at age 16 would have given up and remained at home as invalids. But "Fannie Farmer," as she will forever be known to Americans, was not most girls. She had had the good fortune to be born into a family that valued women's education, and before her stroke had intended to go to college.

Although her handicaps restricted her from living on her own, Farmer pursued an interest in cooking, and recovered well enough by age 30 to enroll in the Boston Cooking School. She was such a star student that she was invited to serve as the school's assistant director—right after her graduation! Two years later, after working even harder on her studies, Farmer became director of the school and began to write *The Boston Cooking School Cookbook*, her 1896 magnum opus.

The Boston Cooking School took an intellectual, scientific approach to food preparation and diet, which led to an elevation of women's role in cooking to that of authorities on proper nutrition for people healthy and sick. Farmer's cookbook was about more than food, too; it took a modern, concise, and scientific approach to nutrition—and people were eager for that, buying four million copies and making Farmer rich. (She'd retained the copyright.)

In 1902 Farmer opened Miss Farmer's School of Cookery, and in 1904 she published what she considered her most important work: *Food and Cookery for the Sick and Convalescent*. She dedicated it to her own mother, who had nursed her through so many years and raised a woman so stalwart that Farmer's last lecture, from a wheelchair, would come just days before her death in 1915.

A Fannie Farmer cookbook used in a 1950s home economics class

ELEMENTARY

The early years of formal schooling that now take place around the world are one of the most mannerly eras of a person's life. Even if a child's parents have taught her the basics of "please," "thank you," and eating with her mouth closed at home, going to school is often the first time that child has to contend with rules outside of her family—and lots of strange new people. From navigating a new building, to meeting new adults and children, to learning how to use and organize new materials, and to venture to the restroom all alone, the world of elementary school can be an awfully strong "culture shock."

Fortunately, the younger we humans are, the more adaptable we tend to be. Elementary-school students learn some big lessons, like how to obey a person they've just met (the teacher), how to share classroom toys and supplies, and how to use strange things like finger paints and pipe cleaners. We are all so accustomed to children leaving for school at age five or six that we sometimes forget this is a relatively modern system, especially for girls. While upper-class boys were educated away from their families in the ancient cultures of Egypt and Greece,

Education is simply the soul of a society as it passes from one generation to another.

—G. K. CHESTERTON

the idea of regularly educating girls in anything other than the domestic arts did not become a part of common life until the 19th century.

Boys who weren't born into rich families also had to wait until relatively recently to get access to regular education. Around the world, working-class and poor families needed children as laborers—a system which may well have led to the current Western school year, in which classes are held from the end of one hard planting season to the beginning of the next.

Respect yourself and others will respect you.
—CONFUCIUS

Humble Heads

IN THE UNITED STATES, many schoolteachers' desks are adorned with mugs, notepads, and myriad figurines depicting apples. "An apple for the teacher" is a sign of respect—students once brought shiny specimens of their best produce to honor their schoolmistresses.

In apple-less cultures there are other ways to honor teachers. In Thailand, in the Wai Kru ceremony early in the school year, schoolchildren present their teachers with bouquets of flowers, each with a specific, academically inclined meaning, and perform a *krab* bow.

In Thailand, as a sign of respect students also make sure that their heads are never higher than their teacher's, whether they are sitting, standing, bowing, or kneeling. Teachers will often sit in chairs and students will kneel or sit. To the Thai, it is a natural outgrowth of their cultural views on age, wisdom, and experience. Children are expected to "look up to" their elders, and teachers exceed their students not only in age, but also in learning. Thailand is a hierarchical society in which parents are above children, bosses above subordinates, and teachers above students.

A Thai teacher instructs pupils from the Hmong tribe.

He who opens a school door, closes a prison.
—VICTOR HUGO

A Longer Week

CLASSROOMS AROUND THE WORLD, whether they're set up in a tent in Pakistan, a walled courtyard in Cuba, or a brand-new school in Switzerland, have many characteristics in common: some sort of special area for the teacher, so she can keep supplies close at hand. Desks and chairs or a seating area for the students to gather. A wall or curtain that allows everyone in the class to see certain instructional materials.

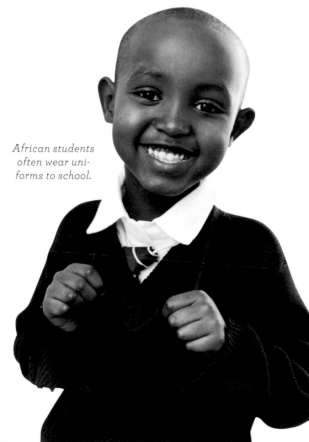

African students often wear uniforms to school.

Classrooms also have time parameters involved in their occupation, and these can vary just like the "common" characteristics. In one country, the school day might begin very early so that students can go home for a meal and siesta, escaping the worst of the midday heat. In another place, the school year runs through all 12 months, while in many Western countries, there is a break during summer (whether that is June through September in the Northern hemisphere, or December through March below the Equator).

Even the school week can shift. In Africa, many schools are open six days instead of the five that they are in most industrialized nations. Some U.S. politicians and school administrators have proposed the same thing, but their reasons—more productivity, less wasted space—aren't necessarily the same as those of their African counterparts. On that continent, the idea that children should be free to go to school, learn, and better their futures is a relatively new one. Children who are able to claim a place in a school are less likely to be sent out to work at ages Westerners consider shockingly young. Sometimes more school isn't a punishment, but a real benefit.

Adults are obsolete children.
—DR. SEUSS

The Children's Garden

ROBERT FULGHUM IS FAMOUS for writing *All I Really Need to Know I Learned in Kindergarten,* which reminds adults that things like nap time, fair play, and reading for pleasure are things that endure for a lifetime. By the time Fulghum wrote his book (which has spawned dozens, if not scores, of imitators), the concept of kindergarten was firmly established in the United States. It's considered a sort of transitional year in which children learn how to communicate, play, and interact with other people after spending their early years at home.

Although both Scottish and Hungarian educators pioneered organized classrooms for children around age five, the idea of *der Kindergarten* ("The Children's Garden") was the brainchild of a German named Friedrich Froebel, who in 1840 opened the first in Schwarzberg-Rudolstadt. Less than two decades later, an American woman of German extraction, Margarethe Meyer-Schurz, opened the first Froebel-based kindergarten in Watertown, Wisconsin—her sister founded the first one in London, England, shortly thereafter.

Today countries all over the world have kindergartens or their equivalent, but interestingly, many of them—including Germany—consider kindergarten part of preschool education, instead of the first year of elementary school as is normal in the U.S. Canada and India have "Junior" and "Senior" kindergartens. In France and many Francophone countries, these years of education take place in what is referred to as *l'école maternelle* ("motherly school").

Using kindergarten blocks teaches lifelong skills.

However, no matter what it's called or how it's institutionally structured, this kind of early education always involves paste, paint, and play in greater or lesser amounts. For many humans, it's the last year in which they have no work to do, deadlines to meet, schedules to follow, or problems to solve until decades later, when they retire.

*The chief reason for going to school is to get the impression
fixed for life that there is a book side for everything.*
—ROBERT FROST

The Perfect Prefect

BOARDING SCHOOLS, once the top option for upper-class parents in solving what to do with children, are less common. Lots of students globally know about boarding schools mainly from the Harry Potter books and movies, in which the Hogwarts School of Witchcraft and Wizardry is modeled on an old-fashioned British "public school," or boarding school with a bent toward "prep": preparing students for university educations.

From the communal dining halls to the sleeping quarters to the occasional outing to the nearest village (Hogsmeade, for a "butterbeer"), Harry and his Hogwarts classmates move about in a school that might, without the magic, be in the middle of Somerset. One of the customs

A prefect's lapel shows off "rank."

adhered to by Potter author J. K. Rowling is that of the "prefect," also known in British schools as "head boy" and/or "head girl."

Prefects of the best sort were students of good character who had extra authority and responsibilities. Naturally, this power could go to the head of an already egotistical type and led to what a British schoolchild might call "priggishness." In the Potter universe, Ron Weasley's brother Bill was known as this sort of "head boy"—someone too rule-oriented for words.

Rowling did provide a more benign counterpart in Prefect Cedric Diggory, a good sport, a kind soul, and handsome, to boot. Alas, such perfection was doomed: Diggory died a hero's death in *Harry Potter and the Goblet of Fire.*

OBJECTS OF ETIQUETTE: Dance Cards Elaborately designed "dance cards," really small booklets, were bedecked with charms and tassels and once hung from the slender wrists of single women whose admirers could use the small attached pencil to reserve a particular style of dance or piece of music during which the couple might properly have (minimal) body contact and private conversation.

UNIVERSITY

Not everyone receives a university education; most of the world's population goes straight from secondary school (if that) to working life. But because college and university years are privileged, they also allow for some types of customs seen in no other sectors of life (and no, we're not talking about keg parties). The unusual amount of leisure time and focus on intellectual achievement during university degree programs (four years for most undergraduates in the United States; three years in England) allows students to philosophize—over pizza; to solve problems like how to get south for spring break; and to create art—like tattoos.

We're joking, but only just. Like the Amish *rumspringa* year taken in the late teens, university time has come to substitute in modern society for the years that might previously have been spent wandering, fighting, or preparing for partnership and family life. Those who have the resources to take a few years for higher education do need to find their way, too; few of them are like Sebastian Flyte in *Brideshead Revisited,* able to retire to a family mansion in the countryside or a family palazzo in Venice whenever the going gets tough. Most undergraduates either flounder while trying to juggle classes with part-time jobs, or cram as many classes in as possible so that a future career will be lucrative enough to pay off student loans.

At least the U.S. students: One of the interesting differences in culture between our nation and the rest of the world is that in most countries, universities are free to all qualified citizens. Without debating the economic policies involved, it's possible to see that systems without large tuition bills change many of the customs involved in gaining a mortarboard.

> *The philosophy of the school room in one generation will be the philosophy of government in the next.*
>
> —ABRAHAM LINCOLN

Education is what remains after one has
forgotten what one has learned in school.
—ALBERT EINSTEIN

Mind the Gap

"MIND THE GAP" IS THE polite British command displayed at railway and subway or "tube" stations around the United Kingdom. No one wants to stumble on the way out of a carriage and onto the platform.

Similarly, no one wants to make the wrong move after finishing secondary school—today, many young Britons who have taken the classes necessary for admission to university delay their entry by at least a year and instead get a job, take supplementary course work, or travel. This year away from formal education is

Well stamped equals well traveled, for students.

familiarly known as a "gap year," signifying the space between two kinds of schooling.

The gap year is a relatively recent phenomenon, although it has historical precedent in the "grand tour" upper-class Westerners once considered essential to a young person's social development. "Grand tours" were at one time a chance for young men to see the world, although later in the 19th and into the 20th century well-chaperoned young ladies were also allowed to visit places like Paris, Rome, St. Petersburg, and even Hong Kong (depending, of course, on a family's resources and contacts).

After the Second World War, people in many countries changed travel and education habits, and in England, where wartime economies like food rationing lasted well into the 1950s, these habits were particularly affected. Even rich families weren't able to send children on elaborate itineraries, yet many students didn't want to go straight from one classroom to another. The "gap year," with its flexible nature, suited the decade in which it became popular—the 1960s. More than four decades later, the "gap year" has migrated across the Atlantic to America, and many young people find that getting a breather helps them make better decisions without stumbling.

It takes courage to grow up and become who you really are.
—E. E. CUMMINGS

A Real Grind

WHETHER THEY'RE CALLED cram schools, "crammers," "grind schools," prep courses, or tutorials, businesses that help students prepare for rigorous high schools, universities, and graduate schools flourish all over the world. In the U.S., many high-school students take special classes to prepare for college entrance exams like the SAT and ACT, while their British counterparts take numerous courses, depending on the number of subjects they've decided to "sit" (take exams in) for their A-levels.

But it's in Asia that cramming courses have been elevated to, if not an art form, at least a commodity. Japan's *Juku,* Korea's *Hagwon,* and China's *Bu Xi Ban* aren't occasional or supplemental to regular education; although they are held in separate facilities and can be extremely costly, these cram schools can take up as much time and sometimes more than "regular" school. The instructional method is rote memorization, i.e. cramming as much information

into a student's head as possible. Some Japanese parents believe that public schools no longer teach rigorously enough and will pay almost any amount to a cram school if they believe it will give their son or daughter a leg up in university admissions or a job interview.

Parents and students alike take cram schools so seriously that teenage suicides and other kinds of violence in Japan and other places have been linked to depression about poor performance in these schools. In 2006 a 16-year-old Japanese boy who had lied to his father about his exam scores tried to get out of the situation by setting his house on fire—and killing several family members. The boy had attended cramming classes every evening, and had been forced by his father to study even later into the night. While hard-driving educational methods fueled Japanese progress for many years, no doubt because of incidents like this, in the 21st century the government and families are taking a longer look at the cram school lifestyle and considering less-structured, more creative alternatives. Of course, one thing that will never change: Parents want the best education possible for their children.

Too much exam cramming can cause fatigue.

Let us celebrate the occasion with wine and sweet words.
—PLAUTUS, ROMAN PLAYWRIGHT, 254 B.C.-184 B.C.

Charmed Lives

STUDENTS ABOUT TO GRADUATE from high school in the U.S. say they have "senior fever," attend proms, and sometimes head off for "beach week" with their friends, but when it comes to post-secondary education high jinks, no country has Norway beat. The Norwegian *Russ,* as students who have just graduated are called, are a national tradition, point of pride, and nuisance in equal measures.

Horned helmets gave rise to russefeiring.

The *russefeiring* takes place from May 1 through May 17 each year, and during those two and a half weeks, the students are supposed to wear their uniform of overalls and caps constantly, without washing them (although most take them off for sleeping—if and when they do sleep). The custom goes back to a time when Norway had no universities, and Norwegian students had to attend Danish universities and wear a set of horns until they passed their first examinations. Now that Norway has its own institutions of higher education, the *Russ* has become a wacky rite of passage, complete with the costumes indicating their intended course of study by color (e.g., blue for economics, red for education, black for engineering), "knots" or "charms" given for outlandish (and sometimes obscene and/ or dangerous) stunts, and crazy "business cards" that students collect and trade.

Not only do students in groups tend to do things that are outlandish, obscene, dangerous, and even illegal (hopefully, not all of them at the same time)—they also tend to use up a lot of money while engaging in these activities. One journalist estimates that the *Russ* period can cost up to 6,000 euros for a single student in Norway, because the students chip in to buy buses that they decorate and kit out according to their peer group's tastes, as well as hold large parties and eat out together at restaurants. Thankfully, the *Russ* tradition has a traditional end, too: On May 17, Norway's National Day, students parade with everyone else—and then start preparing for the next phase of their lives.

FAMOUS GAFFES: Amish DUI in a buggy   Twenty-six-year-old Elmer Stoltzfoos Fisher of Paradise, Pennsylvania, got picked up by the police for a DUI. Fisher was spotted on a Sunday night, slumped over and evidently asleep after consuming enough alcohol to register 0.18 on a Breathalyzer, over twice the legal limit for operating a motor vehicle. The remarkable thing about this was that Fisher wasn't behind the wheel, but behind the reins of his Amish family buggy.

The roots of education are bitter,
but the fruit is sweet.
—ARISTOTLE

A Tiger of a Parade

IMAGINE MARCHING ALONG with tens of thousands of your fellow alumni, wearing an orange-and-black-striped blazer, perhaps sporting a foam tiger hat, and carrying a plastic tumbler of beer. Congratulations! You're a Princetonian attending the annual "P-rade" reunion.

In the United States the oldest and most prestigious undergraduate institutions have a long tradition of meeting post-commencement for gatherings of classmates. Reunions were originally mainly a social conceit meant to foster camaraderie among the young lions (oops, tigers, in Princeton's case) of Harvard, Yale, and the other Ivy League–level schools.

There are more special props and traditions involved in the P-rade than you could shake a stick at—and that stick had better be the special Class of 1925 ebony one topped with a leaping sterling-silver tiger that is ceremonially used by each year's eldest attending alumnus, who is often ferried around campus in a tiger-striped golf cart.

For 25th reunions, classmates receive uniquely patterned tailored "beer jackets," so-called because their earliest versions were designed to be worn over fine woolen suits to prevent suds stains. Although nowadays reunions are a prime opportunity for universities like Princeton to collect donations from former students, the dominant theme for those who return to old haunts is definitely returning to old habits, and drinking more alcohol than usual is a time-honored one at Princeton and other U.S. schools.

Fortunately for teetotalers, the P-rade offers more than booze. There are plenty of adorable babies (and babes) to ogle and coo at wearing outfits of every orange hue imaginable and class signs with clever jingles and poems. The large, noisy, festive Princeton salute to its alumni is over-the-top in every way and demonstrates the American capacity for excess in all things.

An early 20th-century Princeton "tiger" poster

MANNERED LIVES

Emily Post

One of the longest-running dynasties in U.S. history isn't political or industrial, but well mannered. The Post family, which now includes twentysomething Lizzie and her book *How Do You Work This Life Thing?* owes its beginnings to matriarch Emily.

Emily Price was born in Baltimore, Maryland, in 1873 to an architect father and socialite mother who properly sent her to a New York finishing school once the family moved north. Married at 19 to banker Edwin Main Post, Emily bore two sons and lived a well-bred, upper-class existence for a dozen or so years until her husband's dalliances with showgirls resulted in his being blackmailed for so much money that his wife's pride could no longer bear it. The couple divorced in 1905.

The well-bred and well-heeled Emily Post appealed to readers of all socioeconomic levels.

Emily Post found that in order to support herself and her children, she needed work. She began publishing short stories in magazines and even wrote several novels. However, it was not until 1922, when the publisher Funk and Wagnalls approached her about putting together an etiquette manual, that Post found her true calling. She believed that good manners begin with consideration for others, and that the execution of these manners is the best way to succeed in personal relationships as well as in business. Her book, entitled *Etiquette,* was originally written for the newly rich who wanted to live, entertain, and speak like the wealthy. However, the book appealed to a much wider range of readers.

Before her book had been out a month, readers of all socioeconomic levels bombarded her with questions the book had not addressed, and these formed the basis of later versions. The book was especially popular with middle-class women who had not been able to attend finishing school, but who aspired to a refined lifestyle.

PROFESSIONAL

E DUCATION, WE BELIEVE IN THE MODERN WORLD, should be a lifelong pursuit. Never stop learning, never stop growing, never stop making progress. No wonder we're all complaining of fatigue!

In other times, people were more concerned with the lifelong pursuit of food, or physical safety, than with continuing to "learn and grow." But along the way, different kinds of craftspeople, artists, scientists, caregivers, and technicians figured out that in groups they not only learned from each other, but could protect their standards and their fees. The great medieval guilds of Europe are a wonderful example of these groups, but not the first, only, or best. The most important thing about guilds or confraternities is that they allowed skilled workers to share knowledge in preliterate societies (no one was publishing *Stained Glass for Dummies* instructional books when they built Notre Dame de Paris).

Some groups guarded their secrets jealously: One famous example is that dynasty of Italian physicians who invented forceps to aid in

Education is an ornament in prosperity and a refuge in adversity.

—ARISTOTLE

childbirth. Before the family died out, they buried their invention, which was found decades later and resurrected, this time to the benefit of far more obstetricians and mothers-to-be.

As the industrial revolution took hold and printed manuals became easier to teach from and to obtain, guilds lost their power—but their true death knell was the free-market economy, in which the person who could best do the job for the best price, regardless of association with any group, was usually hired. Some of the finer functions of guilds, like adherence to professional codes of conduct, became part of professional schools and training programs.

*Education is an ornament in
prosperity and a refuge in adversity.*
—ARISTOTLE

Technically Speaking

AMERICAN STUDENTS WHO ARE accustomed to high schools with huge sports programs of the kind featured in programs like the TV show *Friday Night Lights* might be astounded to learn that European high schools have no sports programs associated with them. (This doesn't mean, of course, that European high school students don't play sports; their teams and clubs are simply separate from their schools.)

However, there are more important differences between American and European

high schools than whether they have football teams, cheerleaders, or lockers in the hallways. In countries that include England, France, Germany, Italy, and Spain (there are others), secondary schools can be found in three different types: vocational, professional (specific training for white-collar jobs like accounting), and college/university preparatory. More so than their American counterparts—who usually don't start seriously thinking about careers until their final years of high school—European students make decisions at a young age that could set the course of their professional lives.

One example of the European system is the German/Scandinavian *gymnasium,* which is pronounced with a hard "g" and has nothing to do with "gym class" as Americans know it. The *gymnasium* (from the Greek *gymnasion,* or "place of physical and intellectual education") sometimes provides a general (liberal arts) focus, or might have a specific subject, such as modern or classical languages, economics and politics, or mathematics and science.

Students attend *Gymnasien* for different periods of time in Germany, depending on the region in which they live—some states require six years, some eight. However, at the end of the school's coursework all German *Gymnasien* require students to pass *Abitur* exams (Abitur comes from the Latin *abeo* for "leave, go off"). Known colloquially as the *Abi,* this diploma carries a certain amount of prestige, much as graduating with honors does in the United States.

*The best way to find yourself is to
lose yourself in the service of others.*
—MOHANDAS GANDHI

The Great Leveler

THE HISTORY OF ARMIES that are all-volunteer versus armies that are drafted is long and complicated; many countries have had both types, while others have only had one, which is the case with Israel.

Israel's nationhood is extremely recent compared with its long identity as the birthplace of two major world religions and its central geographical importance to the Middle East and Africa. Founded in 1948 by the post-World War II British Balfour Declaration, Israel is now a fully organized modern state as well as a homeland for all Jews (through national law anyone who has a Jewish mother or has converted to Judaism is entitled to citizenship).

Its Israel Defense Forces (IDF) are now fully organized and modern, too—much different from the "volunteer soldier farmers" who fought for Jewish independence before Israel was created.

The IDF as a whole is a study in contrasts: Both modern (the Israeli Army was founded in 1948) and ancient (its roots are in ancient Biblical territory), professional yet nonhierarchical, and aggressive yet socially conscious, the IDF functions as a societal leveler. Every Israeli citizen is obligated by law to serve in the IDF, which

A mid-20th-century Israeli military poster

means that not only does everyone undergo a common experience, but people from all walks of life meet during that experience. That includes females—Israel is the only country in the world that makes national service compulsory for women, although religiously devout women can opt for a "community service" program.

ARCHAIC MANNERS: Tennis Whites Many tennis aficionados know that British player Henry "Bunny" Austin was the first to wear white shorts during a match, in the 1930s—but it was actually his countrywoman Maude Watson who first wore all white, in an ankle-length, bustled ensemble on the court in 1884. Watson's innovation was purely practical; if women had to remain covered, at least white fabric meant no one would have to see them sweat.

Law never made men a whit more just.
—HENRY DAVID THOREAU

The Point Is Moot

PART OF PROFESSIONAL TRAINING and education is practicing what you'll do once certified as a professor, dentist, or junk-bond trader (some professions are more, ahem, professional than others). While future surgeons can perfect their suture gauge on cadavers, future attorneys find it more challenging to get practice in court, since mistakes can be held against them. Legally.

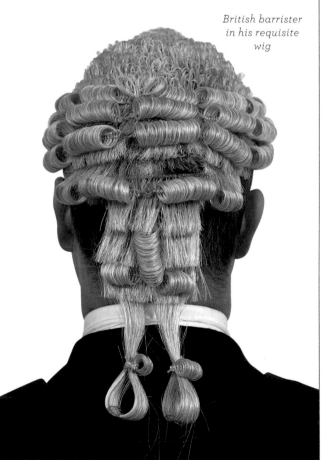

British barrister in his requisite wig

The solution, in U.S. and British law schools, is something called "moot court," an extracurricular and competitive activity in which students hold simulated appellate court proceedings that include written briefs, arguments, and even witnesses, often local actors or the students' friends. In some law schools, especially those that send students to national competitions, moot court rivalries are intense. Law students throw themselves into writing briefs and arguments, often spending as much if not more time on this competition as on their classes.

"Moot court" is not "mock trial"; *moot* is an Anglo-Saxon word meaning "a gathering," usually of important and well-known people. Once the *moot* (from *gmot* or *emot*) had arrived at a decision, that was the last word—which is how we came to today's American meaning of "The point is moot." In American law, a matter is moot if further legal proceedings can have no effect, or it's gone past the reach of the law. That holds for the purely academic "moot court," even if most of us hardly ever refer to anything that way.

*Foolish the doctor who despises
the knowledge acquired by the ancients.*
—HIPPOCRATES

Good Humors

SOMETIMES A GREAT DEAL OF protocol and training go into something that is quite unfamiliar to us—early generations might have said "foreign" or "exotic." But all of these words—unfamiliar, foreign, exotic—really mean the same thing, which roughly translates to "I don't understand that idea/system/method."

Once upon a time, people thought that bathing was unhygienic, that you could turn lead into gold, and that the world was flat; now we know differently, but during the periods in which those things were believed, anyone who held to a different idea was considered suspect. Perhaps one day practitioners of the ancient Indian system of Ayurvedic medicine, which seeks to heal with herbs, nutrition, cleanses, acupressure, and other methods, will no longer be looked at as questioningly by adherents to Western medicine. That is not to say that Ayurvedic practices are without fault (e.g., there have been questions about the use of aconite in herbal preparations) and should not be thoroughly tested by our best modern practices, but it is to say that many of our Western practices, like bleeding sick patients with leeches, using "cupping" to cure respiratory ailments, and "starving a fever" have been shown up as flawed over the years, too.

Ayurveda means "the complete knowledge for a long life," and before Western medicine was introduced to the Indian continent, Ayurvedic medicine was one of the most important healthways known to India. The system, which dates back thousands of years, stresses the *doshas,* or humors (wind, bile, and phlegm, loosely corresponding to air, fire, and water) and believes that when one is too much or too little present, health problems result. It focuses on cleansing the body, thus helping restore both physical and mental harmony. Ayurvedic practitioners are not shamans; they are certified through more than 100 accredited institutions in India, and a bachelor's degree in Ayurveda, Medicine, and Surgery is a five-and-a-half-year course. According to the National Institutes of Health, 80 percent of Indians use Ayurvedic medicine exclusively or in addition to Western medicine, and a 2007 study found that 200,000 Americans had used Ayurvedic treatments in the past year.

7

ON THE
ROAD AGAIN

We travel to get closer to our loved ones—or to get away from them. We travel for business, pleasure, excitement, relaxation, health, and wealth. We fly solo, hitch our wagons, and jump on board. But whether we're headed into the wild blue yonder, bound for glory, or just walking to the mailbox, humans keep going places—and that means we're likely to need rules about where, when, how, why, and with whom we go. Travel involves other people as well as food, clothing, gadgets, commerce, social strata, and all of the other things that have customs, manners, and quirks bound up in their existence. Is there proper etiquette for handling our shoes and Baggies of bottled liquids in airport security lines? How do you tip abroad? How much of the foreign language should you try to learn?

Journeys really are little worlds (or at least societies) of their own. What happens in Vegas, stays in Vegas, they say, and perhaps there the usual rules don't apply. However, that doesn't mean you'll be given an indulgent smile if you eat spaghetti with your hands while sailing on the Queen Mary, or steal someone else's cab in Manhattan. Just as in other parts of life, it's the journey and how you behave on it, not the arrival, that matters.

French travel poster advertises allure of Rome.

ON THE GROUND

HUMAN BEINGS ARE DESIGNED FOR LAND—we can swim, but we can't breathe underwater; we have machines that can fly, but no wings of our own; and when we go to outer space we're just completely untethered without gravity.

The simplest form of transportation for people is walking. Naturally, that means we couldn't be satisfied with walking. We had to try skipping. Jogging. Running.

The most important trip you may take in life is meeting people halfway.

—HENRY BOYE

Our prehistoric ancestors who invented the wheel provided a technology that has still not been bested, judging by the number of scooters, recumbent bicycles, and passenger trains on our highways and byways, not to mention buses and subway cars. If there is a route from point A to point B, humans want to find the shortest version of that route. Many of those vehicles mentioned are becoming faster, sleeker, and more efficient, both to accommodate hectic modern lives and to try and discover alternative forms of fuels.

When trains, subways, and bicycles first came into widespread use, there were no automobiles. People were accustomed to using different kinds of resources, like brute animal strength from horses for coaches, or wind in sails, to accomplish journeys impassible on foot. While there were specific kinds of etiquette involved (e.g., for coachmen and sailors), sometimes those mass-transit models involved the same issues of good manners that the modern engine-powered types did. People in close quarters, be they shipboard or railbound, have to figure out ways in which to tolerate one another's noises, gestures, odors, appearances, and foodstuffs.

Everyone has this sense of togetherness right now.
For example, one guy on the subway today, he wanted to share my pants.
—DAVID LETTERMAN

People Pushers

DON'T BE SURPRISED OR FRIGHTENED if, while boarding a subway car at Tokyo's Ginza station, a hefty gentleman grabs your arm or leg and moves it. He's not trying anything funny; he's probably an *oshiya,* or subway "pusher," hired by one of the transportation system's two main vendors to help keep packed commuter car doors safely closed so that the trains run efficiently.

The oshiya are often hefty because they need to be strong in order to keep cramming

A Tokyo ashiya *tucks commuters into a train.*

people together long after the cars might seem full by other countries' standards. Oshiya are sometimes former sumo wrestlers, but what is most remarkable about them is their extreme deference to and solicitude with the passengers whose bodies they are touching. First the oshiya will courteously help rearrange people's briefcases and "stray" limbs; then, if the train doors still will not close, several oshiya will gather, and one will tell the assembled commuters, "We're going to push, all right?" At that point, three or four of the "pushers" lean into the people closest to the door and heave with all of their might until they can start pulling the doors together, tucking in stray hands, trouser cuffs, and shopping bags as they go. It's a contrast to other systems, such as Washington, D.C.'s, Metro, where people generally fend for themselves when squeezing onto packed cars, and the doors still clamp down on arms, legs, and coats.

The oshiya system is a good example of a custom that couldn't happen in a culture without finely honed and observed standards of behavior (and just because there is such a system doesn't mean there isn't groping, like in other parts of the world, as Japanese women can surely attest). The oshiya are very polite and careful, but so are the passengers. Everyone in Tokyo is accustomed to extremely crowded subway trains and the people who help keep them running, and all are willing to endure occasional discomfort in order to keep getting where they need to go on time.

Life is like riding a bicycle.
To keep your balance you must keep moving.
—ALBERT EINSTEIN

Bells Are Ringing

TRAVEL WRITERS HAVE described the constant *briiiing, brrrring* noise of bicycle bells in Beijing and other Chinese cities. At one point, China produced nearly 200 million bicycles each year, and those bells, rung by people running errands, heading to work, or visiting family, were a ubiquitous auditory backdrop to life in the large, crowded country. More than 1.3 billion people call China home.

But old-fashioned pedal power is changing as China's economy heats up, and the bicycle bells that once kept wheeled street traffic well-regulated are under siege from a new means of transport: electric bikes. While some analysts worry about the Chinese car boom and its effects on air pollution, pedestrians and traditional bike riders are more worried about these inexpensive, plug-in vehicles that lessen environmental damage but are a hazard to slower traffic's health. In 2007 there were 2,469 deaths from electric-bicycle accidents nationwide (in

Common scooter outing in China

which people were hit by those fast, quiet bikes), up from just 34 in 2001, according to government statistics.

The real culprit may not be any one machine in particular, but the economy. Chinese people didn't start pedaling from place to place because the population has a natural tendency toward quaint modes of travel—they rode bikes because the Communists who took power in the mid-20th century found that manufacturing two-wheelers was lucrative for them. Electric bikes also had their first boom in China in the 1960s under Mao Zedong's government but didn't take off until later in the century when city planners noted a haze in the city and started looking for some way to curb the smog. In today's burgeoning Chinese economy, cheap, efficient e-bikes look great to consumers—unless they happen to be in one's path.

Motorbike travel in China's Jiangxi Province

A good traveler has no fixed plans,
and is not intent on arriving.
—LAO-TZU

The Longest Ride

IMAGINE TAKING A 6,000-mile train ride. We're not asking you to imagine it because it isn't possible: You can hop aboard the Trans-Siberian Railway anytime. We're asking you to imagine it because very few people reading this will probably ever brave this system of three rail lines that connect Moscow with the Sea of Japan, covering places along the way from Irkutsk to Ulan-Ude. These 10,000 kilometers span roughly one-third of the globe and are the route of the world's longest continuously operating railroad.

Czar Alexander III built a major Russian railway.

The Trans-Siberian Railway was started by Czar Alexander III in 1891 to connect Russia's capital city with its Pacific port, Vladivostok. It was meant to run straight across the country, but as legend has it, the dictatorial czar accidentally traced a small nick in his ruler. His planners were too terrified to correct the mistake, so the final railroad has a large kink in its route. The railroad was finished in 1916 by Alexander's son Nicholas and was considered so crucial to national security that much of the Russian Civil War of 1917-1920 was about its control.

Today the Trans-Siberian Railway is really a concatenation of four lines: The Trans-Siberian, the Trans-Manchurian, the Trans-Mongolian, and the Baikal Amur Mainline. It takes six or seven days to travel from Moscow to Vladivostok, and that week is considered an experience in communal living, with people of all sorts of ethnicities and walks of life riding together. Each carriage has an enormous hot-water samovar at its end so that passengers can make simple meals and hot beverages between conversations that often consist of a lot of laughing, pointing at objects, and consulting phrasebooks.

FAMOUS GAFFES: Lord Kelvin, full of hot air In 1895 the hubristic Lord William Thomson Kelvin stated, "Heavier-than-air flying machines are impossible." While Lord Kelvin, who was a learned physicist with degrees from Cambridge, argued from what he believed was irrefutable scientific fact, one hopes that he might have been humbled if he had lived past 1907 and seen the results of "flying machines" in warfare during World War I and in travel from the 1920s on. Then again, Lord Kelvin also said, "There is nothing new to be discovered in physics now."

MANNERED LIVES

Eisenhower

*Eisenhower's military acumen helped him
plan the Interstate Highway System.*

Whether commuting, traveling, or just running errands, millions of Americans benefit from the Eisenhower Interstate System. But not many of those Americans know the full story behind why our nation's highways are named after President Dwight D. Eisenhower.

Eisenhower was a military officer before he ever took public office, and it was shortly after his 1915 graduation from the United States Military Academy at West Point that he and his fellow lieutenants found themselves serving in World War I. Afterward, the Army put together an "expedition" to traverse the nation by automobile from Washington, DC to San Francisco—that expedition was led by the new Lieutenant Colonel Eisenhower.

The young officer's sense of how important motor transport could and would be to modern warfare was honed in France where he saw fuel shortfalls and roadway obstacles. So when some of the same problems plagued the 1919 expedition, Lt. Col. Eisenhower decided that he would one day do something about poor roads in his country.

His experience would be magnified when he commanded all U.S. troops in Europe as General of the Army during World War II. He was frustrated by poor roads both in the Allied capture of Tunis and after the D-Day landings, where Normandy's famous roadside hedgerows made advances a nightmare. But it was seeing how smoothly things ran on Germany's more famous *Autobahnen* that convinced Eisenhower that the U.S. needed "good, two-lane highways . . . [in] broader ribbons across the land."

On becoming the 34th U.S. President, Eisenhower immediately pushed for highways, saying, "Our unity as a nation is sustained by free communication of thought and by easy transportation of people and goods." In 1956, he signed the Federal-Aid Highway Act.

*[There are] only two classes of pedestrians in these days
of reckless motor traffic—the quick, and the dead.*
—LORD (THOMAS ROBERT) DEWAR, SCOTTISH DISTILLER, 1864-1930

Planning for Pedestrians

ONE WAY TO DEAL WITH ground traffic is to restrict it to just one type, which is what the Danes decided in 1962 when they created the world's longest pedestrian mall. Decades of streets choked by cars, trucks, bicycles, trams, and pedestrians convinced urban planners in Copenhagen to create Strøget (pronounced "stroll," it means "stripe"). It was so successful it now serves as a model for pedestrian malls in many cities around the world.

Strøget is an amalgamation of five streets: Frederiksberggade, Nygade, Vimmelskaftet, Amagertorv and Østergade and runs through the center of the city between Rådhuspladsen and Kongens Nytorv, the square at the head of the Nyhavn canal. One of the most interesting factors in the mall's success is that it has kept medieval architecture and landmarks intact while filling other spots with everything from department stores to theaters to restaurants to museums. Plus, street performers, drawn to all the foot traffic, provide a live soundtrack.

While many other urban areas would like to emulate the success of Strøget, there are a few other factors in Copenhagen's city structure they should also consider. First, Strøget and most of the surrounding area is built on a level plain that makes walking, cycling, and commuting through its streets and many parks easy. Second, because Copenhagen does not have "single district" zoning (in which one area is for living, one for working, etc.), its residents combine working, living, and recreating together, making the town center its true heart.

No wonder the Danish capital chose to celebrate its 800-year jubilee on Strøget in 1967, serving 800,000 cups of coffee and 100,000 "Town Hall" pancakes on the "world's longest coffee table" set up on the pedestrian mall.

Denmark's Strøget is for all people and purposes.

BEHIND THE WHEEL

AUTOMOBILES TRAVEL THE GROUND just like trains and bicycles, but the combination of an engine that can be used to ferry a single driver anywhere was intoxicating to post-Industrial Revolution society. Although people had some trepidation about "horseless carriages" and their dangers in the early 20th century, by the 1950s "motorcars" had become an ineradicable part of modern life. This was especially true in the United States, where wide-open spaces and post-World War II national prosperity enabled families of varied incomes to own cars.

The man who goes alone can start today; but he who travels with another must wait till that other is ready.

—HENRY DAVID THOREAU

Since those heady days of boat-sized fin-tailed bench-seat sedans, cars and their ilk (delivery trucks, taxicabs, minivans, and SUVs) have spread to virtually every corner of the world. We depend on motorized vehicles to get us to school, to work, to lunch, to vacation spots, to a grandmother's house, and to anywhere else along a road. Even if we believe in the economic and environmental virtues of public transportation, we know that cars are here to stay.

While in some places (Boston, Mumbai, the Indianapolis Brickyard) driving can be scary, none of us could ever travel by automobile if we didn't trust in the basic manners of our fellows. We have to believe that other drivers will respect our boundaries and stay in their lanes, respect hierarchies like who goes first at a crossroads, and respect rules like green means go and red means stop. Each day's commute, whether in a large city or a small town, is an intricate system of transportation etiquette. Yes, even when the person in front of you just won't move fast enough . . .

The civilized man has built a coach,
but has lost the use of his feet.
—RALPH WALDO EMERSON, "SELF-RELIANCE," 1841

Making Tracks

THE MOLLUSKS KNOWN AS SLUGS travel very slowly indeed; if they want to move faster, they have to "hitch a ride"—and that's what the slugs of Northern Virginia do each day to and from Washington, D.C. No, these aren't slimy creatures; the term actually comes from slugging, as in to fill a slot: They're men and women trying to commute affordably and environmentally sensibly in and out of the city where they work.

These people are called "slugs" because they wait in line—often quite long, but very fast-moving—for drivers who have room for one or more extra passengers en route to our nation's capital. Why would anyone want to let a stranger hop in her car? The reason has to do with respect for laws that make each day's morning and evening commute less stressful for everyone.

During certain hours, Route 66 in and out of Virginia has "HOV" lanes open—"HOV" stands for "High-Occupancy Vehicle," meaning that at least two people must be in the car. The HOV lanes opened during the Energy Crisis of the 1970s, when the U.S. government was looking for new ways to curb its dependence on foreign oil. The lanes have stayed because they cut down on traffic problems. Other large U.S. cities have these lanes now,

Signs like these lead to the fast lane in D.C.

too, including San Francisco and Houston. The entire arrangement is a sort of hitchhiking one, with drivers getting cars filled so they can enter the "fast lane," and passengers travel for free.

Slugging might seem very casual, but all participants abide by an unofficial code of conduct that includes "rules" like: No talking unless the driver initiates conversation.

No open windows unless all passengers approve. No money will ever be exchanged or requested. Smoking, drinking beverages, and eating is prohibited, unless the driver permits it. The driver has full control of the radio; passengers may not request a station or volume change. Drivers are not to pick up sluggers en route to or standing outside the line, a practice referred to as "body-snatching."

OBJECTS OF ETIQUETTE: Dusters Not many people still wear the full-length "duster coat" that was once de rigueur attire for automobile travel in the days of open-chassis vehicles. However, the idea of protecting clothing from the elements persists in full-length raincoats that are especially popular in urban areas, where getting on and off of buses and trains can be dirty work.

*...the winner ain't the one with the fastest car.
It's the one who refuses to lose.*
—DALE EARNHARDT, AMERICAN RACE CAR DRIVER, 1951–2001

Fast Times

WHOOOOOOOOOOSH. Zoooooooooooooom.
Traffic on *die Autobahn,* the German version of
a highway, zips by so quickly that if you're not
going quickly too, you're in danger. You might
say "Well, of course; everyone knows that there's
no speed limit on the Autobahn!"

That's actually not true. Even though the
speed limit is higher than any in the U.S., and
even though that limit is regularly disregarded
by German drivers, signs suggesting a recom-
mended speed limit of 130 kilometers an hour
(80 miles an hour) are posted along most autobahns. Urban sections and a few dangerous
stretches sometimes have posted speed limits
as "low" as 100 kilometers an hour (62 miles
an hour). There is also a commonly used rule

A name synonymous with high traffic speeds

of passing: If you are driving in the far left lane
(the fast lane) and a car behind you deploys his
left-hand turn signal, he is indicating that he
wants to pass. Driving etiquette requires you to
move over into the lane to your right in order to
let him pass.

Although Hitler has often been given credit
for the autobahn-type highway, the real precursors were the *AVUS* experimental highway in
Berlin (built between 1913 and 1921) and Italy's
130-kilometer *Autostrada* tollway between Milan
and the northern Italian lakes (completed in
1923). Although Germany's depressed economy
and hyperinflation of the late 1920s prevented
plans for new autobahns from being carried out
at the time, many miles of roadway were built
during the time of the Third Reich. Hitler saw the
construction of autobahns primarily as a military
advantage; its benefit as a job-creation program in
the 1930s was an added plus.

Today's German autobahn system stretches
11,000 kilometers (6,800 miles) across most
parts of unified Germany. Plans to increase
the number and length of autobahns and other
highways have often met with citizen opposition
on ecological grounds.

*Autobahn speed limit sign for 130 kph
(about 80 mph)*

*An agreeable companion on a journey
is as good as a carriage.*
—PUBLILIUS SYRUS, LATIN WRITER

High Beams

ONE OF THE MOST CURIOUS THINGS about manners is that sometimes what works perfectly for a society becomes anathema to it—and then returns again as a virtuous solution. Such is the case with street-based trams, linked sets of passenger cars that run along tracks in the middle of roads in cities including San Francisco, Melbourne, and Budapest.

The word "tram" comes from the Germanic *traam,* or beam, and refers to the earliest way that this form of transportation worked. Horses and other working animals were used to pull passenger carriages along a beam built into a road. The very first "tramway" was built in 1807 to connect the Welsh towns of Swansea and Mumbles. It was followed by lines in New York and New Orleans, which has the oldest continuously operating streetcar system in the world.

The oldest continuously operating electric rail system dates to 1883 in Brighton, England—the predecessor of today's light rail lines that are touted as the most sensible new urban commuter alternative. Trams once ran down the middle of city streets, and once people adapted to driving automobiles, this system interfered with traffic. Today, light rail lines like those in London, Milan, and many U.S. commuter cities are placed in areas convenient for people, but away from busy streets.

Happily, the return to tramways in the form of electric light rail has not only improved the environment for cities where it exists—It's also improved the overall atmosphere, making urban areas easier to navigate.

The streetcars of San Francisco

ARCHAIC MANNERS: Ladies Ride Sidesaddle The "sidesaddle" was developed to help upper-class women ride horseback while maintaining their expensive skirted riding habits; it was considered unseemly for women to wear trousers and to sit astride a horse. Today most female equestrians mount and ride the same as men do, but a few devotees of "side riding" still exist.

*Anytime four New Yorkers get into a cab together
without arguing, a bank robbery has just taken place.*
—JOHNNY CARSON

Ridesharing

A LEFTOVER OF THE EARLY post-Soviet years, *marshrutkas* (a diminutive of the Russian *marshrutnoye taksi*), or minibuses, were intended to compensate for the collapse of public transit systems. These taxis follow a fixed route and seat up to 15 passengers. ("The less oxygen for you, the more money for us," one driver told a journalist.)

To hail a marshrutka, stick out your arm as you would for a taxi. You can't stand on the typical marshrutka, and most drivers wait until they are full before setting out, so one or two might pass before you get a seat.

You pay once you sit, passing your money to the driver through passengers in front of you.

So, it is best to avoid the seats at the very front, otherwise you'll spend your journey passing money back and forth. Unless you are traveling to the route's end, you need to ask the driver to stop. If you speak the language, explain exactly where you wish to be dropped. Otherwise, just shout "as-to-na-VI-tye, pa-ZHA-lu-i-sta" ("Stop, please!") when you see your stop.

Fares are slightly more expensive than on public buses, but are always less than a dollar in the city, and only a bit more for suburban trips. And they are much cheaper than regular taxicabs.

A marshrutka is a public transit option for navigating Kiev's busy roads.

IN AIR OR WATER

IF HUMANS ARE MOST SUITED TO GROUND TRAVEL, it's no wonder that the two other elements that separate us—air and water—became something we had to mythologize. From the power of Neptune and his mighty trident to the grace and awe of Apollo steering his chariot in front of the sun, cultures are rife with stories of ways to overcome the insurmountable sky and the threatening sea.

Those words sound hyperbolic to the contemporary ear because we are used to technology that allows us to reach almost any destination we like—even the moon. We have flying machines and marine contraptions that will take us to the deepest depths and the highest heights. But that doesn't mean getting to those places is easy, any more than it was easy for the Wright brothers to achieve liftoff or the earliest mariners to get through the Straits of Magellan. Our ancestors endured all sorts of discomfort in ship holds of days gone by, often against their will—and now we endure all sorts of discomfort in airplane cabins, often because we want cheaper tickets.

32 USA

Kitty Hawk 1903

I have found out that there ain't no surer way to find out whether you like people or hate them than to travel with them.

—MARK TWAIN

The fascinating thing is that we keep on trying, even if that trying comes in fits and starts according to epoch. One civilization makes great strides in shipbuilding, then suffers a downturn before its innovations can be learned by anyone else. We get so far in understanding outer space, and then lack of funding keeps us from making more progress. Eventually, though, we make strides— small steps for the ancient gods, but big steps for mankind.

I am not afraid of storms
for I am learning how to sail my ship.
—LOUISA MAY ALCOTT, AMERICAN NOVELIST, 1832–1888

Vex-ing Messages

NAUTICAL FLAG SYSTEMS HAVE BEEN around for thousands of years, but the ones used aboard ships now were first developed in 18th-century France and refined in 19th-century England before being standardized as an international code in 1857. That code contained 18 signal flags;

Highly visible nautical flags on a tall ship

today there are 40, representing the 26 letters of the Roman alphabet, 10 digits (0 to 9), three "repeaters" or "substituters," and an "answering" flag that is used to show that a grouping/message has been received.

Most of us never see nautical flags in anything other than their fleet-parade display capability, but these flags—also keyed to an international code—have a serious, practical function. When at sea, only a few different colors can be distinguished quickly and easily—red, blue, yellow, black, and white. The flags' hues are the best contrasts of these colors so that sailors can get an instant understanding of the message.

One-flag signals convey a particular urgency such as "disabled," "fire; keep clear," "stop instantly," or "man overboard"; two-flag signals indicate slightly more complex maneuvering or other urgent messages such as "Permission to enter Harbor is urgently requested. I have an emergency," or "Man overboard. Please take action to pick him up"; three flags communicate such information as relative bearings, and points of the compass; four flags can convey names of ships, etc.; five flags share time or position; six flags are used when signaling points of the compass in latitude and longitude signals. Seven flags (Yes, it goes up to seven!) are for longitude signals of more than 100 degrees.

While most of us see these striking banners only on festive occasions, when all other means of communication fail during a storm or other disaster at sea, nautical flags can mean the difference between life and death.

A woman knows the face of the man she loves
like a sailor knows the open sea.
—HONORÉ DE BALZAC

The Love Boat

IT'S AN IDYLLIC SCENARIO: You and the one you love standing on the deck of a ship, a beautiful sunset reflected in the sea, the captain guiding you through your vows and then inviting you to kiss your sweetheart, who is now, officially, your spouse.

Idyllic, but not necessarily long-lasting: Technically, ships' captains can marry you, but so can your best friend, your favorite uncle, or the lady with three cats who lives down the street—but that doesn't mean your marriage is legally binding. Contrary to very popular beliefs, U.S. sea captains have never been able to perform marriages—unless, of course, those captains are also clergypersons or otherwise legally licensed.

Shipboard weddings can't run on love alone.

However, people believe in the myth of captains performing weddings so strongly that in U.S. Navy regulations there is actually a statute forbidding captains from performing "freelance weddings." Why does everyone persist in holding onto this inaccurate, if romantic, belief? One explanation may be that captains are seen as the supreme authority "on board," and being on a ship is akin to being on a small island with its own customs and laws. Another reason is that captains do register all sorts of events in their log, from births to deaths to—you guessed it—marriages on board.

It would seem to make sense that a captain could perform a wedding ceremony—making it convenient for everyone involved. However, the fact that most captains cannot legally bind two people together in matrimony shows that for many societies, the solemnity of the commitment outweighs any ease gained by giving the captain the authority to perform the ceremony. If you have your heart set on that sunset scenario, be sure—before you board the boat—that there is a licensed minister or justice of the peace waiting in the wings. That way, any vows you whisper to each other will be valid on land as well as at sea.

ARCHAIC MANNERS: The Origin of "Posh" One apocryphal tale of how the word "posh" came to be is that it is an acronym for "port out, starboard home"—the most desirable alignment for England-to-India routed shipboard cabins, available only to the rich, or "posh." However, the term was first recorded as meaning a "dandy" in 1867, and may have a connection to the Romany word *posh,* signifying money. In other words, a dandy was a man who spent a great deal of money on clothes—he was "a posh."

Whenever I see his fingernails,
I thank God I don't have to look at his feet.
—ATHENE SEYLER, ENGLISH ACTRESS, 1889-1990

Space-Age Hygiene

FOR SEVERAL DECADES, space travel has been the province of only highly trained professional astronauts—but all of that is changing in the era of wealthy tourists who are able to drop millions of dollars for a jaunt towards the planets and the stars.

Just as there are good manners and rules of hygiene on Earth, there are also good manners and rules of hygiene to be followed while on board a spaceship anywhere in the solar system. However, those rules are complicated by the fact that everything on a spaceship defies the laws of gravity that keep us all grounded in our on-Earth shoes. Anything that's spilled or dropped can create a big mess that is difficult to clean up beyond the bonds of earth.

Following the guidelines isn't simply for the sake of cleanliness—it's also to make sure that tensions don't build up in tight quarters, something that anyone who has taken an airplane flight or gone on a family automobile vacation can understand is quite important. No one wants "air rage" to develop after hours or days of someone else's sloppy, inconsiderate behavior. Of course, keeping things clean and stress free is more difficult when everything floats, including long hair and fingernail clippings. Women astronauts with long locks often have to spend over an hour shampooing, then more time dabbing hair to get it dry, while fingernail clippings and beard trimmings are captured with duct tape.

The answer to one waste-ful problem: a vacuum toilet that works by creating a tight seal between the user and seat, which requires straps and bars to keep any person in "position." It looks awkward, but previous astronauts say you get used to it, like any other otherworldly adaptation.

Vacuum-seal toilets probably aren't what those wealthy tourists had in mind, but it's still a fledgling industry. Maybe one day tickets to the moon will be sold as "coach" or "first class."

Launch of the space shuttle Discovery.

*If you reject the food, ignore the customs, fear the religion
and avoid the people, you might better stay home.*
—JAMES MICHENER

Mile-High Cuisine

BACK IN THE DAY, airlines recognized that distracting passengers from the anxieties of air travel required fine china, proper cutlery, and well-starched napery.

Notice that sentence didn't include anything about the food. That's because no matter how often frequent fliers choose to comment on their meals (and comment they do, if the web sites devoted to airline cuisine are any measure), they aren't necessarily tasting them. Sure, when you buy a business- or first-class ticket you look forward to a little extra coddling: juice in glass tumblers, a selection of wines, maybe even a cheese plate in miniature if you're flying Air France.

Tightly plated in-flight meals

However, airlines know that while your senses of sight and touch may be fully engaged, your sense of taste and smell are compromised the minute you board. Parched cabin air evaporates nasal mucus, which helps odor receptors function—and up to 80 percent of what we consider taste is actually smell. The dry air affects foods, too—those with a high water content, like caviar, suffer not just from a passenger's inability to taste, but from becoming dried out and unpleasant in texture.

The good news: When you're elbow-to-elbow with a few hundred of your best friends in economy class, you're actually less likely to be bothered by bad smells than while sitting several cubicles over in an office. You're also less likely to be affected by liquor. A wine with strong flavors and high alcohol content will taste lighter and weaker on high (no wonder they call them "the friendly skies").

The bad news: Now that the airlines have also figured this out, they think we'll all be placated with soft drinks and bags of pretzels.

CROSSING

REMEMBER YOUR EARLIEST SOCIAL STUDIES textbook? It showed you how your house sits on your street, how your street connects to other boulevards, how those boulevards make up your town, which towns make up a city, where that city stands in relation to the nearest state line, and so on until the Milky Way. Sometimes it seems that being human is all about lines of demarcation.

Too often travel, instead of broadening the mind, merely lengthens the conversation.

—ELIZABETH DREW

Some of those lines are easy to cross: When you're five or so years old, your parents may watch as you look both ways and cross the street to visit your playmate's house. You may find it a little more challenging to leave your town boundaries once you're old enough to drive, but the truly regulated borders are those between different countries. Territories were once defined by natural boundaries like rivers, lakes, oceans, valleys, mountain ranges, and deep forest or jungle. Once people figured out ways to negotiate those things, groups found new, man-made ways to define land: castles and fortresses, walls and barricades, fences and moats.

Of course, your neighbor's "castle" can be just as impregnable as a medieval tower in terms of how little you may know about her. But even if you long for that neighbor to attend your Tupperware party, it's unlikely that a great deal of trade and commerce depends on your relationship. On the other hand, relationships between nation-states do affect world supplies, and so the crossings that we know best as "borders" have become very important. The laws that govern the spots where we cross from one country to another have also become very important—even when the distance crossed is the width of your childhood street.

He did not care in which direction the car was traveling, so long as he remained in the driver's seat.
—ENGLISH POLITICIAN LORD BEAVERBROOK ON LLOYD GEORGE, 1963

License to Thrill

IF YOU'RE IN NEW YORK CITY or Washington, D.C., and notice a pale blue license plate on the car next to you, watch out: That diplomat might be trying to steal your parking spot, even if it's a permit-only spot.

Technically, these license plates don't come with special privileges. The distinctive blue is used, according to the U.S. State Department, to "identify vehicles as being owned by a diplomatic mission . . . and to indicate to law enforcement officers that the operator of the motor vehicle may be entitled to diplomatic immunity."

However, as any resident of Manhattan's East Side or D.C.'s Georgetown neighborhoods can tell you, just because diplomats aren't supposed to be exempt from parking tickets or other traffic violations doesn't mean that law enforcement doesn't turn a blind eye from time to time. Officially the U.S. State Department does not have the authority to intervene with local officials or to dismiss tickets or fines. Their website warns that, "failure to pay parking tickets . . . or to resolve traffic violations could result in the loss of driving privileges." But asked how many licenses had been denied due to unpaid fines, the State Department declined to comment.

They may appear to be a random assortment of letters and numbers, but the government uses a system for coding diplomatic plates. While this information is not public, a former member of the State Department agreed to confirm generally what they mean. The first letter is a status code identifying the car's

For diplomats, decals allow special treatment.

owner as a diplomat, foreign consul member, U.N. Secretariat employee, or nondiplomatic staff member. These codes define the diplomatic immunity rights of the car and driver.

The next two letters are country codes that the State Department's Office of Foreign Missions created specially for these licenses. Don't bother trying to guess which letters stand for which country using these codes. They have no correlation to the country's name and were designed this way to protect foreign dignitaries and prevent people from targeting vehicles of diplomats from certain countries.

*It is not always the same thing to
be a good man and a good citizen.*
—ARISTOTLE

Homes Sweet Homes

THEY SAY YOU CAN'T GO HOME again—and that may or may not be true. But some people have two homes, or homelands—and what's certainly true is that they can't visit both of them at the same time! "Dual nationals" are people who hold citizenship in two countries simultaneously.

Dual citizenship can happen in a number of ways. A child born in a foreign country to parents who are United States citizens may have U.S. citizenship as well as being a citizen in her birth country. In such cases, upon reaching the age of majority (18), that child has to choose just one country as her own. A citizen might also acquire foreign citizenship through marriage, or acquire a new nationality by naturalization—occasions in which the dual citizenship can be maintained.

While the U.S. government does not encourage dual citizenship, it is allowed, and there

Home Sweet Home

Beloved Currier and Ives print from the 1870s

are people who also pursue it for personal and professional reasons. A Canadian man whose family has strong ties in Spain might want dual citizenship because he wants to spend a great deal of time visiting with his relatives and be able to work in both countries without navigating complicated visa applications and restrictions on how often he must get his passport stamped or how long he's allowed to stay.

People with dual nationalities are required to follow the laws of both countries to which they profess allegiance, but it is generally understood that they owe the greatest loyalty to whichever country they are living in at a particular time.

Nationalism is power hunger
tempered by self-deception.
—GEORGE ORWELL

Brand Nationalism

YOU SEE THEM ON ALMOST any international flight—passengers clutching brightly patterned plastic sacks full of liquor, wine, chocolates, and perfume. They've been to the "duty-free shop" and they're bringing home what they hope are either bargain-priced luxury goods, exotic things they can't get at home, or maybe even both. The goods must be exported intact (they cannot be consumed in the airport), and they are importing them into the destination country under that country's own tax rules.

While people have been crossing borders and bringing home various types of souvenirs for centuries, modern duty-free shops have a short history. The world's first Airport Duty Free was established at Ireland's Shannon Airport by Dr. Brendan O'Regan in 1947 and is still in service. For many U.S. citizens, a stop at The Loop at Shannon Airport during a refueling stop on a flight back home became a cherished tradition, so much so that the stores now have a popular mail-order catalog so there's no need to purchase an airplane ticket to get your goods.

Soon after, a similar enterprise called "Duty Free Shoppers" became a worldwide franchise, and what was originally one nation's effort to push its most recognizable products became a global "trick" for travelers to get large amounts

Temptations at Gatwick Airport's duty-free shop

of alcohol and tobacco purchased. Modern regulations and security considerations have made this more difficult, and so duty-free shops have once again become a sort of last opportunity to see a nation or region's best and most typical goods. France, which claims the status of "the most visited country in the world," does the most seamless job of tempting customers while showing off its industries: Boutiques devoted to everything from Hermès scarves to Cartier jewelry ensure that saving money is the last thing on a traveler's mind as they leave the country.

I fear the carnival of crime
is beginning on our border.
—EDWARD BLAKE

Borderline

NATIONAL BORDERS AREN'T a standardized kind of thing—they can occur in the middle of a salt mine (Austria-Hungary), a mountain pass (Kyrgyzstan-China), or even a busy urban café (Holland-Belgium). But two of the strangest borders in the world have to be those around the cities of Ceuta and Melilla, which are located geographically on the coast of Morocco—but belong to Spain.

That is, they "belong to Spain" according to the Spanish. They are part of what is called The Spanish Protectorate of Morocco. Morocco does not recognize Spanish sovereignty in North Africa. While Spain has erected three-meter-high barbed wire fences around the cities, Morocco does little to enforce obedience to those "borders." Unfortunately, illegal immigration attempts are common and often have tragic results. Many members of the European Union disapproved of Spain's choice to put up these border fences.

Customs officials are gatekeepers to nations.

Bilingual sign meaning "stop for customs"

Although these cities are the only European Union territories on the continent of Africa today, and might sensibly be returned to Morocco, an understanding of their history and development shows that their culture, population, and economies have been tied to European ways for centuries (both were at one time part of the Roman Empire). Ceuta, which has coast in both the Mediterranean and the Atlantic, is very close to the former British colony of Gibraltar, which is also geographically part of Spain. In Ceuta you'll find a rebuilt 15th-century cathedral, shipyards and a fish-processing plant. It takes 90 minutes aboard a ferry to get from the town to mainland Spain. Melilla, which has an old walled city within, was conquered by Spain in 1497 and has been Spanish ever since. Indeed, these border towns have more in common with each other in some ways than they do with their various nations—varied architecture; communities diverse in religion, ethnicity, and culture; and busy commercial ports.

BOUNDARIES

NATIONAL BORDERS AREN'T THE ONLY KIND that can be crossed. Everyone deserves human rights. However, the behavioral boundaries we set for ourselves and others can be quite different, even with contemporary attitudes oriented toward the idea that we're individuals. Many cultures, even those that are now organized as nations with their own distinct identities, believe that community values and rights are more important than family or individual ones.

Some believe there is a right or wrong to this. Others do not. We can't debate this here, nor would we even try—but what we can say is there are still many situations in which people's physical and mental boundaries can be violated by outsiders. Make no mistake; this category is in the chapter about vehicles and transportation deliberately, because it's about distances. Perhaps even more in a world in which we can reach each other almost instantaneously, we need ways to reinforce our separateness.

Natives who beat drums to drive off evil spirits are objects of scorn to smart Americans who blow horns to break up traffic jams.

—MARY ELLEN KELLY

However, some of these "ways" have existed for a long time. Geography has a big effect on society. One group of people may have thousands of acres to roam while another is forced to build upwards to accommodate a population. Those living conditions set up new and different kinds of rules on their own. Ultimately, the interplay of geography, religion, language, technology, and commerce changes some things but leaves others in a sort of alchemy that transcends the very borders people once established.

One morning I shot an elephant in my pajamas.
How he got into my pajamas I'll never know.
—GROUCHO MARX, AMERICAN COMEDIAN, 1890-1977

Pajama Party

POLITE BEHAVIOR involves many rules about clothing, but sometimes those rules don't apply in different cultures. Western citizens eschew being seen in their pajamas, but in Shanghai men in PJs and women in nightgowns are seen almost everywhere: walking the streets, shopping in markets, and lounging around neighborhoods.

Wearing pajamas in public began in the early 1990s, when people traded their Mao suits for more comfortable and fashionable clothes. The Chinese adopted Western pajamas not knowing that they were only supposed to be worn at home, and usually within bedrooms and other private spaces. Both citizens and tourists enjoyed the spectacle: citizens because they thought the pajamas were comfortable and practical, and tourists because watching beautiful Shanghainese women trotting around in nightgowns was alluring.

This practice came about partly because the

Pajamas are day wear for some Shanghainese.

newly solvent Chinese saw Western pajamas as expensive and cool, but also partly because of their own living traditions. Homes and living areas were so small that the idea of changing to walk a few meters across the street seemed silly.

While the government has recently been trying to convince residents of Shanghai (where the custom of pajama-wearing is particularly strong) that being "a civilized resident" means changing out of pajamas before leaving the house, it is meeting resistance from a public that has found nightclothes easy and appealing. In Shanghai, there is not a great deal of differentiation between "public" and "private." Wearing pajamas shows that you have money, style, and an ineffable sense of "cool"; changing into street clothes goes against the "Shanghai style," as ingrained in that city's residents as is the New York City tradition of wearing mostly black.

FAMOUS GAFFES: Reagan, Russia, and "The bombing begins in five minutes"   U.S. Presidents can do almost anything—but they have to be careful when attempting to make jokes. On August 11, 1984, United States President Ronald Reagan, while running for re-election, was preparing a weekly radio address, and during the sound check quipped: "My fellow Americans, I'm pleased to tell you today that I've signed legislation that will outlaw Russia forever. We begin bombing in five minutes." While the joke wasn't broadcast, it was leaked—and the then-USSR was decidedly not amused.

I'd rather sit down and write a letter than call someone up.
I hate the telephone.
—HENRY MILLER

Delhi Dialing

MODERN TECHNOLOGY HAS CHANGED so many rules of good manners that many books on the subject have or will be updated soon to accommodate things like Facebook. What happens when you hit "unfriend"? Do you have to get involved in that long boring conversation about your niece's sweet-16 dress? Should you ignore that odd message from your boss? Many different realms, from work to family to the past, can get mixed up on our laptops and other devices.

But sometimes it's not access to others but access to those devices that determines mode of communication and therefore the manners used. In India, Internet usage is not as high as it is in developed countries because computers are expensive and not available in every home and office. Mobile phones (without data plans) are much cheaper than laptops or BlackBerries. Forget email, forget Facebook, forget Twitter—all of those communication modes cost extra on mobiles. The preferred mode of communication for most Indians? Text messaging.

Turbans and tech in India's Delhi

Text messaging isn't something merely for teenagers in India. All sorts of conversations and transactions take place via Short Message Service (SMS), including business scheduling, shopping, and divorces. Yes, Muslim men in India issue divorce decrees via texts. Under Muslim law, a divorce can be granted via *talaq*—a specific statement from man to wife, which does not have to be said in person.

Because text messaging is so affordable and popular, Indian entrepreneurs have figured out new ways to capitalize on its success. For example, GupShup is a Twitter-like service that operates via SMS, allowing friends to check on each other's status updates without web access. Maintaining friendships is, after all, always good manners.

There is hardly any personal defect which an agreeable manner might not gradually reconcile one to.
—JANE AUSTEN

Grecian Formula

PERSONAL BOUNDARIES ARE A funny thing. Many people find themselves unable to confess a story to their closest friend, yet wind up sharing it with a stranger on a plane. (Where do you think the idea for *Strangers on a Train* came from?)

Similarly, in some countries public manners are warm and friendly, yet still quite formal.

An elegant and typical Greek amphora

Visitors to Greece will sometimes report feeling rather overwhelmed by hospitality. Modern Greek hosts believe in sharing as much food and drink as they possibly can. You should plan on eating every bit of stuffed grape leaves, spit-roasted lamb, and everything else that might land on your plate—but it's also very important to ask for seconds (even if you're stuffed to the gills), as this shows respect for your host and compliments to his or her cooking and entertaining abilities.

Anyone invited to share a table and meal in Greece is considered "part of the family," and guests are treated with great warmth and kindness. However, no matter how much bonhomie you feel while dining and talking with a Greek group, keep in mind that there are boundaries still in place. The Greeks are quite conscious of family ties and honor, and blood-related members of a family are always given precedence in a conflict. Nepotism isn't viewed negatively in modern Greece, and while North Americans might be shocked at the idea of a nephew or aunt getting a position just because of a relationship, in Greece this is considered true courtesy: Putting family first.

Don't be surprised, then, if while meeting with potential business associates in Athens you find yourself shaking hands with several people who share the same surname. The Greeks do not see this as suspect, but as evidence that they've accomplished something together. The family business is the outward sign of true success.

People who know little are usually great talkers,
while men who know much say little.
—JEAN-JACQUES ROUSSEAU

Close Talkers

IN THE POPULAR U.S. 1990s television sitcom *Seinfeld,* one episode highlights the characters' discomfort with a "close talker": a man who stands too close to others while having conversations. Comic Jerry Seinfeld says in the show's opening monologue "Don't you hate these people that talk . . . into your mouth like you're a clown at a drive-through?"

Manhattanites like Seinfeld and his friends might loathe "close talkers," but in other parts of the world conversational distance—and the likelihood of being exposed to a person's halitosis—can vary quite a bit. For example, one Australian man believes that city folk greet each other at the closest distance, while "bushies" (farmers in outlying areas) tend to stand far apart and lean in to shake hands. No matter where or at what distance, these habits are so distinctive that they are studied and known as "proxemics," a term coined by anthropologist Edward T. Hall in 1966 that includes measures for intimate, personal, social, and public distances.

Ensuring a few
degrees of separation

Many cultures have "close talker" proxemics, which means that the usual Hall standard of 1.5 to 2.5 feet can shrink to as little as 6 inches. North Americans reserve this kind of nearness for their absolute nearest and dearest, like spouses, immediate family members, and children. However, in Istanbul, even the most etiquette-conscious Turks draw their faces and bodies close when engaged in conversation.

The irony is, of course, that this proximity in Turkey is most common between men, because for many years, even though Istanbul is one of the most cosmopolitan and sophisticated of cities, it has had a devout Muslim population that believes women other than one's closest relatives must be avoided. While things are changing in modern Turkey, expect that men may stand closer to other men, giving unknown women a wider berth.

OBJECTS OF ETIQUETTE: Bicycle Racks Cyclists face the problem of theft whenever they must leave a bike outside. The solution is to attach the bicycle to a sturdy, unmovable object like a fence or a tree. In many urban areas around the world, metal bike racks, bolted to sidewalks, are the solution, offering cycling proponents a way to secure their means of transportation.

MANNERED LIVES

Lady Bird Johnson

When you drive through a city or down a highway and see landscaping or banks of flowers instead of concrete or monotony, thank Lady Bird Johnson. Mrs. Johnson, born Claudia Alta Taylor, was the First Lady of the United States from 1963 to 1969 when her husband Lyndon Baines Johnson was President. ("Lady Bird" was a childhood nickname bestowed on the wren-like little girl by her nanny.)

Lady Bird Johnson, a lifelong Texan and environmentalist, launched a campaign called "Beautification" in 1965. "Beautification" included legislation and public campaigns on rural and urban environmentalism, national parks conservation, antipollution measures, water and air quality improvement, landscaping, and urban renewal. Her initial effort was the creation of the Committee for a More Beautiful Capital: Two million daffodil and tulip bulbs, 83,000 flowering plants, 50,000 shrubs, 137,000 annuals, and 25,000 trees were planted around or near the public buildings to create "masses of flowers where the masses pass."

Lady Bird Johnson during her years as First Lady of the United States

Johnson also lobbied for development of the National Mall where the various Smithsonian museums were located; it was her influence that convinced art collector Joseph Hirshhorn to donate his collection to the Institution. She encouraged the Job Corps to expand the professional skills it taught to include landscaping; gave impetus to the continuance of a Pennsylvania Avenue redevelopment, an idea begun by President Kennedy; and created the Jacqueline Kennedy Garden and the Children's Garden on the White House South Lawn.

After her husband's decision not to run for reelection, Johnson was happy to return to her family home in Stonewall, Texas. She focused on the indigenous plants and wildflowers of that region as well as of the rest of the country, and in 1982 created the nonprofit National Wildflower Research Center. In 1995 the center expanded into a new 42-acre facility. In 1998 the center's board unanimously decided to rename it the Lady Bird Johnson Wildflower Center.

CARRYING

SOME PEOPLE FIND IT IRRITATING to tote anything other than what can fit in the pockets of their clothing, but let's face it: Pockets are a human accommodation to our need to carry baggage. Upright *Homo sapiens* is a remarkable creation, but has no way to store extra food and water needed at regular intervals; the body cannot provide us with shelter, let alone currency, identification, chewing gum, and lip balm.

Sooner or later, even those espousing a "hands free" lifestyle will need to bring home groceries, move possessions across town, or pack for a vacation. Changing our individual "footprint" can also change how we behave and how others treat us (as any woman in the third trimester of pregnancy will tell you). Are we carrying something because it's near and dear to us—like a totem—or because we've been ordered to do so—like a military rucksack? Do we hold it in our hands, our arms, or on our backs? Are we carrying something because it makes us stand out, or because it makes us look like everybody else?

Don't forget planning: You wouldn't want to reach the North Pole, open your duffel bag, and find it filled with swimsuits and flip-flops. That's part of manners, too. If you arrive with the wrong gear, someone else has to help you out. Even if they do so cheerfully and willingly, it changes things. The bag we pack can also say a lot about us—is it a designer original? Or a hand-me-down with a broken zipper? Cultures pay attention to baggage (it can be mental, too) because it can be something that causes a chain reaction. Think of the old rhyme "For want of a nail . . . " It starts with someone not having enough tiny bits of metal, and ends with an entire kingdom being "lost."

> *Our deeds still travel with us from afar, and what we have been makes us what we are.*
>
> —GEORGE ELIOT

She cannot see an institution
without hitting it with her handbag.
—SIR JULIAN CRITCHLEY, ENGLISH CONSERVATIVE POLITICIAN

Pardon Mon Sac

THE FRENCH BASICALLY invented "luxury brands," the high-priced and fashionable items that people across the world crave. It's difficult to pinpoint the beginning of human fascination with things made to order, but certainly the French couture industry helped develop "name brands": Think of Chanel, Dior, Hermès . . .

The House of Hermès, opened in 1837 as a leather-goods shop, is one of the oldest brand-name businesses in the world. The Hermès dedication to quality and detail brought a large following among the European upper classes for whom horses, riding, and carriages were de rigueur. Hermès made its first bag, for

Monaco's Prince Rainier III and Princess Grace

carrying saddles, in 1900—but when a relative complained about the lack of decent women's handbags in the early 1920s, the company first produced its soon-to-be-iconic *sacs des femmes.*

Today the Hermès "Kelly" bag (named after its most famous owner, Princess Grace of Monaco, née Grace Kelly of Philadelphia) and "Birkin" bag (inspired by 1960s British supermodel Jane Birkin) can be seen on the elbows of some of the chicest and most famous women.

It's ironic that the Hermès Birkin is oversize, as the French are quite conscious of personal space and rarely carry large, sloppy overstuffed totes. Briefcases are slim, and women's purses are trim and carried close to the body.

The chic Hermès purse named for Grace Kelly

How full of trifles everything is! It is only one's thoughts that fill a room with something more than furniture.
—WALLACE STEVENS

Go-Anywhere Gear

RECENTLY MERCHANTS HAVE touted a jacket that converts into a sleeping bag and outerwear that can hold as much as a carry-on suitcase (even folded business shirts in a pocket).

For modern travelers tired of lugging equipment, these "innovations" must seem heaven-sent—but there's actually a venerable tradition of bringing civilized comforts to less-than-comfortable places. One example is British "campaign furniture," which peaked in the 18th and early 19th centuries when masters of cabinetry like Hepplewhite and Chippendale made full suites of tables, chairs, beds, settees, and even cradles for the English army to take to battlefields.

The pieces were also called "knock-down furniture," because although they were made

Simple yet functional portable chair

Campaign furniture at South African peace talks, 1902

by craftsmen to look as traditional as possible, each desk and divan could fold flat or otherwise be taken apart and sometimes packed into specially configured trucks. Surviving articles are marvels of innovation made possible by hinges, screws, and springs.

There were imperial overtones—implying that no officer would stoop to native chairs—but we're also reminded that soldiers yearn for touches of home. Just as U.S. soldiers overseas long for Pizza Hut and McDonald's, British cavalrymen of 1825 might have been cheered by a "proper" dining chair.

*It is the unseen, unforgettable, ultimate accessory of fashion
that heralds your arrival and prolongs your departure.*
—COCO CHANEL

Message in a Turban

TURBANS, WHICH LOOK BOTH quaint and exotic to Westerners, had a practical beginning: The long strips of cloth wrapped (sometimes quite intricately) around the head were meant to keep the head cool and protected from the sun. The turban is referred to in the Bible, and by early Islamic times, people in desert climates including parts of the Middle East, North Africa, and South Asia, adopted the headdress. One of its predecessors (really, a part of many modern turbans) is the *amamah,* a strip of cloth wound around the head to shield the lower portion of the face from wind and sand.

Many types of turbans and methods of wrapping them now exist, from Afghanistan's *lungee* to India's *pagri* to the peaked *kaffiyeh* turban affected by PLO leader Yasir Arafat. However, North Americans who associate the turban with people from the Middle East should recall that Native Americans also wore head wraps, sometimes constructed from animal furs and hides.

Baptized members of the Sikh religion (which is totally separate from the Islam and Hindu faiths) wear the turban as an identifying garment. Sikhs—both male and female—forego cutting all body hair, so most of them have large topknots that are covered by the turban, which represents what Sikhs call "the five Ks;" *kesh, kanga, kara, kachera,* and *kirpan.* The *kesh* is uncut hair; the *kara,* an iron bracelet, and the *kachera,* a special type of loose-fitting cotton underwear. The *kanga,* a wooden comb, and the *kirpan,* a bronze dagger, are actually worn inside of the turban.

Neither the kanga nor the kirpan is used; they are spiritual reminders. The kanga is a reminder to care for and tidy one's hair, and the kirpan is a reminder to protect the innocent in times of conflict.

Sikhs with signature turbans and uncut hair

I hope I'm not a tourist attraction—I'm sure that they come here really because St. Andrews is just amazing, a beautiful place.
—PRINCE WILLIAM

Tourist Trap

SOME LUGGAGE CARRIES MESSAGES far larger than its actual size. The perfect example might be the all-too-ubiquitous "fanny pack" that many U.S. citizens swear by on their travels. (There are many names for this; the British often call it a "bum bag," since the term "fanny" means something different there.)

The "fanny pack" is a modern version of a working waist pouch (usually for ammunition or tools like a fisherman's lures and hooks) and a secure "money belt" long favored by safety-minded travelers. Although the words "fanny" and "bum" imply that the packs are worn with the sack-like pouch in back, over the buttocks, most proponents of these bags keep the zippered pouch in front for safety.

Waist bags peaked in the 1980s and 1990s, and when combined with shorts, puffy white leather sneakers, and sun hats, became a

An obvious tourist in New York City

Fanny pack brimming with travel essentials

much-parodied "look" for American tourists. Of course, it's one thing to wear a uniform of a sort at places like Disney World and the Grand Canyon; it's another to gear up in the same garb when gawping at Pompeii or the Great Wall of China. Americans thought they were being comfortable and practical; people in other countries thought they were awkward, gauche, and unwilling to adapt to other customs. The luggage manufacturers started making different small bags, and fashions changed.

As always, fashions also change back: A 2011 *Wall Street Journal* article heralded the revival of what top-line designers are trying to call "the belt bag."

GETTING & SPENDING

Money changes everything. Money makes the world go 'round. Money—no, wait, the *love* of money—is the root of all evil. Money can't buy me love. Show me the money. It doesn't matter if any or all of these clichés about money are true; the very fact that there are so many of them shows us that humans find the concept of money important.

We've already seen that the things humans value, like family, education and communication, tend to have customs and manners around them. It's no different with money. Very few people are able to produce or find everything necessary to survival, and so from the earliest times humans have had to engage in trade with each other: One person had meat from a recent hunt, another had berries from recent scavenging, and they realized both could have some of each.

Money did change everything when it eventually became clear to early humans that sometimes when you were out of berries, you could still obtain necessities by giving the other person a mutually agreed upon currency such as shells, which had no intrinsic value, but which could be traded for other things. Thousands of years later, we're all still wondering who is supposed to "shell out" for what . . .

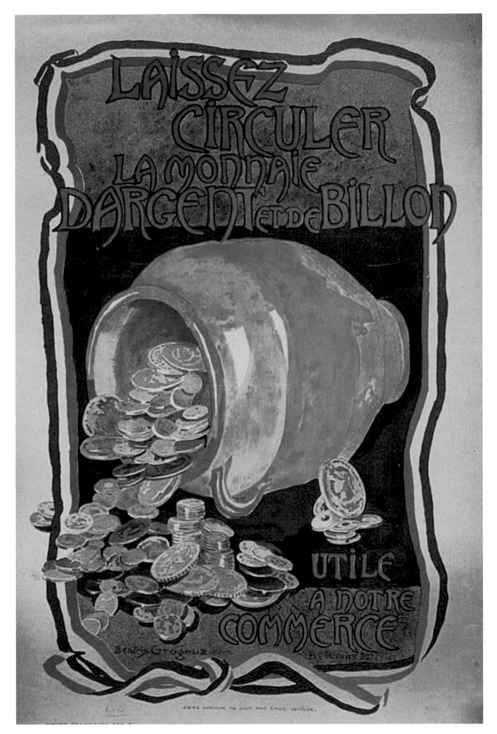

French poster encourages circulating "silver and nickel coinage."

CURRENCY

NYONE WHO SAYS "I DON'T CARE ABOUT MONEY" should recall that the thing almost everyone takes when leaving the house is a purse or wallet. You may not care a lot about money, but you do care about it to a certain extent because of what it allows you to do: board a train, buy milk or lottery tickets, get a haircut or a newspaper. Most of the time those things require payment through currency—something that is circulated as a medium of exchange.

Currency might take the form of those shells mentioned previously, polished stones or beads, or most common, bits of metal that have evolved into coins and pieces of paper that have evolved into bills. Originally, coins represented the actual value of the metal that made up their weight, but over time as monetary systems became more sophisticated, inexpensive and plentiful metals could be made into coins.

> *You have to be very rich or very poor to live without a trade.*
>
> —ALBERT CAMUS

One of the reasons that paper money came to Europe was because plentiful Swedish copper was not worth much, so coins created with it were very heavy. Paper currency, also known as banknotes, was for several hundred years tied to gold and silver standards, meaning that governments held supplies of those metals supposedly equivalent to the amount of money they printed.

Gradually, national treasuries ceased using gold and silver standards, with the United States being the last to give up the gold standard, in 1971. Paper currency still exists, of course, but it is just as likely to be bypassed for plastic today: People use credit, debit, and automatic teller machine cards in situations that once required cash, from fast-food drive-up windows to subway fares.

*The best way to find yourself is to
lose yourself in the service of others.*
—MOHANDAS GANDHI

Keep the Change

THE PRACTICE OF TIPPING, or leaving gratuities for service workers, is always fraught with anxiety for travelers, as the amounts and customs can differ greatly from place to place. Many people in the United States carry wallet-sized laminated cards that give different tip amounts for different dollar amounts.

While a tip is, by definition, money that is freely given on top of a bill and is never a legal requirement, it can be a serious misstep not to leave one, especially in places like the U.S. where waitstaff are often paid a low hourly wage with the expectation that their collected tips will "make up" for the poor pay. Unfortunately for consumers, tips aren't just for restaurant workers any more: They're often expected by everyone at the hair salon, contractors, delivery people, babysitters, and baristas. Few North Americans blink an eye at tip jars.

However, there are just as many cultures in which tipping is not expected. In most Asian and Western European countries, service gratuities are customarily added to bills or are completely unknown. Germans have an unobtrusive custom of "rounding up" any bill to the next highest number and simply telling a waiter *"Stimmt so,"* which literally means "It stays that way," or "Keep the change." Occasionally in less formal situations a person might say to the waiter *"Als Trinkgeld,"* or "For drinking money."

Money may not buy happiness, but it can damn well give it!
—FREDDIE MERCURY, BRITISH LEAD SINGER OF ROCK BAND QUEEN

The Money Dance

SOME TRADITIONS SEEM AS IF they must be older than they actually are, which is the case with what some cultures call "the money dance" and others "the dollar dance." Both of these phrases refer to the custom of having a bride dance with as many guests at her wedding reception as possible, each of whom pins cash or an envelope with money it to her gown. The DJ plays a slow song that allows friends and relatives to "catch" the bride and contribute to the new couple's "nest egg."

Variations of "the dollar dance" include having the bride carry a purse into which the money is placed, and having money "attached" to both the bride and groom. Since the custom often takes place in the U.S. at Italian and Polish weddings, people sometimes believe that it came over from "the old country" along with ancestors. However, historians say that these dances originated in Polish settlements in the U.S. in the early 20th century as a way for community members to get young couples off on the right foot. (Speaking of "the right foot," at Hungarian and Portuguese weddings, the bride puts her shoes in the middle of the dance floor and they are passed from guest to guest to be filled with money.)

Many etiquette experts find this custom vulgar, believing that gifts of money should be

Delighted bride after a "money dance"

given discreetly in wedding cards so that no person at a party feels obliged to contribute. While it is generally agreed that accepting an invitation to a wedding reception means you should bring a gift, that gift should be of the guest's choosing. (We won't even attempt to discuss wedding gift registries here . . .)

OBJECTS OF ETIQUETTE: Coasters While pub towels (and their companion bar mats, made of cardboard) are made to soak up excess liquid, coasters are designed to keep liquid from reaching wood and fabric. Manufactured from materials including woolen needlepoint, cork matting, leather, and stone, these round or square mats protect a host or hostess's furnishings from stains.

If you give money, spend yourself with it.
—HENRY DAVID THOREAU

Red Envelopes

IN CHINESE CULTURE, red is the color of good luck and is also thought to guard against evil spirits. That's why *hongbao*—long, narrow paper packets—are always a bright shade of crimson. Hongbao, colloquially known in English by the less interesting phrase "red envelopes," are made for presenting gifts of money at weddings, birthdays, and especially during the Chinese New Year celebrations, the most important Chinese festival, when citizens get to enjoy a much-deserved, multiday public holiday.

Red envelopes are often decorated with gold characters for different kinds of events. Traditionally these symbols were the only decoration, but in recent decades all sorts of hongbao have been produced, including many with popular cartoon characters for children and many with the year's animal avatar (rabbit, ox, dog) depicted, too.

The amount of money is less important than the giving for Chinese New Year and birthdays, but at weddings, when the envelopes are opened and amounts are recorded on a ceremonial scroll, the contents of red envelopes can be significant. Certain amounts of money are to be avoided; for example, numbers beginning or ending in a 4 are avoided because *sì* (four) sounds similar to *sǐ* (death). Even numbers (except number four!) are considered much better than odd numbers, with the numeral 8 especially being very lucky. Few Asians use paper checks, so the contents of red envelopes are almost always cash—never coins, which are considered unclean. The paper money included should always be new, crisp, and unwrinkled—anything else looks bad. Hongbao are presented and received with two hands, which is particularly important to remember since these envelopes are often given from an elder like a parent or boss to a child or employee. Respect and humility are considered paramount on these occasions. After all, she who receives a red envelope will someday be giving one.

Crimson hongbao *with lucky eights*

Decorative lions in lucky Chinese red

MANNERED LIVES

Letitia Baldrige

Letitia Baldrige earned her prominence as 20th-century etiquette doyenne based on her career in government protocol. Baldrige, who grew up in Omaha, attended Miss Porter's School in Connecticut and graduated from Vassar College.

Baldrige served as personal secretary to the Ambassador at the American Embassy in Paris, traveled to Rome with Ambassador Clare Booth Luce and became the first director of public relations—and the first woman executive—at Tiffany and Company.

Letitia Baldrige: social secretary extraordinaire and queen of protocol

Baldrige's roots in politics and protocol were strong. In 1961 she came to Washington with President John F. Kennedy and his glamorous young wife Jacqueline. Jacqueline Bouvier Kennedy's determination to bring a worldly feel to Washington, D.C., and the White House meant that her social secretary Baldrige was challenged by new situations and people. While she almost always rose to the occasion, it was Baldrige's lapses (like the time she introduced the Ambassador from Pakistan as the Ambassador from India) that truly led her to prominence as a spokesperson for real manners: "There are major CEOs who do not know how to hold a knife and fork properly, but I don't worry about that as much as the lack of kindness," she said. "There are two generations of people who have not learned how important it is to take time to say 'I'm sorry' and 'please,' and 'thank you' and how people must relate to one another."

Today, the octogenarian Baldrige runs a consultancy with a business partner that advises prominent executives, government officials, and academicians on the basics of true good manners in both public and private life.

For devil's sake, don't give bribes.
—MOTHER TERESA

Here's a Tip

WHEN MANY WESTERNERS hear the term "baksheesh," they think of bribery conducted by robed men in alleyways. While at one time baksheesh represented bribes—really, a form of payment for services rendered, even if that payment was sometimes higher than it should have been—today it is better understood.

Baksheesh comes from a Persian word meaning "present," and has long been a part of daily life in Middle and Near Eastern countries. While shady back-alley dealings and corruption can be part of baksheesh, it's actually a more complicated and meaningful economic system than many outsiders might understand. Baksheesh can mean giving alms, or charity, which is one of the Pillars of Islam. Street beggars often cry "Baksheesh!" Unlike Western cultures, which regard begging as a nuisance, in Muslim societies, giving money to one of these people is considered a sign of piety. Baksheesh

Baksheesh can span alms to gratuities.

can also mean what Westerners call "tipping," and in countries like Turkey, the word *baksis* now means "gratuity." Just like in other societies that tip people who provide services, baksheesh means 10 to 15 percent of a bill.

Finally baksheesh is also used to get favors, or as an outright bribe, in a region rife with government corruption, and it isn't just aimed at tourists: Citizens are sometimes expected to give money to officials when trying to get a permit or special attention. Although foreign visitors may be put off by official baksheesh, it isn't necessarily easily understood or condemned. It's more a closely integrated part of the fabric of life in a part of the world that has different standards than ours.

SERVICE

I T'S NEARLY IMPOSSIBLE FOR ANYONE TO AVOID needing someone else's services once in a while. Even if a homestead had a whetstone, for example, occasionally the owners might want to avail themselves of a knife sharpener's skills.

A knife sharpener—or a dentist, or an actor—provides something intangible, something that people can't do or easily acquire for themselves. Service professionals are dependent on finding clients to whom they can sell their intangibles. There are many variables in a service economy, such as shifting demand according to factors like population change and weather—for example, ski resorts and beach towns that shut down in off-seasons.

The lessons taught in great books are misleading. The commerce in life is rarely so simple and never so just.

—ANITA BROOKNER

Many service professionals operate somewhere near the middle of what economists call the "service-goods continuum," with the service end being teaching (pure service) and the goods end being salt (pure commodity). A custom tailor provides a service—measuring and sewing—as well as a product—a new suit. A café provides ambience as well as coffee.

The people who provide services can be considered upper-class professionals like physicians, attorneys, and university professors, as well as working-class tradespeople like manicurists, short-order cooks, and soldiers. Interestingly, nearly everyone in the world eventually needs both "upper-class" services (e.g., examinations by a doctor) and "working-class" services (a car oil change). Shouldn't we all, then, treat each other with equal respect?

Go, and never darken my towels again!
—GROUCHO MARX, IN THE FILM *DUCK SOUP*, 1933

Your Towel, Sir

EVERYTHING'S BIGGER IN VEGAS, and that includes the vending options placed out by bathroom attendants. At high-end clubs and restaurants, men and women can find everything necessary to a night of fun (depending on how each person defines that term) from cigarettes to breath mints to colognes to hairspray to lip gloss to antiperspirants and more. The attendants, who usually work for a low hourly wage, compete for tips—usually it's understood that if the attendant hands you a paper towel, you should leave some change in his dish.

Essentially, bathroom attendants are housekeepers for their domains, and sometimes clean them as well as keeping supplies like soap and toilet paper stocked. However, they're often employed in expensive nightclubs for seamier reasons: to keep patrons from engaging in drug-taking or sexual acts in restrooms that would not only make other customers uncomfortable, but might result in legal problems for the management.

At least that's the case in modern Western places. Farther east, in more old-fashioned cities like Vienna and Moscow, bathroom attendants hark back to a time in which a lady or gentleman might truly be in need of a spritz of perfume or

Bathroom attendant doles out supplies for tips.

a bit of pomade before returning to an elaborate formal meal.

Of course, patrons don't always realize that the bathroom attendants are there for more than just wiping down sinks and passing out lollipops, and resent their presence. The solution is not to use their services. If a washroom attendant offers you a towel or mint, you are under no obligation to tip unless you accept, or have utilized the products in the bathroom. Even so, if you have benefited from the cleanliness and safety of the facility a tip is certainly in order.

ARCHAIC MANNERS: Tradesmen's Entrances Grand entryways were built for grand entrances; the people who constructed the manor houses of the English countryside and the mansions of Newport were awaiting visits from dukes and Vanderbilts, not chimney sweeps and carpet salesmen. So they deliberately built "tradesmen's entrances" around the back of these homes where no aristocratic noses would have to be put out of joint by seeing a plumber's wrench or a butcher's van.

Ask not what you can do for your country. Ask what's for lunch.
—ORSON WELLES, AMERICAN ACTOR, DIRECTOR, PRODUCER, AND WRITER, 1915-1985

Towers of Tiffins

AT MIDDAY IN MUMBAI, thousands of towers of tin-covered plates are collected from private homes, delivered to downtown offices, then re-collected and returned for the next day's lunches by a group of specialized workers known as *dabbawalas*. Literally, this means "person who carries a box," but these industrious souls are sometimes also called "tiffin wallahs," after an English term for a light afternoon snack or meal.

Ironically, this entire system of meals and boxes came about because the British, when occupying India, often disliked local food. An Indian entrepreneur, Mahadeo Havaji Bacche, invented the tiffin distribution business back in 1890, and by the 1950s and 1960s the tiffin wallahs were delivering some 200,000 *dabbas,*

Distinctively painted metal dabbas, *or tiffins*

or lunch-boxes, a day. The lunch boxes used to be stackable metal containers, but now most often are insulated soft-sided lunch bags.

While reliance on *dabba* has diminished with the advent of fast-food restaurants and feminism, there are still about 160,000 home-cooked lunches delivered every day in Mumbai—and only one is misdelivered every two months, or just one in six million! This led *Forbes* magazine to award the dabbawalas (who have a union) a "6 Sigma" performance rating, a term used in quality assurance if the percentage of correctness is 99.9999999 or more.

Part of the secret to success of the "tiffin wallahs" is their system of color coding used on the top of each tiffin box. The home address, office address, railway stations of delivery and pickup are all crunched into a small series of letters and numbers, painted by hand. Almost all of the *dabbawalas* come from the same village of Pune outside of Mumbai—and some are fourth-generation dabbawalas.

Tiffin wallah (aka dabbawalla*) with deliveries*

What a dust have I rais'd! quoth the fly upon the coach.
—THOMAS FULLER, ENGLISH WRITER AND PHYSICIAN, *GNOMOLOGIA*, 1732

Come to Dust

SOMETIMES STEREOTYPICAL images of a particular job have a basis in historical fact. When you hear the words "chimney sweep," you probably think either of a small, soot-faced boy, Dick Van Dyke in a top hat in *Mary Poppins,* or both—and neither is entirely wrong. Early chimney sweeps were, sadly, often little boys who could fit into the chimney cavities and brush out accumulated soot. Accidents, illness, and abuse at the hands of "master sweeps" were sadly common for these children.

The age of sweeps changed in the 18th century when Joseph Glass of Bristol invented the cane-and-brush contraption that is still in use today (along with the Continental ball-brush-and-rope system), but unfortunately it took until 1840 for it to become illegal to employ anyone under the age of 21 as a chimney sweep.

Once "sweeps" became older, they also became more of a brotherhood and began to affect similar costumes and habits. They were often seen (and photographed, once that technology was available) wearing gentleman's top hats and frock coats, because they accepted cast-off clothing from undertakers—very practical, because it was all black. Their offbeat combination of formal attire and smudged cheeks might have been part of the reason that seeing a chimney sweep on your wedding day became a harbinger of luck.

However, some things never change. Lewis Carroll once wrote a line of verse: "Golden lads and girls all must / Like chimney sweepers come to dust." Chimney sweeping remains a dirty job, and chimneys still need to be swept, but today chimney cleaning is considered a trained profession, and the people who do it need to know not just how to remove soot but also how chimneys work, are built, and can be repaired.

Chimney sweeps still use forms of these tools.

A good lifeguard will mostly stay dry,
if using prevention.
—ANN LAWTON

Coast Guards

VISITORS TO SYDNEY, AUSTRALIA, rarely pass up a chance to spend some time on Bondi Beach, the Malibu of down under (most Aussies would prefer to say that Malibu is the Bondi of the United States!). The beautiful beach is, despite its sometimes placid appearance, home to some of the most vicious riptides known to humans—so it's a good thing it's also home to the Bondi Beach Lifeguards and Lifesavers.

Both of these groups—one professional, one volunteer—developed as sea bathing became more and more popular in the late 19th and early 20th centuries. The Bondi Surf Bathers' Life Saving Club was formed in 1907, the world's first, and its red-and-yellow quartered caps with chin ties are still worn today. Swimmers could venture into the waters knowing that there was literally someone watching their backs.

The "Black Sunday" tragedy of 1938 at Bondi Beach reinforced the need for lifesavers: Three freak waves overwhelmed the beach, and hundreds of people who had been lounging were swept away. The lifesavers rescued 300 of them.

Today the all-volunteer Lifesavers are joined by the Bondi Beach Lifeguards, a group of 35 professional lifeguards who patrol the beach 365 days a year and are known familiarly as "The Boys in Blue" due to their pale-blue-and-black shirts and swimsuits.

Australian lifeguards vigilantly patrol the surf at Bondi Beach in Sydney.

NEGOTIATION

NEGOTIATION IS THE BASIS OF COUNTLESS PERSONAL INTERACTIONS and a large part of topics covered elsewhere in this book, like diplomacy. But negotiation assumes a different tone when money is involved. Even though many of today's business negotiations involve parties who have full stomachs and well-padded wallets, all negotiations trace their lineage back to two early humans arguing over who would get the most food.

From a Harvard Business School video study of negotiation styles of 15 different affluent cultures, it seems some of those early arguments must have been quite interesting. Overall, the study found that the Japanese were most polite, the northern Chinese asked the most questions, the Israelis interrupted one another frequently, and the Brazilians were most aggressive. None of this information was collected in order to discover or reinforce any kinds of stereotypes, and it is not shared here for that purpose, either—instead, it shows how many gaps there are to be overcome in bridging communication styles to conduct successful negotiations in a modern world that has become increasingly interdependent.

The truth doesn't sell. It is high in supply, but low in demand.

—ERIC SCHAUB

Not only are different cultures different in terms of bargaining-table behaviors: They're also different in the things that they find most important, the things that motivate them. For example, everyone knows that U.S. citizens value time above everything else, and are always interested in moving on to the next thing, so many international businesspeople will make "the Americans" wait when engaged in important transactions. Meanwhile, in societies like China, the Philippines, and Mexico, where nepotistic relationships are quite common, the motivation to save face and family honor is quite high. Everyone wants to win, but what winning means changes from country to country, and it shouldn't be assumed that everyone considers success to be the same thing.

Money can't buy love,
but it improves your bargaining position.
—CHRISTOPHER MARLOWE, ENGLISH DRAMATIST, 1564-1593

Bargain Hunting

THE VERB "TO HAGGLE" IS SO OFTEN used in tandem with "bazaar" and "souk" that native English speakers might believe it is an Eastern word. Not so: "Haggle" derives from the Middle English *haggen,* which in turn derives from the Old Norse *hoeggva.* Haggen meant to chop or hack, and over time as people began to dispute exchanges, they began referring to "chopping" a price (hence the name of a popular U.S. supermarket chain, Price Chopper). "Haggling" came to have a specific meaning, that of arguing over an item's cost. In other words (pun intended), haggling, or bargaining over the price of goods, is not something unique to the East.

That has to be said, because Westerners who visit souks in Morocco and other countries often are shocked by all of the negotiating going on there. It's true that in modern American and European life, few prices can be changed—and often when they are up for negotiation, as for new automobiles, that is not much to the customer's advantage. But markets that allow bargaining exist not just in Morocco, but in Syria, China, Thailand, Egypt, and Turkey. In many markets, prices of items from bags of spices to carpets to machinery can be changed, depending on factors from supplies, to amount purchased, to weather, and so on.

Preparing to haggle at a Moroccan souk

Haggling can be an intimidating process, especially if you are visiting a country where you don't speak the language, and merchants know this. The most important thing to remember is that the first price quoted is never, ever, the expected end price. Travel experts will tell you that your counteroffer to the first price should always be less than half; usually 66 percent less than what the seller wants. From there, the two of you can go back and forth until you're both satisfied with the price—and even if the seller acts angry and disappointed, if he or she accepts that price, it's fine. But let the buyer beware: Never agree to a price you're not willing to pay, or try to back out of a purchase once the price has been set. Both will lead not to haggling, but to real argument.

Do what you can, with what you have, where you are.
—THEODORE ROOSEVELT

Final Offer

ONE OF THE BASIC TENETS of business in the West is "Always be ready to walk away." If you know you will survive without winning a contract or a position or an argument, then you can proceed from a place of greater honesty and strength. Right?

Wrong. At least when it comes to business negotiations in Russia. Russian business etiquette is, at least currently, a mix of northern European love of bureaucracy and organization and southern European love of discussion and collaboration, which is fitting considering its geographic range.

Russians take negotiations very seriously, and are often put off by the less-formal tone that U.S. business partners use, preferring punctuality, set goals, and compliance—in keeping with the northern European side of things. On the other hand, Russians are quick to look for leeway in contractual arrangements, in keeping with their southern European side. This means that although the Russians like set goals, they don't like fixed contracts—and they may turn the process of negotiating a contract into something quite long and drawn out.

Unfortunately, signing on the dotted line isn't the end of things for Russian businesspeople. They often continue to press for a better deal even after copies have been made and distributed—and if that tactic doesn't work, they may even ignore some of the contract's term. This isn't merely a bullying maneuver, although it may certainly seem like that. It's because Russians base their negotiations on trust, and believe that if they trust someone, that person will agree to their demands.

Although this may not make negotiating with Russian counterparts easier, it might make it more understandable. Knowing that no offer is final means that you might want to think differently about the contents of an agreement.

St. Basil's Cathedral towers over Moscow.

I have noticed that people who are late are often so much jollier than the people who have to wait for them.
—E. V. LUCAS, ENGLISH ESSAYIST AND WRITER

Late for Dinner

ONE OF THE MOST FRUSTRATING things about doing business in Spain for North Americans and British people is that meetings can go on and on. And on. There are several reasons for this, all of which can make a big difference in successful negotiations with Spaniards.

The first is that the business day is considerably different in Spain from the business day

Waiting for dinner companions in Spanish hotel

in North America or northern Europe; the midday siesta affects not just business hours, but also people's staying power. Spanish colleagues who actually take a rest after lunch may not feel as fatigued as their counterparts who keep to an 8-to-5 or similar schedule.

Second, for most Spanish people, meetings are not about making decisions, but rather about discussion and information gathering. In other words, the slow pace has nothing to do with the stereotype of a *mañana* attitude, and everything to do with caution—something that is quite understandable given the country's turbulent history of the past century. (The civil war of 1936-39 tore the country apart and it only made the transition to democracy after the death of longtime dictator Francisco Franco in 1975.)

The third factor in long Spanish meetings has to do with interpersonal style. The Spanish generally prefer to do business with people they know well, and if there are few chances for lunches, dinners, and other social occasions, meetings can be drawn out so that the Spanish tea feels more comfortable with new colleagues. Easy personal interaction and "chemistry" can be more important than expertise, in some situations. While dinner outings can take place extremely late relative to a typical North American evening meal (even a 10 p.m. start is common), these meals are actually an opportunity to become better acquainted with Spanish counterparts and ultimately shorten the daytime "business" meetings.

*Dinner was made for eating,
not for talking.*
—WILLIAM THACKERAY

Dinner, Interrupted

IF YOU'VE EVER WATCHED a French film with a dinner-party scene, you'll probably remember that the conversation was quick, lively, and intense.

The difference is that the French—whose conversational style is always rapid—don't change just because they're engaged in business or other types of negotiations. Although formal and polite, the French will be direct and probing, asking lots of questions. The French treat business discussions like intellectual exercises, making arguments from a position of logic and analysis.

This means anyone engaged in business discussions with the French will be judged on her ability to demonstrate her intellect, and that includes debate, sometimes of confrontational ideas. For North Americans accustomed to being judged on their ideas, rather than on their ability to defend their ideas, this may be

Lively French dinners like this one can be noisy.

difficult—especially because the French will continue to use a rapid-fire delivery to defend their own ideas, including lots and lots of interruptions. Both men and women at different levels of seniority may jump in and ask questions or contradict someone.

North Americans are usually taught not to interrupt. Allowing the person speaking to finish his sentence and complete a thought is very good manners. Not only are French interruptions jarring to this sensibility, the focus can change in the middle of an argument. While the French find such digressions productive, if a visitor's usual way of negotiating is more linear, this can be confusing.

STAFF

TODAY WE TALK OF "EMPLOYMENT" AND CONSIDER all able-bodied adults to be free to pursue . . . working for someone else. Of course, self-employment has grown in popularity during the new-media boom of the late 20th and early 21st centuries, but eventually many self-employed entrepreneurs are successful enough to hire their own employees.

People didn't always have options in choosing for whom they would work. When a baby was born, everyone knew whether or not that baby would grow up to be a king, a philosopher, or a peasant, based on where it was born, who its parents were, and what resources were available. Very few people had any choice at all about their future work or for whom it would be done. Most farmed, and lived by family hierarchies. The farms were controlled by a thane or vassal, who collected products and gave "the cream of the crop" to a local noble, who in turn paid a tribute to the nearest royal. Eventually, some people became artisans, others developed professions, and still others remained farmers. Those were the lucky ones: Less fortunate people became slaves with no personal freedoms whatsoever.

> *The secret of life is honesty and fair dealing. If you can fake that, you've got it made.*
>
> —GROUCHO MARX

It has taken a long time for the modern system of choosing a profession to develop, and it's not a surprise to learn that there were many bumps along the road to fair working conditions and just compensation. It's also no surprise that there have been many misunderstandings about common courtesy and manners in the workplace over the years, because many organizations involve employees at different levels with different sets of skills and different backgrounds.

The finest clothing made is a person's skin, but,
of course, society demands something more than this.
—MARK TWAIN

Code and Tie

THAT GAILY PATTERNED TIE—yes, the one with the martini glasses and crossed golf clubs—that you just wrapped up for Father's Day has ancient and far-off roots. Men's ties aren't simply a bit of sartorial splendor, meant to add color to otherwise drab business suits. They are badges of honor that once denoted status and membership (to more than the nearest country club).

Neckerchiefs first became popular during the 17th-century Thirty Years War, when Croatian mercenaries sported small red knotted scarves. Their name for themselves, *Hrvati,* combined with the French name, *Croates,* to result in a new name for the scarves: "cravats." These soft, folded neck coverings still exist for some dapper gentlemen, and also morphed into narrow stocks, bowed solitaires, and wide-flapped ascots.

However, the modern necktie developed and has lasted because of practical reasons. As the Industrial Revolution took hold in Europe, men (or at least the women dressing them) who

The cravat has ties to Croatia.

were heading to offices and meetings could not spend too much time on pleating and folding (let alone laundering and ironing) found that a one-piece length of fabric worn looped and knotted was the simplest way to finish off their costumes. Different knots (the Windsor, the four-in-hand, etc.) add distinction—but it's the different fabrics that really allow tie wearers to signal things to the public. British regimental and school ties, with stripes running from left shoulder to right hip, were supposed to be purchased and worn only by members of particular units and graduates of the "right" schools.

And therefore never send to know for
whom the bell tolls; it tolls for thee.
—JOHN DONNE, ENGLISH POET, 1572-1631

You Rang?

MOVIES AND TELEVISION SHOWS that feature Victorian and Edwardian manor houses with full complements of servants often "show" the system of bells, pulls, and buzzers that could summon the correct staff member as needed. Bell pulls, often elaborate needlepoint tapestry creations, hung in morning rooms and libraries, while dining rooms often had a small handbell or discreet buzzer built below the surface of the table.

How historical! How fascinating! Thank goodness no one does that any more . . .

Wait. Even people in lowly positions are not expected to jump to anyone's call around the

Utilitarian servants' bell

A lady summons with a bell pull.

clock (except, perhaps, for new parents) but if we think we're free from being summoned, all we have to remember is the telephone.

Put aside the telephone's uses for speaking with loved ones and getting help in emergencies. At the office, the telephone—and email, and instant messaging, and any other forms of intra-staff communication—is the summoning bell. Think about it: When your boss calls, do you dawdle, or do you pick up the receiver smartly? Whose emails do you answer first? When it comes right down to it, we respond to the summons . . .

ARCHAIC MANNERS: Maid's Quarters When homes had live-in staff, the "maid's quarters" could be anything from a cupboard beneath the stairs to an upstairs garret—but these quarters would certainly be smaller, plainer, and less plush than anything the owners of the house occupied, designed for a single female employee. Today homes that are built with an area for a staff member usually have a spacious bedroom with an en suite bath.

Oh dear, what a pity.
Nannies are so hard to come by these days.
—ANONYMOUS, THE SUNDAY LONDON *TIMES* MAGAZINE, 8 JUNE, 1975

Super Nannies

THE MOST SOUGHT-AFTER NANNIES, graduates of England's prestigious Norland College, wear distinctive full-length wool coats, felt monogrammed hats, and white gloves.

"Norland Nannies" (the College prefers "Norland Nurses") have been trained for positions with the finest families (or at least wealthiest, because these nannies command good salaries) since 1892. Emily Ward, the Victorian child care expert who founded the school based on some of Friedrich Froebel's principles of early-childhood development, not only wanted her students placed with the best families—she wanted those families to know that her students were the best: "Put a silver-backed hairbrush on your dressing table when you arrive, that way you won't be taken for one of the servants."

Only 40 graduate each year, and each immediately has her pick of positions on yachts, at large country homes, and in exotic places. The College's early and long-held commitment to standards demonstrates true professionalism. Students learn every aspect of child care, including cooking from scratch, sewing simple toys, and even how to drive on black ice. They wear that above-mentioned uniform, which includes exceedingly dowdy brown lace-up shoes, plain ear studs, and minimal makeup.

Norland Nannies in their distinctive uniforms

Coffee, which makes the Politician wise,
And see through all things with his half-shut eyes.
—ALEXANDER POPE

A Real Estate

WE OFTEN FORGET ABOUT the origins of things quite basic to our lives. A good example: Coffee. It isn't a wild plant any more; it has to be carefully cultivated to provide the millions of bags of beans that can be found around the world at any given time. Those beans are grown on what is commonly known in other countries as a "plantation."

Since the end of the Civil War and the abolition of slavery in the United States, the term

Coffee plantation in El Salvador

"plantation" has connoted a past lifestyle with no relevance to the modern age.

However, in other parts of the world, the word "plantation" is less loaded. Many large-scale agricultural operations in South America, Africa, India, and Australia are considered "plantations" in the word's original sense of being a place where a crop is planted and maintained. These estates—tracts of land—are not staffed by slaves, but they are usually run by a "plantation manager" who oversees everything from crop yields to human-resource issues to climatology.

This isn't to say that wrongs, excesses, and injustices never happen on modern plantations, but it is to explain that there is no slight to American politics involved if a South African friend mentions that he's just taken a new job as a coffee plantation manager.

COLLEAGUES

Anyone who has ever spent a long morning in the office listening to the person in the next cubicle over snapping her gum, whining to his mother on the phone, or slurping his coffee knows that one's colleagues greatly affect the quality of one's work life. However, to the snappers, whiners, and slurpers out there, we'd all just like to say, "Mind your manners, please!"

Unfortunately, direct confrontation can have dire consequences in an office environment, especially in close quarters (see "space rage" in Chapter Seven). Letter after letter has been written to and published by advice columnists over the years about how to convince a coworker to bathe, discourage a colleague from malicious gossip, or retaliate against the guy from the mailroom who keeps calling you "honey." If you read that last sentence and thought "*Hmmmm*, are those about good manners, or are those matters for Human Resources?" then you have hit the reason why those advice columnists get so many letters of this ilk: No one is exactly sure where to draw the line between common courtesy and litigation when daily work is involved.

Naturally, because few of us actually leave our personal lives at the door, there are all sorts of pitfalls that have to be negotiated even when our fellow officemates are as quiet as mice. Sexual, religious, political, and economic overtones can cause miscommunications and bruised feelings—and that's without any of the actual work being accomplished. Also, even when we do succeed in keeping our home life outside of the office, when you spend all day every day with the same group of people, office life starts to look uncannily like family life—and family life has its own separate set of customs, manners, and quirks.

> *Perfect freedom is as necessary to the health and vigor of commerce as it is to the health and vigor of citizenship.*
>
> —PATRICK HENRY

*Women are the only oppressed group in our society
that lives in intimate association with their oppressors.*
—EVELYN CUNNINGHAM, AMERICAN JOURNALIST, 1916–2010

Woman's Work

THE JAPANESE "SALARYMAN," with his determined loyalty, excessive stress, and after-work drinking habits, has been depicted—or really, caricatured—in numerous media, but his female counterpart, the "office lady," or "OL," is less well known. The OL (pronounced "o-eru") is a fixture of almost every Japanese office; in fact, another term for OLs is *shokuba no hana,* or "office flower."

Being an "office flower" is really the OL's function. Generally between the ages of 18 and 30, an OL typically lives at home with her parents and is unmarried (more on that in a moment). Thousands of young OLs flood Tokyo's trains early in the morning, because they usually commute in about an hour. They try to arrive at their offices before the salarymen-types (some of whom, today, are women) get there in order to prepare for the day. Regardless of the OL's own personal clothing style preferences, once at the office she will change into conservative attire—often a navy blue skirt and vest with a white blouse, although as long as the outfit is a dress or skirt and fairly demure other types are acceptable, too.

The OL's main job is to be pleasant and to bring tea or other soft drinks as required to meetings. That's it! Some OLs do a small amount of paper pushing, but their real function is to help maintain an overall positive tone. While OLs can and do remain in the same office for several years, once a young woman reaches 25 or so, her boss and colleagues will begin discreetly hinting that it is time for her to get married, and even going so far as to set her up with someone else on staff or with a matchmaker if things do not seem to be progressing. An old-fashioned Japanese slang term for an unmarried woman of 26 was "Christmas cake" because the cake was considered stale and unwanted once Christmas was past. However, following an equal employment opportunity law enacted in the late 1980s, more and more Japanese women are pursuing careers and delaying or foregoing marriage altogether. According to the *Wall Street Journal,* Japanese government data show that about one third of women ages 30-34 remain unmarried compared to only 8 percent in the mid-1970s.

A part of this strangeness of dress is that it links the biological body to the social being, and public to private.
—ELIZABETH WILSON, AMERICAN ACTRESS

No Veiled References

THERE ARE DIFFERENT WORDS for women's quarters depending on which part of the Arab and Middle Eastern world in which you're traveling. Harem, zenana, seraglio. Most of the words' roots refer to keeping something safe, and due both to cultural practices and Islamic religious beliefs, many people in these regions feel that it is important to keep women—including girls, and sometimes even young children of either sex—safe from prying eyes.

These are all secluded places for women. The number of women who use them and the degree of seclusion provided depend on many factors. Men, especially those from outside the family, rarely enter into these quarters. Instead, women gather for socializing and domestic tasks, including cooking, laundry, and child rearing. The secluded nature of the space also allows its inhabitants the freedom to chat and laugh freely, without fear of harsh restrictions.

Because special hidden living spaces for women have existed for hundreds of years in the Middle East, even today when some countries no longer legally segregate female members of the household, some customs surrounding their previous status stick. Of course, in countries like Saudi Arabia and Iran, women are still legally obligated to wear heavy, all-covering

Veiled mother cradles her child in Afghanistan.

veils out in public—and their secluded quarters still exist, too.

Therefore, it's easy to see why people conducting business in this region are advised not to ask after a Middle Eastern colleague's family, especially his wife and daughters. Men with traditional views might be offended, especially if one of them thinks that he is being interrogated (e.g., how many wives he has). Even if the colleague holds more Western-style beliefs about religion and gender politics, he will have been used to a society in which talk of family is considered private and off-limits to outsiders. The safest thing is to say nothing about family.

OBJECTS OF ETIQUETTE: Velvet Ropes   Are they designed to keep people out, or to keep others in? Sometimes "velvet ropes," usually sectioned for easy reconfiguration, are all about keeping order. They're used to form orderly lines in cinemas, theaters, and department stores so that those who arrive early hold on to their advantage.

I'd rather see America save her soul than her face.
—NORMAN MATTOON THOMAS

Saving Face

THERE'S BEEN A penchant for Scandinavian mystery novels among the reading public in the past few years, and if you've ever picked up a thriller by a Swedish author, you know that our northern neighbors are more than a little stoic in the face of adversity. Detectives, nosy neighbors, and quirky young scofflaws—they're all portrayed as being mostly calm and unruffled by the bloodiest of crime scenes and the nastiest of courtroom battles.

Truth is said to be stranger than fiction, but in the case of Swedish demeanor, the two are pretty much aligned: People all over the country maintain the same poker-faced reserve whether greeting the mail carrier, shopping, or in the office. Although Sweden is one of the most egalitarian societies on earth, with a workplace made up of 48 percent women and a corporate style that might be considered

Malmö, Sweden's "Turning Torso" skyscraper

more collaborative than adversarial, most Swedish people are still formal enough to believe that in group situations members of a company should remain unemotional.

Of course, just because they don't show emotions in group settings doesn't mean that Swedes have none. Far from it (as anyone who has engaged in Swedish parties or festivals can attest)! An unofficial rule of Swedish professional culture is that employees maintain decorum with superiors and subordinates, but are allowed to "let down their hair" with peers. One of the important courtesies this underscores is the Scandinavian dislike of boasting or putting oneself forward in an unseemly way. By complaining to and discussing office politics only with people on a similar level, there is less chance of unmannerly conflict.

FAMOUS GAFFES: Alain Levy In March 2003, music company EMI's chief executive Alain Levy said that he had cut the artist roster in Finland down from 49 artists, as he didn't think there were that many people in the country "who could sing." When his local executive pointed out that up to that point, EMI had commanded a 20-percent share of the local market, everyone feared Levy had "done a Ratner": A British phrase referring to a speech executive Gerald Ratner made, which almost ruined his company.

A cake, long in shape but short in duration,
with cream filling and (usually) chocolate icing.
—ANONYMOUS, *THE CHAMBERS DICTIONARY*, 1993

Cake for All

As we've noted elsewhere, offices all over the world tend to function a bit like substitute families. People spend six to ten hours a day at full-time jobs, and that can wind up being more time than they are able to spend at home with their real family members. Within offices, coworkers' interactions can mimic family dynamics, for good and bad. "Siblings" squabble over drawer space, "office spouses" seethe with resentment over missed lunch dates, and everyone vies for parental (i.e., the boss's) favor.

Celebrations can be particularly tricky (no wonder the sniping between members of the Dunder Mifflin Party Planning Committee on NBC-TV's popular sitcom *The Office* makes us laugh so hard), because everyone wants the attention that comes with them, but very few people can be bothered to take the steps needed to make them happen. Of course, in a very small outfit with just a few employees, making sure each person's birthday is observed can be fairly painless.

The obligatory office birthday party

However, for organizations with several dozen or more members or for divisions of larger companies, things can get trickier. Remembering to tote in a cake and its accoutrements (plates, napkins, forks, etc.) is bad enough, but what if there are ten birthdays in April but none again until July? A popular solution in U.S. offices is to celebrate all the birthdays that fall in a particular month on a single day. Everyone gathers, "Happy Birthday" has to be sung only once, and everyone gets a slice of cake. Maintaining the birthday list often falls to an executive assistant who may then have to deal with occasional requests from highly sensitive people to ignore their birthdays. While most adults recognize the date as an occasion to let themselves and others enjoy a celebration, some people entertain the notion that a birthday is their private secret. It may be their prerogative, but why deprive colleagues of a little cake?

MANNERED LIVES

Judith Martin, AKA Miss Manners

Judith Martin writes as "Miss Manners," and with that nom de plume and her trademark upswept hairdo, you might think she's all shtick. Hardly. Mrs. Martin, who was born and bred in Washington, D.C., and educated at Wellesley College, is exactly as advertised: A properly raised gentlewoman whose personal decorum matches her public persona.

Martin worked at the *Washington Post* for many years as a journalist covering the capital's

Judith Martin: arbiter of American manners since 1978

social scene as well being the drama and film critic. In 1978 she began writing a column called "Miss Manners"—which quickly gained syndication around the country—advocating a return to civility after the late 1960s and 1970s in which traditional mores had been challenged.

Readers responded in droves to Martin's new column, asking everything from which fork to use for salad to how to handle romances, workplace dilemmas, and even hospital etiquette. She handled every answer with both aplomb and wit, her humor leavening her solutions. No wonder her colleague George F. Will calls her "The National Bureau of Standards."

Martin has not slacked off in the 21st century; as its first decade drew to a close, she had just published her first title, coauthored with her newlywed daughter Jacobina Martin, about negotiating the minefield of modern weddings. Now that both of her married children (the Martins also have a son) have become parents, Martin does not rule out the possibility of their writing a book about child rearing—in which she may have a say as grandmother, of course.

COMPETITORS

DEPENDING ON HOW YOU LOOK AT THINGS, we start competing the moment we are born. Of course, at that time we're not necessarily competing with others, but we're working to get attention so we can breathe, eat, and be cared for in all of the ways that we humans, with our prolonged infancies and childhoods, need. Each human baby requires a certain amount of air, water, food, and space. Given the reality that there's only a certain amount of air, water, food, and space overall, then it's really no wonder we're competitive!

By the time we're old enough to engage in currency-driven trade and commerce, we know that competition exists in realms beyond those of our basic needs. Just because you have enough to eat doesn't mean that you wouldn't like more or more-refined foods; just because you have enough money to survive—or even to thrive—doesn't mean

The business of America is not business. Neither is it war. The business of America is justice and securing the blessings of liberty.

—GEORGE F. WILL

you don't want more. There's no way to predict human material desires, and even if there were, doing business isn't just about making money; as we've seen in previous parts of this book, winning at the bargaining table can have as much to do with honor, family survival, and satisfaction as it does with the bottom line.

Competition has both less and more in common with courtesy than any other topic in this book: Less, because as they say, "All's fair in love and war"; more, because as we all know, in modern business your opponents usually live to fight another day. Might as well acknowledge that everyone wants to come out on top and be as considerate and scrupulous as possible while battling your way there.

People being vulgar and rude to one another
in contrived stressful situations is TV's bread and butter.
—LYNNE TRUSS, *TALK TO THE HAND*

Round of Applause

BABIES TEND TO CLAP THEIR HANDS together spontaneously, often when they're excited about something. Perhaps that's the earliest impetus for what we now call applause.

We know that ancient Romans had many ways of expressing group kudos, including snapping fingers, tapping fingers into a hollowed palm, and waving the ends of togas. They also had applause "ringers," who would respond on cue to calls of *"Valete et plaudite!"* (Praise and acclamations!), very much like the person who holds up "Applause" signs in TV studios today. The Roman custom was taken up in Europe, specifically by the French, who called groups of professional applause makers "claques."

People applaud for all sorts of occasions now—even in church, where applause for a musical performance such as a solo hymn was once viewed as too much attention focused on the human instead of the divine. The one place where modern people tend not to applaud is between movements of instrumental musical pieces in a live performance, a tradition that seems to date from composer Richard Wagner's day, when his works were premiered in Germany, and the "Bayreuth hush" would descend upon spectators.

Since applause is quite common, it shouldn't strike Westerners as particularly odd that their Chinese colleagues will often open a meeting—particularly a large conference—with a round of applause. No one has done anything yet, true; but the Chinese believe it courteous to acknowledge that everyone has arrived and is ready to begin.

FAMOUS GAFFES: Burden of privilege   President George W. Bush said in a 2001 radio address, "In the long run, the right answer to unemployment is to create more jobs." The unconscious obviousness of this statement was not the first time President "43" (his father, former President George H. W. Bush, is referred to in the family as "41") had had a slip of the lip and angered many Americans struggling with joblessness and an economic downturn.

Punctuality is the virtue of the bored.
—EVELYN WAUGH

The Waiting Game

EVERY CULTURE HAS different ways of dealing with time and punctuality, and every culture has different ways of dealing with "the competition." Sometimes the two are combined.

Life in Indonesia is vastly different from life in the industrialized West. The nation is made up of literally thousands of islands, which means that there is often the need to travel over water for even routine errands. It is also the world's fourth most populous country, so there are millions of people waiting to run those errands. Indonesia is also the most wholly Muslim nation, with about 88 percent of people there adhering devoutly to that religion's creed, requiring them to pray five times daily along with special pre- and post-prayer cleansing rituals. Since many Indonesians live quite simply—without electricity, running water, and other conveniences—sometimes they have to be patient.

No wonder this culture has a concept called *jam karet,* or "rubber time," indicating that time is elastic rather than fixed. What does this mean for people trying to accomplish business dealings with

Elaborate wayang golek *rod puppet from Indonesia*

An Indonesian shadow puppet made of leather

Indonesians? Meetings will always begin late. However, just because your counterparts in Jakarta don't show up or start the meeting on time doesn't mean that you have the same leeway: Westerners are supposed to be punctual and patient regardless of how many minutes tick by in the boardroom.

Yes, this can be seen as a power play—but it's more than that. It's also a tactic based on the Indonesian overall mindset, in which negotiations are based on building relationships and not on determining outcomes. Business relationships build over time. This is one "waiting game" that can pay off in the long run.

*Winning is everything. The only ones who remember
when you come second are your wife and your dog.*
—DAMON HILL, BRITISH RACING DRIVER

Going for the Win

SOMETIMES RESIDENTS OF Cape Town, South Africa, refer to their burg as "the Mother City" because they like to joke that it takes nine months for anything to get done there. All levity aside, South Africans tend to be very laid-back in their commercial dealings. While this might partly be due to the tranquility of their beautiful location, it's also due to intense political and cultural change over the past few decades. Once segregated by rigidly enforced apartheid policies, South Africa has emerged from its once-divided past as a multicultural "Rainbow Nation" with a population equally entitled in the eyes of the law, and one that is diverse not just racially, but ethnically, culturally, and socially, as well.

Even if you know very little about South Africa, you may have seen the popular 2009 film *Invictus* starring Morgan Freeman and Matt Damon, who portray South African President Nelson Mandela and captain of the Johannesburg Springbokke rugby team François Pienaar respectively. The movie tells the story of how Mandela (called "Madiba," his clan name, by people of color in South Africa) urged Pienaar to coach his team to a victory at the Rugby World Championships in 1995. The way in which Mandela did that is an excellent example of the South African predilection for "win-win" outcomes in business.

Basically, the cheerfully persistent Mandela refused to take "no" for an answer from anyone, believing that true racial equality would benefit all of his countrymen—not just those with dark complexions. His can-do spirit has filtered down to all levels of government and trade in his country: In negotiations, South Africans now take their time (although hopefully not nine months!) and come to a final decision slowly, attempting to ensure that all parties will be satisfied.

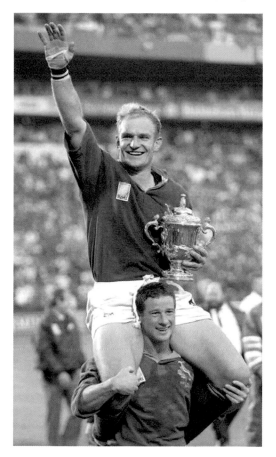

François Pienaar with rugby's World Cup trophy

*A bank is a place that will lend you money
if you can prove that you don't need it.*
—BOB HOPE

A Good Account

MANY PEOPLE AROUND the world make jokes about how things are rather disorganized in Italian culture and business, but the old saw about how it took a dictator to make the trains run on time neglects the important role Italy has played in developing the way we all do business in the 21st century.

That doesn't mean that Italians developed all of these important business innovations in the 20th century—far from it! The Italians have had a long history and a very long time to develop aspects of their food, culture, and business practices. For example, Italy played a significant role in refining the world's banking system. They didn't invent banking, which actually dates back thousands of years to ancient Assyria and can be found mentioned in the Code of Hammurabi, but they did initiate the first international banking exchange in Genoa in 1156. Late in the 13th century, Italian banking progressed further, as the powerful de Medici family helped to found the first product- and industry-specific banks, which are now considered forerunners of today's credit unions.

Cosimo the Elder founded the Medici dynasty.

Another Italian contribution to the world of business that continues to make a difference in the modern marketplace is the now seemingly simple concept of double-entry bookkeeping. In this type of bookkeeping, an accountant maintains two columns of figures, one for debit (Latin for "he owes") and one for credit (Latin for "he trusts"). This allows merchants to double-check their transactions: If at any point the sum of debits does not equal the corresponding sum of credits, an error has occurred. It follows that in order to tally correctly, the sum of debits and credits should be zero.

Obviously, the Italian culture had a great role to play in the Western development of "money economies," or those that are set up to exchange currency instead of bartering valued items or commodities for services. Another pivotal development that enabled this type of economy to not only stay afloat but also to thrive was the system of insurance that began to evolve in late 14th-century Genoa just as banks were growing. When it comes right down to it, the Italians really know how to do business.

Acknowledgments

All books are collaborations, a fact I am even more aware of
since this is my first as sole author.
My thanks are due:

To the manners mavens who have inspired me since childhood,
including Emily Post, Amy Vanderbilt, and Judith Martin.

To the National Geographic Society, whose publications
encouraged me to look at how people around the world conduct themselves.

To the people at the National Geographic Society whose ideas and encouragement made
this book and its predecessor possible, including Barbara Brownell-Grogan, Susan Tyler Hitchcock,
Lisa Thomas, Marianne Koszorus, Meredith Wilcox, Sanaa Akkach, Linda Makarov, and many
others. Special thanks to my very smart and patient editor, Susan Straight, who shepherded the
process and provided feedback through multiple rounds of outline and manuscript.

To my indefatigable and savvy agent, Erin Cox.

To friends who have cheered me on through this book's writing, including Christine McCarthy,
Barbara Nordin, Laura Goldberg, Meredith Hindley, Melissa Klug, Julie Klam, Erin McHugh, Joe
Wallace, Karen Palmer, Kara Sirmans, James and Cheryl Cricks, and Kamal and Laurie Beyoghlow.

To my family, especially my father and mother for their support, my daughters,
Claire and Eleanor, for their patience, and my husband, John, for his unwavering love.

Say Please & Thank You in Many Languages

	PRIMARY COUNTRY	SPEAKER POPULATION	TOTAL COUNTRIES
MANDARIN	China	840,000,000	31
SPANISH	Spain	329,000,000	44
ENGLISH	U.K., U.S.A	328,000,000	112
ARABIC	Saudi Arabia	221,000,000	57
HINDI	India	182,000,000	20
BENGALI	Bangladesh	181,000,000	10
PORTUGUESE	Portugal	178,000,000	37
RUSSIAN	Russian Federation	144,000,000	33
JAPANESE	Japan	122,000,000	25
GERMAN	Germany	90,300,000	43
LAHNDA (PANJABI)	Pakistan	78,300,000	8
TELUGU	India	69,800,000	10
VIETNAMESE	Vietnam	68,800,000	23
MARATHI	India	68,100,000	5
FRENCH	France	67,800,000	60
KOREAN	Korea, South	66,300,000	33
TAMIL	India	65,700,000	17
ITALIAN	Italy	60,600,000	34
URDU	Pakistan	60,600,000	23
TURKISH	Turkey	50,800,000	36

Being able to say "please" and "thank you" at the appropriate time in the local idiom can warm the hearts of strangers. That's because language is more than just rules of grammar and mechanics of pronunciation; it's a way to create a positive connection with other human beings.

The list below contains the words for "please" and "thank you" in selected languages from among the most commonly spoken languages in the world. In cases where the languages are written in non-Roman characters, we've included those characters as well as a phonetic version of the phrase in Roman letters. Most of these are the polite versions of the expressions for "please" and "thank you"; for colloquial expressions as well as for pronunciation, consult a language-specific dictionary or an online pronunciation guide.

Language name, country, and speakers used by permission, © SIL International, Ethnologue, 16th Edition, 2009.

PLEASE	CHARACTER(S)	THANK YOU	CHARACTER(S)
qǐng nǐ	請	xièxiè	謝謝
por favor	-	gracias	-
please	-	thank you	-
min fadlak/lau samaht	من فضلك	shukran	شكرا
kri-paa ho-gee	कृपया	dhan-ya-vaad	धन्यवाद
pleez	দয়া করে	d'oh-noh-baad	ধন্যবাদ
por favor	-	obrigado	-
pazhalsta	Пожалуйста	spaseeba	Спасибо
kudasai	ください	arigato	ありがとう
bitte	-	danke	-
kirpā karkē	ਕਿਰਪਾ ਕਰਕੇ	dhannavād	ਧਨਵਦ
santos-impinçu	దయచేసి	dhanyavaadaalu	ధన్యవాదాలు
làm ơn	-	cảm ơn	-
krupaya	कृपया	dhanyawad	धन्यवाद
s'il vous plaît	-	merci	-
chebal	제발	kamsahamnida	감사합니다
tayavuceytu	தயவுசெய்து	naṉṟi	நன்றி
per favore	-	grazie	-
meharbaanii	ی مہربان	shukriya	یہ شکر
lütfen	-	teşekkür ederim	-

	PRIMARY COUNTRY	SPEAKER POPULATION	TOTAL COUNTRIES
GUJARATI	India	46,500,000	20
POLISH	Poland	40,000,000	23
MALAY	Malaysia	39,100,000	14
UKRANIAN	Ukraine	37,000,000	27
MALAYALAM	India	35,900,000	11
KANNADA	India	35,300,000	3
PERSIAN	Iran	31,400,000	29
FILIPINO	Philippines	25,000,000	1
HAUSA	Nigeria	25,000,000	13
TAGALOG	Philippines	23,900,000	8
ROMANIAN	Romania	23,400,000	20
INDONESIAN	Indonesia	23,200,000	6
DUTCH	Netherlands	21,700,000	12
THAI	Thailand	20,400,000	5
PASHTO	Pakistan	20,300,000	9
UZBEK	Uzbekistan	20,300,000	14
AZERBAIJANI	Iran	19,100,000	17
IGBO	Nigeria	18,000,000	1
OROMO	Ethiopia	17,300,000	4
SERBO-CROATIAN	Serbia	16,400,000	28
KURDISH	Iraq	16,000,000	32
NEPALI	Nepal	13,900,000	5
SOMALI	Somalia	13,900,000	13
MALAGASY	Madagascar	7,500,000	4

PLEASE	CHARACTER(S)	THANK YOU	CHARACTER(S)
pleez	મહેરબ ની કરીને	aabhaar	આભ ૨
zadowalać	-	dziękuję	-
tolong, silahkan	-	terima kasih	-
bood laska	Будь ласка	duže diakuju	Дякую
dayavaayi	ಡಯವಾಯಿ	nanni	ನನ್ನಿ
dayavittu	ದಯವಿಟ್ಟು	t'ank-you	ಧನ್ಯವಾದ
lotfan	لطفا	motashakkeram	ممنون
1. paki 2. maki	-	salamat	-
bismillah	-	na gode	-
paki	-	salamat	-
rog	-	mulţumesc	-
persudikanlah	-	terima kasih	-
behagen	-	dank u	-
kawe	กรุณา	kawp khun	ขอบคุณ
mehrabani Wokray	ی مهربانی وک	manana	مننه
iltimos!	-	rahmat!	-
zähmät olmasa	-	täshäkkür ediräm	-
biko	-	ndalu	-
gammacciis	-	galatóm fat	-
zadovoljiti	-	hvala	-
memnûn bûm	-	spas/ teşekkür	-
kripaya	कृपया	dhanyabaad	ढन्यबाद्
i samah saheb	-	abalmari	-
azafady	-	misaotra (indrindra)	-

Manners Mavens: In Their Own Words

PTA-HOTEP
From *Teaching of Ptahotep*,
transliteration after Devaud 1916,
using Papyrus Prisse as principal source

Then he addressed his son:/Do not be proud on account of your knowledge,/but discuss with the ignorant as with the wise./The limits of art cannot be delivered;/there is no artist whose talent is fulfilled./Fine words are more sought after than greenstone,/but can be found with the women at the grindstone.

If you meet an opponent in his moment/A director of heart who is superior to you,/bend your arms and bow;/do not take up your heart against him,/for he will not be swayed for you. You can belittle bad speaking/by not clashing with him in his moment;/it will mean he is called a fool,/when your self-restraint has subdued his excess.

If you are a man at a sitting/at the table place of one greater than you,/take whatever he causes to be set before you,/do not stare at what is before him,/do not pierce it with many glances

Pressing it is an offence to the ka./Do not speak to him until he has requested:/you never know what may displease./Speak when he questions you,/and your speech will please./A great man, when he is at a meal,/behaviour following the command of his ka,/he will give to the one he favours,/that is the night-time behaviour that happens/only a fool complains about it.

CONFUCIUS
From *The Analects of Confucius*

XV.21: The Master said, "The superior man is dignified, but does not wrangle. He is sociable, but not partisan."

XVII.24: Tzu-kung asked, "Has the superior man his hatreds also?" The Master said, "He has his hatreds. He hates those who proclaim the evil of others. He hates the man who, being in a low station, slanders his superiors. He hates those who have valor merely, and are unobservant of propriety (*li*). He hates those who are forward and determined, and, at the same time, of contracted understanding."

XVI.10: Confucius said, "The superior man

has nine things which are subjects with him of thoughtful consideration. In regard to the use of his eyes, he is anxious to see clearly. In regard to the use of his ears, he is anxious to hear distinctly. In regard to his countenance, he is anxious that it should be benign. In regard to his speech, he is anxious that it should be sincere. In regard to his doing of business, he is anxious that it should be reverently careful. In regard to what he doubts about, he is anxious to question others. When he is angry, he thinks of the difficulties his anger may involve him in. When he sees gain to be got, he thinks of righteousness."

ERASMUS
From Erasmus, *The Manual of a Christian Knight*

Thou mayst compare therefore a man properly to a commonalty, where is debate and part taking among themselves. Which commonalty for as much as it is made of sundry kinds of men gathered together, which be of diverse and contrary appetites: it cannot be avoided but that much strife shall arise therein, and parts taken often times, unless the chief rule and authority be in one. And he himself be such a fellow that will command nothing but that which shall be wholesome and profitable for the commonwealth. And for that cause it must needs be that he which is most wise should most bear rule. And he needs must

obey that least perceiveth or understandeth ... Thou mayest account for the chief lords certain affections and them of the body: but yet not all things so beastly. Of the which kind is natural reverence toward the father and mother, love to thy brethren, a benevolent mind toward thy friends and lovers, compassion upon them that be vexed with adversity or cumbered with sickness, fear of infamy, Man is compared to a commonwealth or realm, where is king, lords and the common people. The king obeyeth the law only. Reason is king in a man.

JONATHAN SWIFT
From *Treatise on Good Manners and Good Breeding*

First, a necessary part of good manners, is a punctual observance of time at our own dwellings, or those of others, or at third places; whether upon matter of civility, business, or diversion; which rule, though it be a plain dictate of common reason, yet the greatest minister I ever knew was the greatest trespasser against it; by which all his business doubled upon him, and placed him in a continual arrear. Upon which I often used to rally him, as deficient in point of good manners. I have known more than one ambassador, and secretary of state with a very moderate portion of intellectuals, execute their offices with good success and applause, by the mere force of exactness and regularity . . . Ignorance of forms cannot properly be styled ill manners; because forms are subject to frequent changes; and consequently, being not founded upon reason, are beneath a wise man's regard. Besides, they vary in every country; and after a short period of time, very frequently in the same; so that a man who travels, must needs be at first a stranger to them in every court through which he passes; and perhaps at his return, as much a stranger in his own; and after all, they are easier to be remembered or forgotten than faces or names.

BENJAMIN FRANKLIN
From "Poor Richard's Almanack"

Having frequent occasions to hold councils, they have acquired great order and decency in conducting them. The old men sit in the foremost ranks, the warriors in the next, and the women and children in the hindmost. The business of the women is to take exact notice of what passes, imprint it in their memories (for they have no writing), and communicate it to their children. They are the records of the council, and they preserve the tradition of the stipulations in treaties a hundred years back; which, when we compare with our writings, we always find exact. He that would speak rises. The rest observe a profound silence. When he has finished and sits down, they leave him five or six minutes to recollect that if he has omitted anything he intended to say or has anything to add he may rise again and deliver it. To interrupt another, even in common conversation, is reckoned highly indecent. How different this is from the conduct of a polite British House of Commons, where scarce a day passes without some confusion, that makes the Speaker hoarse calling to order; and how different from the mode of conversation in many polite companies of Europe, where, if you do not deliver your sentence with great rapidity, you are cut off in the midd'e of it by the impatient loquacity of those you converse with and never suffered to finish it!

The politeness of these savages in conversation is indeed carried to excess, since it does not permit them to contradict or deny the truth of what is asserted in their presence. By this means they indeed avoid disputes; but then it becomes difficult to know their minds or what impression you make upon them. The missionaries who have attempted to convert them to Christianity all complain of this as one of the great difficulties of their mission. The Indians hear with patience the truths of the gospel explained to them, and give their usual tokens of assent and approbation. You would think they were convinced. No such matter. It is mere civility.

First, a necessary part of good manners, is a punctual observance of time at our own dwellings, or those of others, or at third places; whether upon matter of civility, business, or diversion; which rule, though it be a plain dictate of common reason, yet the greatest minister I ever knew was the greatest trespasser against it; by which all his business doubled upon him, and placed him in a continual arrear. Upon which I often used to rally him, as deficient in point of good manners. I have known more than one ambassador, and secretary of state with a very moderate portion of intellectuals, execute their offices with good success and applause, by the mere force of exactness and regularity . . . Ignorance of forms cannot properly be styled ill manners; because forms are subject to frequent changes; and consequently, being not founded upon reason, are beneath a wise man's regard. Besides, they vary in every country; and after a short period of time, very frequently in the same; so that a man who travels, must needs be at first a stranger to them in every court through which he passes; and perhaps at his return, as much a stranger in his own; and after all, they are easier to be remembered or forgotten than faces or names.

ISABELLA MARY BEETON
From *Mrs. Beeton's Book
of Household Management*

In conversation, trifling occurrences, such as small disappointments, petty annoyances, and other every-day incidents, should never be mentioned to your friends. The extreme injudiciousness of repeating these will be at once apparent, when we reflect on the unsatisfactory discussions which they too frequently occasion, and on the load of advice which they are the cause of being tendered, and which is, too often, of a kind neither to be useful nor agreeable. Greater events, whether of joy or sorrow, should be communicated to friends; and, on such occasions, their sympathy gratifies and comforts . . .

. . . we should store our memory with short anecdotes and entertaining pieces of history. Almost every one listens with eagerness to extemporary history. Vanity often co-operates with curiosity; for he that is a hearer in one place wishes to qualify himself to be a principal speaker in some inferior company; and therefore more attention is given to narrations than anything else in conversation. It is true, indeed, that sallies of wit and quick replies are very pleasing in conversation; but they frequently tend to raise envy in some of the company: but the narrative way neither raises this, nor any other evil passion, but keeps all the company nearly upon an equality, and, if judiciously managed, will at once entertain and improve them all.

**SAMUEL GOODRICH
(AKA PETER PARLEY)**
From *What to Do and How to Do It,
or Morals and Manners Taught by Example*

This is doing to others as we would have others do to us, in the familiar intercourse of life. Politeness is, therefore, not only a mark of refinement, of good breeding, but it is a duty. It consists in paying a deference to the feelings of others, in trifles; whether we eat or drink, or whatever we do, we should avoid coarseness, vulgarity, and everything in looks, movements, words and actions, that may offend those around us. We should adopt the best manners of the society in which we live; if certain rules, even supposing them to be arbitrary or artificial, are in force there, we are bound, as far as we understand them, to follow them whenever they are not wrong. There is no surer mark of a coarse and ill-regulated mind, than a refusal to observe the courtesies, civilities, and decent ceremonies of the society in which a person lives. All these are soon learned and there is no excuse for their neglect.

Politeness forbids rude words, rude looks, and everything that betokens a lack of respect to the company present; politeness would carry the gentle and kind spirit of christianity into all the intercourse of society.

FANNIE FARMER
From *The Boston Cooking-School Cook Book*

Before **Sweeping Old Carpets,** sprinkle with pieces of newspaper wrung out of water. After sweeping, wipe over with a cloth wrung out of a weak solution of ammonia water, which seems to brighten colors.

Platt's Chloride is one of the best **Disinfectants.** Chloride of lime is a valuable disinfectant, and much cheaper than Platt's Chloride.

Listerine is an excellent disinfectant to use for the mouth and throat.

To Make a Pastry Bag. Fold a twelve-inch square of rubber cloth from two opposite corners. Sew edges together, forming a triangular bag. Cut off point to make opening large enough to insert a tin pastry tube. A set comprising bag and twelve adjustable tubes may be bought for two and one-half dollars.

Smoked Ceilings may be cleaned by washing with cloths wrung out of water in which a small piece of washing soda has been dissolved.

For a Burn apply equal parts of white of egg and olive oil mixed together, then cover with a piece of old linen; if applied at once no blister will form. Or apply at once cooking soda, then cover with cloth and keep the same wet with cold water. This takes out the pain and prevents blistering.

FREDERICK DOUGLASS
From the speech "Self-Made Men."
Address before the students of the Indian Industrial School, Carlisle, Pennsylvania

. . . another element of the secret of success deserves a word. That element is order, systematic endeavor. We succeed, not alone by the laborious exertions of our faculties, be they small or great, but by the regular, thoughtful and systematic exercise of them. Order, the first law of heaven, is itself a power. The battle is nearly lost when your lines are in disorder. Regular, orderly and systematic effort which moves without friction and needless loss of time or power; which has a place for everything and everything in its place; which knows just where to begin, how to proceed and where to end, though marked by no extraordinary outlay of energy of activity, will work wonders, not only in the matter of accomplishment, but also in the increase of the ability of the individual . . . Work is not often undertaken for its own sake. The worker is conscious of an object worthy of effort, and works for that object; not for what he is to it, but for what it is to him. All are not moved by the same objects. Happiness is the object of some. Wealth and fame are the objects of others. But wealth and fame are beyond the reach of the majority of men, and thus, to them, these are not motive-impelling objects. Happily, however, personal, family and neighborhood well-being stand near to us all and are full of lofty inspirations to earnest endeavor, if we would but respond to their influence.

EMILY POST
From *Etiquette*

Detailed directions for dinner giving

The requisites at every dinner, whether a great one of 200 covers, or a little one of six, are as follows:

Guests. People who are congenial to one another. This is of first importance.

Food. A suitable menu perfectly prepared and dished. (Hot food to be *hot,* and cold, *cold.*)

Table furnishing. Faultlessly laundered linen, brilliantly polished silver, and all other table accessories suitable to the occasion and surroundings.

Service. Expert dining-room servants and enough of them.

Drawing-room. Adequate in size to number of guests and inviting in arrangement.

A cordial and hospitable host.

A hostess of charm. Charm says everything—tact, sympathy, poise and perfect manners—always.

And though for all dinners these requisites are much the same, the necessity for perfection increases in proportion to the formality of the occasion . . .

. . . It used to be an offense, and it still is considered impolite, to refuse dishes at the table, because your refusal implies that you do not like what is offered you. If this is true, you should be doubly careful to take at least a little on your plate and make a pretence of eating some of it, since to refuse course after course can not fail to distress your hostess. If you are "on a diet" and accepted the invitation with that stipulation, your not eating is excusable; but even then to sit with an empty plate in front of you throughout a meal makes you a seemingly reproachful table companion for those of good appetite sitting next to you.

ILLUSTRATIONS CREDITS

Getty Images; 132, Library of Congress, #3b49487; 133 (LE), Dani Simmonds/Shutterstock; 133 (RT), Neil Stanners/iStockphoto.com; 134, DEA/G. Dagli Orti/Getty Images; 135, Hulton Archive/Getty Images; 136, Library of Congress, #3c09978; 137, urfin/Shutterstock; 138, Tim Graham/Alamy; 139 (LE), MarinaMariya/Shutterstock; 139 (RT), Luba/Shutterstock; 140, Anyka/Shutterstock; 141 (LE), jaimaa/Shutterstock; 141 (RT), Igor Plotnikov/Shutterstock; 142, Indigo/Getty Images; 143, Svetlana Larina/Shutterstock; 144 (LE), A. W. Cutler/National Geographic Stock; 144 (RT), Brendan Howard/Shutterstock.com; 145, AP Images/Dana Felthauser; 146 (LE), Christopher Futcher/iStockphoto.com; 146 (RT), Jurjen Draaijer/iStockphoto.com; 147, Eric Vandeville-Vatican Pool/Getty Images; 149, "Clap Handies" art by Blanche Fisher Wright from *The Real Mother Goose,* Rand McNally & Co., 1916/www.oldbookart .com; 150 (UP), Natalia Gaak NWH/Shutterstock; 150 (LO), Roxana Bashyrova/Shutterstock; 151, Song Speckels/iStockphoto.com; 152, Lisa Thornberg/iStockphoto.com; 153 (LE), Yvette Chin/iStockphoto.com; 153 (RT), Nenov Brothers Photography/Shutterstock; 154, Joseph F. Rock/National Geographic Stock; 155, jumpingsack/Shutterstock; 156, Library of Congress, #24855; 157 (LE), taelove7/Shutterstock; 157 (RT), taelove7/Shutterstock; 158, Konstantin Sutyagin/iStockphoto.com; 159 (LE), The Bridgeman Art Library/Getty Images; 159 (RT), Title page art by Blanche Fisher Wright from *The Real Mother Goose,* Rand McNally & Co., 1916/www .oldbookart.com; 160, docent/Shutterstock; 161 (LE), Kharidehal Abhirama Ashwin/Shutterstock; 161 (RT), Mary Ann Shmueli/iStockphoto.com; 162 (UP), Wayne Johnson/Shutterstock; 162 (LO), badits/iStockphoto.com; 163, H. Edward Kim/National Geographic Stock; 164, bekir gürgen/iStockphoto.com; 165, Nikola Bilic/Shutterstock; 166, Gema Blanton/iStockphoto.com; 167, Ruth Black/iStockphoto.com; 168, Michael Yamashita; 169, rook76/Shutterstock.com; 170 (LE), Chepe Nicoli/Shutterstock; 170 (RT), AP Images/Eduardo Verdugo; 171, tatniz/Shutterstock; 172, Nancy Louie/iStockphoto.com; 173 (LE), Juanmonino/iStockphoto.com; 173 (RT), Stephen Bisgrove/Alamy; 174 (LE), Vasil Vasilev/Shutterstock; 174 (RT), Chung Sung-Jun/Getty Images; 175, mimirus/Shutterstock; 176, Albert Campbell/iStockphoto.com; 177, clearandtransparent/iStockphoto.com; 178, Mary Evans Picture Library/Alamy; 179 (LE), patty_c/iStockphoto.com; 179 (RT), darios/Shutterstock; 180 (LE), Smart-foto/Shutterstock; 180 (RT), Joe McNally; 181, AP Images/Mark Baker; 183, Library of Congress, #3b48996; 184, TRINACRIA PHOTO/Shutterstock; 186 (LE), Gordana Sermek/iStockphoto.com; 186 (RT), Y. C./iStockphoto.com; 187, art info/The Bridgeman Art Library; 188, Melissa Carroll/iStockphoto .com; 189 (UP), Milorad Zaric/iStockphoto.com; 189 (LO), vita khorzhevska/Shutterstock; 190 (LE), Attl Tibor/Shutterstock; 190 (RT), pic4you/iStockphoto.com; 191, Debbie Woods/iStockphoto .com; 192 (LE), Molodec/Shutterstock; 192 (RT), Deborah Cheramie/iStockphoto.com; 193, Sean Locke/iStockphoto.com; 194, vizualbyte/iStockphoto.com; 195, Mary Evans Picture Library/Alamy; 195, Elena Pal/Shutterstock; 196, Bob Thomas/Getty Images; 197 (LE), Gustaf Brundin/iStockphoto.com; 197 (RT), Sam Falk/New York Times Co./Getty Images; 198, Jim Jurica/iStockphoto.com; 199, Three Lions/Getty Images; 200, Monkey Business Images/Shutterstock; 201, David R. Frazier Photolibrary, Inc./Alamy; 202 (LE), ranplett/iStockphoto.com; 202 (RT), robootb/Shutterstock; 203, Alena Ozerova/Shutterstock; 204 (LE), Philip Dodd/iStockphoto.com; 204 (RT), Edward Moss/Alamy; 205, RetroClipArt/Shutterstock; 206 (LE), David Berry/Shutterstock; 206 (RT), Becky Stares/Shutterstock; 207 (LE), Flashon Studio/Shutterstock; 207 (RT), Andrzej Tokarski/iStockphoto.com; 208, Troy Kellogg/Shutterstock; 209, Library of Congress, #18449; 210, Library of Congress, #3c15059; 211, Stephen Coburn/Shutterstock; 212, kaarsten/Shutterstock; 213, Poster depicting an Israeli military montage, c.1955 (colour litho), Israeli School, (20th century)/Private Collection/DaTo Images/The Bridgeman Art Library International; 214 (LE), Trinity Mirror/Mirrorpix/Alamy; 214 (RT), Erhan Dayi/Shutterstock; 215, Lucy Baldwin/Shutterstock; 217, Library of Congress, #3g12499; 218, patrimonio designs limited/Shutterstock; 219, Iain Masterton/Alamy; 220 (LE), Lou Linwei/Alamy; 220 (RT), Henry Iddon/Alamy; 221, Emperor Alexander III (1845-94) (oil on canvas), Shilder, Andrey Nikolayevich (1861-1919)/State Central Artillery Museum, St. Petersburg, Russia/The Bridgeman Art Library International; 222, Galerie Bilderweit/Getty Images; 223, Fritz Hiersche/iStockphoto.com; 224, paul prescott/Shutterstock; 225, Stephen Finn/Shutterstock; 226 (LE), ICP/Alamy; 226 (RT), Becky Stares/Shutterstock; 227, Adam Jones/Getty Images; 228, Norbert Derec/Shutterstock.com; 229, Ray Roper/iStockphoto .com; 230, Frances L. Fruit/Shutterstock; 231, viviamo/Shutterstock; 232, Joe Raedle/Getty Images; 233 (LE), Shmeliova Natalia/Shutterstock; 233 (RT), Fedor Kondratenko/Shutterstock; 234, rook76/Shutterstock.com; 235, Steve Broer/Shutterstock; 236 (LE), Library of Congress, #3b50463; 236 (RT), Library of Congress, #03148; 237 (LE), alexmillos/Shutterstock; 237 (RT), Travelshots.com/Alamy; 238 (LE), Mike Hauf/iStockphoto.com; 238 (RT), iStock inhouse/iStockphoto.com; 239, hkeita/Shutterstock; 240, Justin Guariglia/National Geographic Stock; 241 (LE), manley099/iStockphoto.com; 241 (RT), David R. Gee/Alamy; 242, evangelos kanaridis/iStockphoto.com; 243, Tom Merton/Alamy; 244, Hulton Archive/Getty Images; 245, Becky Stares/Shutterstock; 246 (LE), Simon Cowling/Alamy; 246 (RT), AF archive/Alamy; 247 (LE), The Art Archive/Alamy; 247 (RT), Maxim Blinkov/Shutterstock; 248, Roberto Cerruti/iStockphoto.com; 249 (LE), Maximilian Weinzierl/Alamy; 249 (RT), Sam Cornwell/Shutterstock; 251, Library of Congress, #3f04057; 252, Tomislav Forgo/iStockphoto.com; 253, argonaut/Shutterstock; 254, Larry Lilac/Alamy; 255 (LE), HomeStudio/Shutterstock; 255 (RT), Eugene Sim/Shutterstock; 256, John McGrail/Time & Life Pictures/Getty Images; 257 (LE), Tom Freeze/Shutterstock; 257 (RT), Song Speckels/iStockphoto.com; 258, Song Speckels/iStockphoto.com; 259, Roy Botterell/Getty Images; 260 (LE), Wikipedia; 260 (RT), Cbenjasuwan/Shutterstock; 261, Timewatch Images/Alamy; 262, Don Arnold/Getty Images; 263, Dimitar Sotirov/Shutterstock; 264 (LE), SeDmi/Shutterstock; 264 (RT), Gary Yeowell/Getty Images; 265, Dimon/Shutterstock; 266, Krista Rossow/National Geographic Stock; 267 (LE), Filip Fuxa/Shutterstock; 267 (RT), New Year's Eve, fashion plate from "Art, Gout, Beaute," published in Paris, December 1923 (pochoir print), French School, (20th century)/Bibliotheque des Arts Decoratifs, Paris, France/Archives Charmet/The Bridgeman Art Library International; 268, RetroClipArt/Shutterstock; 269 (LE), Tatiana Popova/Shutterstock; 269 (RT), Duncan Walker/iStockphoto.com; 270 (LE), Library of Congress, #3g08784; 270 (RT), Phil Holmes/Shutterstock; 271, Eleanor Bentall/CORBIS; 272 (LE), Luis Marden/National Geographic Stock; 272 (RT), Alan Egginton/iStockphoto .com; 273, rudall30/Shutterstock; 274, amana images inc./Alamy; 275, Lynsey Addario; 276, SecondShot/Shutterstock; 277 (LE), Monkey Business Images/Dreamstime.com; 277 (RT), Katrina Brown/Shutterstock; 278, Photo by Kay Chernush, courtesy United Features.com; 279, Ivan Bajic/iStockphoto.com; 280, Digital Vision/Getty Images; 281 (LE), Andy Green/iStockphoto.com; 281 (RT), sutikno tikno/iStockphoto.com; 282, Philip Littleton/AFP/Getty Images; 283, Portrait of Cosimo di Giovanni de Medici (oil on panel), Italian School/Private Collection/The Bridgeman Art Library International; 285, Library of Congress, #0573.

Index

An Uncommon History of Common Courtesy

Bethanne Patrick

Published by the National Geographic Society

John M. Fahey, Jr., *Chairman of the Board and Chief Executive Officer*

Timothy T. Kelly, *President*

Declan Moore, *Executive Vice President; President, Publishing*

Melina Gerosa Bellows, *Executive Vice President; Chief Creative Officer, Books, Kids, and Family*

Prepared by the Book Division

Barbara Brownell Grogan, *Vice President and Editor in Chief*

Jonathan Halling, *Design Director, Books and Children's Publishing*

Marianne R. Koszorus, *Design Director, Books*

Lisa Thomas, *Senior Editor*

Carl Mehler, *Director of Maps*

R. Gary Colbert, *Production Director*

Jennifer A. Thornton, *Managing Editor*

Meredith C. Wilcox, *Administrative Director, Illustrations*

Staff for This Book

Susan Straight, *Editor*

Sanaa Akkach, *Art Director*

Nancy Marion, Caroline Couig, *Illustrations Editors*

Linda Makarov, *Designer*

Rachael Jackson, *Contributing Editor*

Allison Smith, *Translations Supervisor*

Tracy Baetz, *Picture Legends Writer*

Judith Klein, *Production Editor*

Marshall Kiker, *Illustrations Specialist*

Jodie Morris, Noelle Weber *Design Assistants*

Elizabeth Weiss, *Editorial Intern*

Manufacturing and Quality Management

Christopher A. Liedel, *Chief Financial Officer*

Phillip L. Schlosser, *Senior Vice President*

Chris Brown, *Technical Director*

Nicole Elliott, *Manager*

Rachel Faulise, *Manager*

Robert L. Barr, *Manager*

The National Geographic Society is one of the world's largest nonprofit scientific and educational organizations. Founded in 1888 to "increase and diffuse geographic knowledge," the Society works to inspire people to care about the planet. National Geographic reflects the world through its magazines, television programs, films, music and radio, books, DVDs, maps, exhibitions, live events, school publishing programs, interactive media and merchandise. *National Geographic* magazine, the Society's official journal, published in English and 33 local-language editions, is read by more than 40 million people each month. The National Geographic Channel reaches 370 million households in 34 languages in 168 countries. National Geographic Digital Media receives more than 15 million visitors a month. National Geographic has funded more than 9,600 scientific research, conservation and exploration projects and supports an education program promoting geography literacy. For more information, visit www.nationalgeographic.com.

For more information, please call 1-800-NGS LINE (647-5463) or write to the following address:

National Geographic Society
1145 17th Street N.W.
Washington, D.C. 20036-4688 U.S.A.

For information about special discounts for bulk purchases, please contact National Geographic Books Special Sales: ngspecsales@ngs.org

For rights or permissions inquiries, please contact National Geographic Books Subsidiary Rights: ngbookrights@ngs.org

ISBN: 978-1-4262-0813-3

Printed in the United States of America

11/QGT-CML/1